A
Chameleon's
Tale

A Chameleon's Tale

True Stories Of A Global Refugee

Mo Tejani

PAIBOON

PUBLISHING

Published by

Paiboon Poomsan Publishing
582 Amarinniwate Village 2
Nawamin 90 (Sukha 1) Bungkum
Bangkok 10230
Thailand.
Tel: 662-509-8632; Fax: 662-519-5437

Paiboon Publishing
PMB 256, 1442A Walnut Street
Berkeley, California 94709
USA.
Tel: 1-510-848-7086; Fax: 1-510-666-8862

Info@paiboonpublishing.com
www.paiboonpublishing.com

Printed in Thailand.

ISBN 1-887521-65-8

To

Bapuji, my father,
who taught me not to fear the unknown;

Ma, my mother,
who had plenty of love to go around
for all the family and all other animals;

Clare, my English teacher,
who started me off in the world of books;

Julian, my geography teacher,
my first travel mentor,
and a close friend for forty years;

All the chameleon traveler friends of mine,
wherever you are;

And to Zubin, an up and coming young
traveler of the next generation.

Contents

Acknowledgements

This book has been sitting in my head for years. That it has finally come to fruition is due to the many friends I have known in my travels who have encouraged me to put on paper all the storytelling that goes on at campfires on the road.

As the youngest of nine siblings, I have been fortunate to have family members who paved the way of adventure for me. I am grateful to each and every one of them, and their spouses, for the love and support they have given me over the years—and the warm beds and meals when I most needed them.

A special thank you to my brother, Bahadur, for his sensitivity, and for opening my eyes to the world of books and knowledge.

A very special thanks goes to Benjawan Poomsan—an author, dancer, and traveler in her own right—who, as my publisher, has always been there, willing to explore new literary frontiers in her desire to make sure that people who have led unorthodox lives will be heard.

A different, but just as important kind of thanks to my editor, Richard Baker, who has been meticulous in his craft, patient and gracious with his time in the editing sessions. He has been an excellent 'mirror' during my deliberations in the writing process.

Then there is the talented group of friends I have had the privilege of knowing at the Writers Club and Wine Bar in Chiang Mai, Thailand. A warm thanks to my friends Bob Tilley—author, journalist, and the genial host; Andrew Forbes—author and historian with a great sense of humor; Geoff Walton—an editor with a flair for the perfect phrase at the right time; David Henley—photographer, for his guidance; and to Joe Cummings—author, musician, and Lonely Planet guidebook writer. To all of you my heartfelt gratitude for the time you took to read my manuscript and give useful comments.

In California . . . to Alene Terasaki, who has always been on the same wavelength as me; and to Robert Shannon and Mike Baser for the marvelous trips to places with spellbinding views.

In Bangkok . . . to Jim Algie and Cameron Cooper for their 'out of the box' brainstorming sessions; to Alan Watson and Craig Roach, the founders of the infamous giggle factory get-togethers; to Hanz Matla for his humorous e-mail responses to my chapters; to Marleen Vanderree for the kind hospitality; to Amir Tejani for the animated family discussions and insightful comments on the book; and to kind and caring Shanya Attasillekha, always ready to buck me up every time I faltered.

To all of you I say a very big thank you for being my friends and inspiration.

Prologue

I was kicked out of Uganda in 1972 for being a brown-skinned Asian. This was the country I had lived in from the age of two until I was 21. In 1971, Idi Amin, a boxer turned soldier, promoted to major by the colonial British, overthrew Milton Obote, the first prime minister of Uganda, in a *coup d'etat*. Within a year, he ordered the expulsion of 80,000 Ugandan Asians, giving them ninety days to leave the country. They were forced to leave with no more than fifty British pounds in their pockets. Amin trampled my country into the ground for the next eight years.

I lost my home. My family—Shia Ismaili Muslims, the people of the Aga Khan—was forced apart and exiled to countries we had only heard of. Some of my friends went to different countries and continents, never to be heard from again. My country was no longer my own.

That was the first time I became a chameleon.

Thrust into the 1970s England of racial tensions, strikes, and skinheads, I buried myself in studies at the University of East Anglia in Norwich and, for the next two years, attempted to understand the land I had been exiled to. In Uganda I had been brought up to believe that the Brits were best, and anything that came from the UK had to be good. The more I learned about the British and their bloody Empire, the angrier and lonelier I became. One night, at three a.m., drunk in the streets of London, I punched a British bobby harassing a non-English-speaking old Asian lady whose only crime was looking at job bulletins for menial work to pay the rent. My friends dragged me away and we ran for a taxi before he could call for help or chase us down.

Albion College in Michigan offered me a scholarship in the summer of 1974. I was on the plane within a week and never looked back. Now I was a chameleon for the second time. Less shocking this time.

Oriental spiritualism was one of the fads in America during the 1970s. The white suburbanites in Michigan wanted me to be their spiritual yogi. The black folks on the other side of the tracks thought I might be their Muslim brother from Africa. The American Indians from the Midwest adopted me as a kindred soul. Me? I just wanted to be free of all the categorical boxes that people caged me in to feel more comfortable around me. Unfortunately, the boxes followed me east and west, everywhere I went in America. So I ran away, south of the border, armed with Spanish language books.

That was the third time I became a chameleon. Much easier now.

Overland from Mexico to Argentina, I searched for a place in the Aztec, Mayan, and Incan sun, void of time and space, where the brown *campesinos* would let me blend in as one more brown *compañero* looking for peace in the vast Andes. At first the boxes were only names—'gringo' to 'Indio' to 'Hindu'; then they became ideological boxes—*communista, revolucionario, hermano*. In Peru, the day I was contemplating a permanent home in Ollantaytambo, the army tanks rolled into Cusco, three miles away, to crush the emerging Sendero Luminoso (Shining Path) secessionist movement. I hid in the home of an American Peace Corps volunteer, shaved off my beard, and carried on south when it was safe to hit the road again.

That was when I realized I was doomed to be a global chameleon.

On Christmas Day, 1978, I received an invitation to join the Peace Corps as an English teacher in Thailand. I had three months to prepare. I replied that the pre-requisite American citizenship would take at least two years. They expedited my application in two months and sent me a diplomatic passport and an airplane ticket. Would Asia give me the home that had eluded me so far? After all, India, where my father was born and bred, and whose people spoke my mother tongue, was just around the corner from Thailand. Would I be able to get rid of the boxes there? Weren't Thailand's neighbors Malaysia and Indonesia home to large populations of Muslims? Would I be able to live in those places some day? What new boxes and names would I have to adapt to this time? Would Thailand bring me a step closer to my quest to be rid of the boxes once and for all?

1. Volunteer Blues

If you want to lift yourself up,
lift up someone else.
Booker T. Washington.

"**You ain't getting on** that plane to Bangkok until you shave off that Che Guevara beard and the Fu Manchu mustache, too," said the Peace Corps recruiter at San Francisco International Airport.

Apparently, in Thailand, only villains in movies and street gangsters wore hair on their face—not the sort of image the Washington, D.C. headquarters wanted to project about its Peace Corps volunteers, the "ambassadors of goodwill."

What the hell, I could do this. I had just spent the last six months jerking around with bureaucracy; had a dozen friends of mine go through the wringer to be my work and character references. Heck, I'd even had my Peace Corps suitability psyche-tested for three days in alienation games at 'staging' in Frisco by so-called cultural experts (who, incidentally, had just passed my roommate, a Bible-thumping ex-missionary from Louisiana as "eminently suitable" for Buddhist Thailand). Yes, I could do this. I could handle looking as clean-shaven as a baby's bottom, even though it had been years since I'd used a razor. Except for that time in Peru, of course.

I cut myself all over, shaving in the airport bathroom, and landed at Bangkok's Don Muang Airport in March, 1979 looking more like Scarface than 'Ambassador Goodwill.' On the airport runway, the welcoming committee, made up of petite Thai ladies in silk sarongs, showered 35 giant Americans with garlands of jasmine. They cringed when they got to me, Mr. Band-Aid.

At Phuket Teachers' College, six months into my two-year Peace Corps service, I grew back my beard and Fu Manchu mustache, chuckling to myself when the college director gave me special facial exemption, since I was to act as a wise, old, bearded Indian guru in my English students' play that semester. The bearded-guru scam lasted half the year. No one questioned my movie-villain looks anymore. In fact, one of my female English students thought that I was the only English professor in the whole of southern Thailand with a sexy, distinguished beard.

In 2001, when I was back at Peace Corps headquarters in Washington, I overheard a recruiter insisting on the phone that "no beards" was official Corps policy for male volunteers going to Muslim Morocco. A quarter of a century since I'd been forced to give my own beard the chop, the no-beards policy is still enforced in Muslim countries where men chat with their brethren using such phrases as 'by the beard of Allah' and 'in the name of the Prophet's beard.'

ങ

On our second day of Peace Corps orientation in the steaming Thai capital, we muddled our way through temples and noodle shops equipped with a small booklet of Thai phrases written in phonetic

English. No speech tones in the booklet. No explanation that many Thai words had five different meanings depending on the tone you used. No wonder the Bangkokians giggled every time one of us *farangs* ('white foreigners') ventured to speak Thai. For lunch, Jenny ordered a plate of 'knees' thinking she was ordering white rice. Same word for both, just different sound and tone. The eighteen-year-old waitress laughed her head off, whispering to herself, *"farang baa"* ('crazy foreigner': a label that no foreigner ever escapes, and one that gives them freedom to get away with murder, even today).

That same night, at our hotel, my Mexican-American roommate, Ignacio, sneaked in two girls at three a.m. I woke up to the sound of gorgeous gigglers. We giggled our way to daylight. I learned more Thai from those two gorgeous gigglers in five hours than I did in a week of plowing through Peace Corps booklets. Our assimilation into Thai culture was happening faster and in more creative ways than the Peace Corps had imagined. *Vamos hombre*!

Ignacio never made it past Bangkok. He giggled more and more with new gorgeous gigglers every day. So the Peace Corps put him on a plane back to Arizona. They called it "early termination" for inappropriate volunteer conduct. I was luckier. I learned quickly how to giggle with discretion in the Thai culture.

During orientation, Peace Corps staff warned us that flesh-revealing clothing was culturally insensitive and unacceptable in Thailand. Needless to say, we believed it as gospel truth. None of us had been to the girlie bars of Patpong or Soi Cowboy, where the lack of clothing revealed different sensitivities. Not yet, anyway.

One afternoon, I was in Lumpini Park at dusk. I ran into a lone Thai teenager who asked, *"Farang*, where you go?"

"Just out for a walk," I replied.

He rattled off some Thai, which I didn't understand. He spoke no more than ten words of English. Then he came right up to me and pinched my hairy arm, wanting to know (through gestures) why mine was so hairy and his arm, the same shade of brown, was so hairless. I laughed with him. Encouraged, he then took off his shirt, and signaled me to take off my mine so we could compare armpit hairs. I took off my shirt and displayed my armpit, smelly from the Bangkok heat. He was amazed that my hair was black and soft like his, but much thicker. Now we laughed out loud together. He dared me to drop my pants to compare pubic hair. I dared him to do the same. On the count of three, we did so together for a quick flash. He gave me a thumbs-up sign, which I reciprocated. Now we were howling. Before we went our separate ways into the gathering Lumpini night, he gave me the traditional *wai*, pointed to his pubic hair and mine, and said in broken English, "Same same but different."

Weeks later, when I finally plucked up the courage to reveal my Lumpini story in our Thai-language classroom, no one believed me. The Thai teachers thought I was making up the story just to get a laugh. Perhaps I should have changed the setting to Patpong on a Saturday night, not Lumpini Park on a weekday evening. Might have been more credible then. *Mai pen rai.* 'Never mind.'

Nowadays on Khao San Road, the backpacker haven in Bangkok, you see tons of T-shirts and tank tops with the same saying, 'Same Same But Different,' printed in bold letters. They sell faster than sticky rice and mango at a food fair among the thousands of travelers wandering through Thailand.

ß

Later we moved up to Nakhon Nayok, two hours from Bangkok, on the edge of the northeastern Isaan region. The town had two traffic lights, both of them on the main road near the hotel where our group of 35 volunteers was housed. In a primary school (closed for the summer holidays) we continued our Thai-language and culture classes, six days a week, six hours each day. I plunged into the language, thrilled to discover that glottal sounds, impossible for my fellow volunteers to pronounce, rolled off my tongue easily. As did the reading of the Sanskrit-based alphabet. I was borrowing heavily from my mother tongue, Gujarati, a Sanskrit Indian language. Classes went on for the next twelve weeks, by the end of which, some of my Thai teachers were my drinking buddies.

Living with an Isaan family for a week in one of the nearby villages was a mandatory part of the training that most of the group were very nervous about. I wanted longer than a week, antsy to get away from the volunteers, most of whom were reluctant to speak Thai outside the classroom. At my request, Ajaan Uthai—my teacher and the dedicated head of the language program—found me an Isaan family in a distant village where no other volunteer was assigned. Dinner every evening was on the wooden floor of the living room, which doubled up as a bedroom for four at night. At our first meal together—sticky rice with curry and crispy chicken (actually field mice, I found out later)—my family were amazed that I could eat with my hands. I let on that Indians—the easiest box the family could identify with—like Isaan people, eat with their hands, too. This confused them even more, since they had been told that Americans always ate with a knife and fork. We laughed. We learned. We moved on.

Bathing in the outhouse under the stars, with cold water drawn from a ground well, brought back days of my youth in Africa. Some nights, I would pretend that the half moon above me was a Ugandan moon, as the cicadas chirped their African songs all around me. Other nights, I sneaked out with Jom, the son who was almost my age, on his motorbike. This was Peace Corps grounds for 'early termination.' Racing along rice-field dykes in the dark, we met up with village girls at a pre-arranged rendezvous.

My host father gave me my own water buffalo, aptly called Dum ('Black'), to take care of. One day, I rode him from the village into Nakhon Nayok to go to language class. The townsfolk cheered me on, clapping and smiling. At school, I tied Dum up around a post, just like I'd seen the Lone Ranger do with his horse, Silver, on television. Ajaan Uthai whispered to me that it was not proper behavior for a volunteer. He urged me to refrain from bringing the Isaan language (closer to Lao when compared to Bangkok Thai) and traditions into the classroom.

Now I was confused, and made a fuss. Wasn't I being culturally sensitive and integrating with my family by doing chores like taking care of Dum? After all, once training was over, most of the 35 volunteers were to be assigned for two years of service to remote towns and villages all over Thailand. So why all the fuss? Bangkok, the Big Apple, or should I say the Big Mango, was certainly not my idea of the Peace Corps experience.

The Peace Corps' American staff came down hard on me: "Too many questions. Do as you're told unless you want to end up like Ignacio."

Apparently, the three-month training period was yet another suitability test before I could be sworn in as a volunteer by the US ambassador for Thailand at the fortress-like embassy on Wireless Road in Bangkok. Go with the flow, Mr. Ambassador of Goodwill. Hang in there. The swearing-in ceremony was only three weeks away. You see, by now I was already in love with rural Thailand. Maybe this could be my new home, after all.

I managed to convince Ajaan Uthai to let me stay on with my Isaan family for the rest of the training period, assuring him that I was learning Thai faster than most of the other Americans in my group. But I had to give in to him that Dum, my buffalo, could no longer be my Silver.

When training was over, my adopted family and I shed tears. Father assured me that Dum would be there when I came back to visit. Jom assured me that Goong, a village girl I had fallen for, would also be waiting for my return. As a farewell gift, Mother gave me a leather strap with six Buddha amulets on it to wear next to my belly to protect me from evil Isaan spirits.

ભ

Twenty years later, I met up with Ajaan Uthai in Khon Kaen, the regional capital, while working on a rural development project. We reminisced about the old training days when I used to wake him up at two in the morning to practice Thai over 'late night' munchies. He finally confided how proud he was of me when he heard me speak the northeastern dialect with my Isaan family during my farewells at the village. Too bad his American bosses didn't agree. Mai pen rai.

In 2004, at his retirement party, after thirty years of dedicated service to the Peace Corps, Ajaan Uthai asked me if Dum was still alive. Sadly, I told him that Dum had passed away a few years before from old age.

ભ

After swearing to the American ambassador that I would uphold the Peace Corps mission—right hand held high like a witness in a courtroom—I was sent to Phuket in southern Thailand to serve as an English instructor, curriculum writer, and teacher trainer. My body was divided into two halves, one for each of two institutions: Phuket Teachers' College, and the Prince of Songkhla University, Phuket campus. Both student groups were training to be English teachers. I was to teach English literature to the first group (since no Thai teacher wanted this course) and 'tourism English' to the second. The good news was that, since the distance between the two institutions was at least six kilometers, they gave me a motorcycle to get around on. Not only was I in paradise, but now I was mobile, too.

Phuket is an island, Thailand's largest, facing the Andaman Sea. The southerners there are dark brown like me. It was still an undiscovered paradise back then. The town itself had one nightclub and a few five-star hotels. I became friends with a second-generation Indian Sikh family who had a tailoring business on Thalang Road. The boys, Ravin and Narin, became my Phuket mentors. On Sundays I watched Bollywood movies with the whole family while Mom served plate after plate of samosas with tamarind chutney dip. Ravin and Narin's mother called me *"mera betah,"* her adopted Indian son from Africa. Another name to add to my list.

Patong Beach at that time had only one disco and a few guesthouses. The rest of Phuket's beaches—Kata, Kamala, Rawai—were untouched, with miles and miles of soft white sand lined with palms and the occasional group of bamboo huts. Promontory Point (Laem Phrom Thep), a scenic piece of land jutting into the Andaman Sea, was where honeymooners and lovers watched the sunset colors drip into the waves lapping against the rocks below.

A ten-minute walk from the Point over the adjoining ridge brought you to Nai Harn Beach, a blue-water cove with superb snorkeling just off of its white sand. The only hut overlooking the cove belonged to a *chao lae*, a local fisherman. I tracked him down to see if he would rent me the hut every weekend for the next two years.

"*Khaek* ['Indian'] from America teaching Thai students?" he said, incredulous.

I showed him my teacher ID.

He laughed and gave me a *wai*.

I thought he was brushing me off as a lying idiot. Instead, he said it would be his honor to give the hut rent-free to someone who looked just like him but had come from so far away to teach English to his people. Now I was sure I was living in a dream. I spent numerous weekends snorkeling at this isolated cove, playing with fish in the silent clear blue of the Andaman Sea.

Today, this once pristine cove is a full-fledged marina where yachters pay hefty fees to park their boats above the now dead coral. So I've been told.

Fear of destroying a cherished memory made me sure I would never go back to Phuket again.

I was wrong.

CB

In the two-bedroom faculty housing assigned to me on campus, somehow I ended up with Ajaan Marut as a roommate, a man who literally lived the life of a monk. Like the Buddhist monks, he had his head shaved and ate all his meals before noon. However, unlike the Buddhist monks, he did not wear orange robes, live in a *wat* (Buddhist temple), or "beg for a living"—his words for the daily alms ritual in which monks accept food from citizens in return for blessings. Instead, Ajaan Marut taught English at the college to earn his food, and also chaired the committee for the Ministry of Education's ethics curriculum.

Marut, as I soon found out, was no ordinary 'monk.' A few years before, he had made a living as a go-go dancer in a strip joint in Germany. One day, sick of all the sex and debauchery, he returned home to Thailand, shaved his head, and adopted the lifestyle of a monk.

"Why? Was the sex that bad?" I asked when he told me his story.

"No, not at all. I liked it so much that I had to give it up. Now I look back on it and think of all the time and money spent chasing women just to have an orgasm that lasted less than a minute."

"Is that how you view sex now?"

"Too much effort, too little pleasure," he replied.

He did have a valid point, but not one I was ready to accept at the horny age of 28.

Every time I asked him to go to a movie or out drinking with me, he'd always reply, "Been there, done that," then tap his forefinger to his forehead and add, "In here."

In our wooden house, he couldn't stand the mess in my room, so whenever I wasn't around, he'd clean up after me. The living-room floor, where we always ate, had to be spotless. My room needed an overhaul every few days. Finally one day, he said to me, "Teach me how to be dirty?"

"What? What do you mean?"

"I realize I am too preoccupied with cleanliness," he said. "I want to be like you. I want to have a messy room. I want to be able to eat dinner after playing sports without thinking it a mortal sin not to take a shower beforehand. Will you teach me?"

I was speechless for once.

The year was 1980. I was ranting and raving one afternoon to Ajaan Marut about America's disastrous history of foreign policy; its bloated defense budget; how the cost of one B-52 bomber could cover Thailand's entire education budget. On and on I rambled for over an hour. Marut listened, quiet and patient, interrupting only to ask for clarification on certain issues.

When I was spent and exhausted, he finally got up and asked, "Are you finished?"

I nodded with a sigh.

"Thank you," he exclaimed.

"For what?" I asked.

"For teaching me so much about America's history and foreign policy." He paused. "Now, I have one question for you."

"What?" I was curious now.

"Even though I learned so much from you during this last hour, has anything changed for the better?"

I looked baffled. I had no idea what he was getting at.

"What I mean is, has America changed because of your anger? Will the production of B-52 bombers stop because of your speech? Yes, you feel better for complaining about it. But is the world better than it was an hour ago?"

I stopped to consider the shocking simplicity of his statement and realized that he was right.

Once again, he had me speechless.

ɔ

Some time later, while traveling through Malaysia, I was thrilled to be eating Muslim food again: mutton curries with *sambal* chutney wrapped in banana fronds that I hadn't seen since Africa. I was surprised that Monk Marut, who had decided to join me on the trip at the last minute, went everywhere with me. He ate Muslim food (still before noon), visited mosques, played snooker at billiard halls, and even went bikini spotting with me at Batu Ferringhi Beach on the island of Penang. We became close on that trip. We made quite the pair: African Mojo and Monk Marut in Muslim Malaysia.

Later, Marut went to Bangkok but never came back. I looked all over for him. My inquiries at the college and at the ministry in Bangkok led nowhere. He had just disappeared. I was devastated. Angry too, that no one at college seemed to care much either. Guess they thought he was too weird for their categorical boxes. Like me, he was a chameleon.

ɔ

Monk Marut exposed me to the dark side of the Thai Ministry of Education through his work with the ethics committee in Bangkok. He talked about the internal bickering, the domineering male egos, the whoring junkets to beach resorts, and much more. It just so happened that during my last two months in Phuket, I had been seeing a gorgeous 28-year-old honey-skinned bargirl from Patong Beach—let's call her Noi—who spoke better English than most of the Thai English teachers at the college. She was yearning to get out of the bar trade, but didn't quite know how or what else she could do to make a reasonable living. I was yearning to help her find a way out.

During our romance, I was invited to a ministry conference (read: three-day junket) at Cha-Am Beach to review some new curricula ideas.

For three solid weeks, we rehearsed Noi's role as an instructor in English language at Prince of Songkhla University (Phuket campus). She had graduated with a Masters in English from Ann Arbor, Michigan. Yes, it was my Masters degree and my post-graduate alma mater that she adopted.

With just days remaining before the trip, we went shopping and I bought her a fabulous formal dress and matching shoes. The stage was all set when I managed to wangle her a last-minute invitation to Cha-Am. Looking back on it, the situation reminds me of the film, *Educating Rita*, with an Indian Michael Caine and a Thai Julie Walters on Patong Beach.

There were only three other women present at the meeting, all older ladies who retired early each night. The ministry's macho types hovered around Noi like roaches over a bowl of sugar. When they asked her about her experiences in Michigan, she embellished the stories I had recounted to her in my hut at Nai Harn Beach. When they asked her if she could come to work with them in Bangkok, she became coy and said she was hoping to get a scholarship to do her Ph.D in Linguistics in Europe. She had them eating out of her hands, both sticky rice and curricula reform.

Noi went through a confidence metamorphosis at Cha-Am. Back at Patong, her spirits soared and her goals became more ambitious. Within weeks, I became a fling of the past as she moved on to a rich Swede building hotels in Patong and wooing her on sailboats on the Andaman. One evening, out of the blue, she showed up at the Teachers' College in a big car with tinted windows. "*Pai tiaow mai? Noi ja liang.*" 'Let's go out, have a night on the town. On me.'

She wined and dined me at the newest five-star hotel in Patong, courtesy of her Swedish boyfriend.

Could this really become home for me, I wondered that night.

Some years later, I heard through my Phuket grapevine that Noi had left the 'sugar daddy' business, opened up her own dive shop, and was minting money catering to tourists.

Way to go Rita!

ଓ

Then there was the saga of Ajaan 'Kii Mao' (loosely translated as the 'drunken' professor) at the Teachers' College. He had befriended me only because I was the *farang* from America. He couldn't figure out why I wasn't willing to find him a white girlfriend, since he would do the same for me with any student of my choosing. His problem was that he just couldn't help but spend his monthly paycheck on booze and women instead of his wife and children. So the wife came up with a plan. Each month, on the morning of payday, at six a.m., while Ajaan Kii Mao was still sleeping off the hangover from the night before, the wife would park herself in front of the administration building and insist that the payroll clerk hand over her husband's salary to her and not her husband. The college director, feeling sorry for her family, approved it the first month, thereby setting a precedent for the next few months.

Ajaan Kii Mao settled down a bit during this period, as he would have lost too much face among his colleagues to make an issue out of it with the director. Then, one payday, desperate for cash for his vices, Ajaan Kii Mao determined to show up at the cashier's window before his wife. He went gallivanting the night before with money borrowed from me, made his way home, changed into his pajamas, and passed out in the living-room. At dawn, he snuck out of the house to furtively collect his paycheck. That morning, the buzz among the early birds was very loud. There was Ajaan Kii Mao in front of the administration building, perched on a bench, with no shoes and his pajamas on, fast asleep in the fetal position and snoring to high heaven.

It wasn't too much longer before Ajaan Kii Mao was transferred to a desk job with the condition that two-thirds of his salary would be sent directly to his wife each month. Chalk one up for gender equality, Thai style. Broke most of the time, he soon gave up on the idea of making me his pimp for *farang* girlfriends. That was one new name I couldn't accept.

∞

The head of the English department at Phuket Teachers' College was, to put it bluntly, a fat Chinese-Thai old hag—let's call her Jai Dum: 'Black Heart'—who had been teaching the same rote lessons from the same books for the previous thirty years. She threatened that students who left their desks to pee during class time would be caned with a bamboo stick; I took the same students on English-vocabulary walks through bamboo forests and rubber plantations during class time. She wanted me to teach Shakespeare to the southern Muslim students; I ended up teaching Somerset Maugham's stories about Muslim Malays for two semesters. She thought that corporal punishment would instill discipline. Damned if she was going to let some upstart American, one who didn't even look like an American, change any of that. I fought her every step of the way, suppressing the unpleasant memories from my own secondary school in Africa. We rubbed heads against each other all the time. She called me "*Khaek khai roti*" ('Indian selling chapattis'; yet another name to get used to) behind my back. I called her an old Chinese witch. We avoided each other whenever we could.

One day, during the last month of my first year, Rachanee, a dark-skinned student who was head of the English Club, ran into class, tears dripping down her cheeks. When she showed me the bruises on her arm from Jai Dum's bamboo cane, I was livid. My African school days came rushing back. I shivered involuntarily as the flashback came alive. . . .

Most Monday mornings, for some petty schoolboy prank, I was sent to the headmaster's office for punishment. The headmaster, a defrocked Irish priest, would close the black curtains in his office, lock the door, turn off the lights, order me to pull my pants down, and then whip me with a rattan cane all over my buttocks till they were red with blisters. Much as I fought back the tears, a few drops usually spilled.

In my head now, I heard the swish of the cane as it swooped down on Rachanee's arm. I lost my *jai yen* 'cool heart' and stormed into the college director's office with Rachanee in tow. The poor girl was trembling with fear. The director heard me out, didn't even look at Rachanee's wounds, and calmly said that he'd take care of it. I had my doubts.

From that day on, Jai Dum never laid a hand or cane on another student again. At least, not till I left, because she also made sure that I would not work at the college for my second year. Some excuse about not having enough courses for me to teach.

For my second year, I was transferred to Chiang Rai Teachers' College, up north. This, so that no one would lose face: not the college, not the department head, certainly not the Peace Corps, and yes, not even me. Screw the students; they didn't count anyway. Maybe this wasn't home, after all.

ℭঙ

In the early 1980s, during the northern 'winters' of Chiang Rai province, the opium poppy in bloom was a sight to behold. Fields and fields of pink and violet flowers stretched to the horizon. Hmong and Akha hilltribe women, clad in traditional embroidered dresses and sporting silver nose rings, harvested the oozy black juice that dreams are made of.

This was the southern point of the Golden Triangle, that legendary intersection of Thailand, Laos, and Burma. These were the opium fields that financed the border drug lords and the resistance movement to the Burmese military junta.

I suppose I was due for another adjustment, and this one encompassed the entire length of Thailand, from the tropical beaches and sea gypsies of the Andaman Sea to the mountains and hilltribes of the Triangle. Having almost mastered the fast southern accent, I now had to start all over again with the sing-song Lanna dialect of the north. The provincial town of Chiang Rai itself was even smaller than Phuket, with no disco and one movie theater that piped in the English soundtrack for *farangs* in a special room—for a higher price, of course. (One time, during a boring Western movie, I even spotted two Thai translators—male and female—up in the projector room, doing live translation from English to Thai, over the theater's PA system. No wonder John Wayne spoke Thai in such an effeminate voice.)

The Teachers' College gave me a motorcycle and an apartment for myself, with a large green gecko and a yellow frog as bathroom tenants. The college had an attitude to English teaching that was open to new ideas, and they were keen to make me feel at home. At first, my students couldn't get enough of their new teacher, the human language lab, even though our English Club met thrice a week after classes.

One evening, I was riding my motorcycle over the bridge into Chiang Rai town from the college. It had been one of those frustrating days when I couldn't get through to a single student. In English Literature class, we had been studying Robert Frost's famous poem "The Road Not Taken," and the poetic language was proving too far removed from reality for my Thai students to care about or empathize with Mr. Frost.

At the bridge, the last rays of the sun reflected off the Kok River. Young boys and girls led their water buffaloes from plowing the rice paddies back home along various routes to their different villages nearby. The scene, though serene, was a common sight for me every evening when I returned home from the town.

Returned home?

That was it! That was the ticket. I stopped on the bridge and gazed more intently at the boys and girls and the buffaloes. Eureka! I now knew what to do to get my students to understand the meaning behind Mr. Frost's poem.

The next day in class, I handed out the following assignment: "Think back to when you were growing up in one of the local villages. It is evening and you are returning home from the family rice field with your buffalo, Dum, who is your responsibility. Every day you take the same path home. You see the same things on the way. Today, however, you decide to take Dum on a different path. What do you see? Write a short essay on all the things you notice on this different route home."

The students went crazy with words for the next few days. These very same thirty students who repeatedly fell asleep in class, or chatted and doodled cartoons through boredom, now hunkered down with their journals, fighting over the six Thai-English dictionaries and one thesaurus they had to share between them.

Three students got an 'A' for their essays. First time ever. A few turned in additional poems of their own. Not of Mr. Frost's caliber, but certainly a very good start. Two even wrote out in great detail (with the usual grammar and spelling mistakes) what "The Road Not Taken" now meant to them. They became my peer teachers in class the next day. Mr. Frost was now alive and well in the province of Chiang Rai, thanks to my old friend Dum and the Kok River.

03

Few would argue with the statement that Thai food is probably one of the most delightful culinary experiences in the world. But, like all good things in life, it can be taken for granted and even become boring in abundance. So it happened that, after months of gorging on scrumptious spicy Thai food, I woke up one Sunday morning in Chiang Rai craving a big juicy hamburger, with all the toppings, in a sesame-seed bun. American food had not left its mark on me except for pizza, spare ribs, and real burgers. Back then, there were no fast-food joints in Chiang Rai. You were lucky if you found Heinz mayonnaise or slices of Kraft cheese in the town's biggest supermarket. So, as I trudged off to Khun Lek's home-cum-mini-restaurant for my usual daily breakfast of rice with pork omelet and hot chilli sauce, I wondered how I could get my hands on a prime burger with golden fries and ketchup without having to make the overnight bus trip to Bangkok.

Lek and her family had adopted me and three other *farang* volunteers as part of their extended clan. Together we had helped her through Grandma's cremation, and had celebrated the youngest daughter's tenth birthday with songs, games, and a cake that had more icing than cake. Her Burmese husband, Patrick, and I played air guitar to Jimi Hendrix tapes.

So that Sunday morning, when I suggested the idea of me cooking up a hamburger with fries in her kitchen, she smiled and opened up her pantry to watch me go at it. I got hold of two of my *farang* friends and we turned the morning into a burger party at Lek's, just like Sunday morning football games back in Michigan. Patrick brought out his guitar and off we went: "Country road, take meeee home. . . ."

Although the town-wide search for sesame-seed buns and dill pickles was unsuccessful, we managed to cook up a hearty American brunch of juicy meat patties, hot dogs, humongous fries, garden salad, and lots of hot sauce. Watching the men cook up a feast— not a typical kitchen scene in a Thai home—Lek giggled her way throughout. But her eyes were peeled on every move we made.

Days later, word got around fast that Lek was now cooking up burgers for anyone who missed them. Within weeks, Lek's spicy burgers with special Thai sauce, topped with cucumbers and homegrown lettuce, became a life line for expats and an exotic treat for adventurous Thais in Chiang Rai. Every once in a while, she'd give me a free burger meal as her new business boomed.

ⓒ

The upside of living in a small town is a family like Lek's taking you in as one of their own; the downside is that your life is no longer your own. Everyone in Chiang Rai knew when I ate, when I shat, and what color underwear I was wearing during each shit. Growing up in a three-bedroom Indian home with eight siblings meant that privacy was impossible. But my years of living in Britain and America had forced me to respect the Western perception of privacy to the point where I made it my own. I do recall a couple of incidents where a lack of privacy in Chiang Rai really got to me.

During my first fortnight in Chiang Rai, whenever I went to eat my favorite lunch—sticky rice with *nam prik ong* (spicy minced beef)—at my regular restaurant near work, all the neighborhood kids would stop whatever they were doing and gather around the entrance to watch the *farang* eat. They would peep at me from behind the door, giggling and gossiping at every move I made. I felt like a monkey in the local zoo. Trying to shoo them away in English or Thai had no effect. The restaurant owner couldn't be bothered to chase them away either.

Finally, one day, while eating Isaan-style barbecued chicken with sticky rice, instead of putting the rolled up balls of rice into my mouth, I shoved one up each nostril and one in each ear, then ran towards the kids, screaming at the top of my lungs, hands waving wildly. They had just seen their first *farang* sticky-rice ghost, and fled faster than a *jing jok* gecko darting for a fly. Outside the restaurant, I stopped and laughed. The trick must have gotten to the kids that lunchtime because, from then on, they never came back to gawk at me while I was eating.

Another time, when I had just about had it with people wanting to practice their five broken words of English with me, or go through my belongings, or ask me if I knew their cousin in California, I zipped off to Bangkok overnight. I got into a *tuk-tuk* and, as we sped around the congested Victory Monument—five roads converging into a giant roundabout with a huge phallic obelisk in the middle—I let off a deep-throated scream at the top of my lungs. I was thrilled to be back in a big city where nobody knew who I was, where I came from, and especially what color underwear I wore. My scream of joy at my newfound, temporary anonymity was drowned out by the traffic and the chaotic din, and nobody, not even the *tuk-tuk* driver, blinked an eyelid. Still, I felt so free and relieved, as if huge boulders had been lifted off my shoulders.

From then on, whenever I left my small town for the metropolis, I always made it a point to warn the taxi, *tuk-tuk*, or bus driver that I was about to let out a piercing scream of joy and to please not be upset or perturbed by it. They just smiled knowingly and went on with their driving. I was really beginning to feel at home in this country. *Farang baa*!

⋈

Gobbling up all the delicious spicy food on the streets and in the markets, it was only a matter of time before 'Montezuma's revenge,' or 'Thai tummy,' finally caught up with me. There came a time when my farts and belches just wouldn't stop. The cramps had me doubled up in the street, and I would wince with pain. The doctors in Bangkok had a field day exploring every single orifice in my body. After a plethora of enemas and endoscopies, enough to last a lifetime for a herd of elephants, the doctors diagnosed my condition as unknown and mysterious—they had NABCAYFF ('Not A Bloody Clue About Your Foul-Smelling Farts').

So, the Peace Corps, despite my desperate protests about how all my English students were counting on me to get them through their exams, put me on the next plane to Washington, D.C. and Walter Reed Hospital. I was yet another medevac—'medical evacuation' volunteer. It was a November morning in 1980 when I arrived in D.C., and the temperature had dipped to minus ten degrees. The ice on my black mustache formed tiny stalactites. Somehow, within the space of 72 hours, I had been beamed, "Star Trek" style, from tropical Kok River sunsets to the frozen Potomac.

After more probes, poking, prodding, and poop tests, the medical diagnosis in D.C. was not much better than 'NABCAYFF.' The doctor proclaimed the mysterious Asian disease as IBS— irritable bowel syndrome. The cure? A healthy diet. To make matters much worse, the Peace Corps "medically terminated" me, despite protests from my country director and my own pleas. 'Too costly to send you back for just five more months of service' was their attitude. I was devastated. Once again, someone in power had taken a home away from me. *Mai pen rai?*

Mai pen rai, my ass. I was mad and pissed off at the world.

෩

While growing up in East Africa, the first American I became close friends with was a Peace Corps volunteer by the name of Scott from Tucson, Arizona. Back then, he opened my eyes to the world of Jack Kennedy, J. Edgar Hoover, and the first moonwalker, Neil Armstrong. Many years later, in America, I traced him with the help of a kindly Arizona telephone operator, and we hiked down the Grand Canyon together.

During my training days at Peace Corps, when Ajaan Uthai asked me why I chose Thailand, I paused. The diplomatic answer about serving the world's poor as my God-given American duty sounded phony, so I told him the truth. Thailand is halfway between Kathmandu and Bali, two 'paradises' I had fantasized about traveling to. Both were places I might potentially call home. I hadn't counted on Thailand itself being added to that list. Ajaan Uthai laughed and pushed me harder to excel in his language. The pride on his face when I attained the highest language score in eighteen years of Peace Corps history, after only ninety days of training, said it all. I never forgave the Peace Corps for taking away a place I called home. Just like I never forgave Idi Amin for taking away my beloved Uganda.

In 1990, I was chosen to become deputy director for the Peace Corps in Honduras, the year after NSC officer, Colonel Oliver North, was convicted for lying under oath to the US Congress about how funds for the illegal "Contra" guerrilla war against socialist Nicaragua were not provided from drug money and sales of arms to Iran. That same year, the program in Honduras—a country less than half the size of Texas—grew into the largest Peace Corps operation in the world. Coincidence? I don't think so.

In 1993, I assigned six volunteers—against the will of my superiors—into "La Mosquitia," the 'Amazon basin of Central America.' They were to work with the Mesquite Indians, some of whom had been co-opted as Contra guerrillas. I had hoped to undo, in some small measure, the damage done by American personnel, money, and guns to the people of that region. Only then, as an American citizen carrying a US diplomatic passport, did I dare to ask myself the question: Why is it that, every year, America sends some 6,000 unsuspecting 'ambassadors of goodwill' to the four corners of the world to clean up the mess that American politicians make?

Is it just mere coincidence that, in every part of the world where America fought a physical or ideological war, there followed an influx of 'damage control volunteers' to promote American goodwill? From the Congo to Chile. From Somalia to the ex-Soviet republics. Wasn't Thailand one of them during the Vietnam War? Was I one of those 6,000 unsuspecting, duped ambassadors of goodwill, too?

2. Refugees

*In my experience, going home is
the deepest wish of most refugees.*
Angelina Jolie.

"Refugee, where are you running to?" said the soldier standing next to a guava tree on the dusty road. Immediately I went into my shell, as if hypnotized.

Shudders ran through my body any time I heard the word 'refugee' spoken around me. Demons that lay hidden in the corners of my brain raised their ugly heads. Images that I had pushed deep down came surging forth, till they were swimming in front of my eyes.

In Africa. . . .

A guava tree in front of our house in Madras Gardens where, every afternoon after school, as children, both brown and black, we played tree games till our mothers called us home for dinner. . . .

In the pink twilight, crocodiles fighting over dead black bodies dumped in Lake Victoria by Idi Amin's soldiers. . . .

A screaming Indian girl in a Punjabi dress crushed by Ugandan tanks storming down Kampala Road; her oily braided ponytail severed from her head by the grinding tank treads, the only taunting reminder of her existence. . . .

"The Brits and the Indians are playing ping pong with us. Nobody wants us," my brother kept saying as we shuffled from embassy to embassy, seeking refuge. . . .

In England. . . .

Enoch Powell ranting in the House of Commons that the Tory government's acceptance of the Ugandan Asians into Britain was "a drastic policy mistake." These Asians had no real links to Britain, he claimed. They were either born in India or had retained close connection with India. They certainly had no connection with Britain by blood or residence.

And a piece of graffiti I remember seeing on a station wall in Southall, South London, in 1974: "Skinheads, beware of Pakistani hockey sticks bashing your heads!"

In America. . . .

A Californian cop, mistaking me for an illegal Mexican 'wetback,' handcuffed me while I was searching for my lost wallet in my own garden at my Balboa Beach apartment.

In Wyoming, pick-up truck passengers taking rifle shots at me hitchhiking on Interstate 80, yelling "Run, Injun, run!" as I scurried into the bushes. . . .

I came out of my reverie and saw the soldier leaning on the trunk of the guava tree. But this wasn't Africa. The guava tree was not in Kampala at all.

I looked around me. Near a Buddhist temple in front of a barbed-wire fence, thousands of Vietnamese people were milling around trucks distributing food and water rations. I was in a refugee camp somewhere in Thailand.

How did I end up here?

Events in Southeast Asia, moving faster than the cars zooming on the Californian highway I had been living next to, took me there. But I am getting ahead of myself.

cs

In early 1981, I was meditating on the sands of Balboa Beach in southern California, pining for my life back in Thailand. America was swarming with yogis from the Orient. With the Vietnam War finally over, people had gravitated towards the spirituality of the East. Kundalini yoga and Zen Buddhism were in vogue. Carlos Castaneda would publish his fourth volume on the teachings of Don Juan, recommending peyote dreams as the answer to self-discovery. Americans were desperate to heal their wounds after the shenanigans of Watergate and Vietnam. Some were searching for enlightenment through yoga and the chakras, imagining their bodies to be a spiritual temple. I was one of them.

My meditation took me back to the rice paddies and Buddha statues in Thailand. I wondered what Monk Marut and Noi in Phuket, on the other side of this ocean, were doing. Did they remember me? Who was taking care of my buffalo Dum in Nakhon Nayok? Would I ever see Thailand again?

My trance was broken by screams in a foreign language; sounds I recognized.

I opened my eyes and thought I was dreaming. Freaking out before me on this serene Californian beach was a little Hmong girl dressed in hilltribe costume with silver bracelets and earrings. She held a bottle of Coke in her hand. Her mother, also in full hilltribe garb, was soothing her in the Hmong language.

I rubbed my eyes. Were they playing tricks on me? Mountain people from Laos on a southern California beach? How did they get here? What were they doing here? Refugees like me?

Then it all started coming back to me.

In August 1975, the same year that America finally pulled out of the Vietnam War, Laos fell to the communist Pathet Lao. Over the next few months, thousands of Hmong, who had fought for the CIA in the war against communism in Laos, traversed the Mekong River and escaped into Thailand, fearing for their lives. Riddled with guilt, the US government began an instant relocation to America. The first few planes plunked some 2,000 of them (from the Ban Vinai refugee camp on the Thai-Lao border) in southern California, of all places.

Uprooted first from their remote and primitive mountain villages into overcrowded Ban Vinai—a makeshift camp with no water or food—these 2,000 Hmong were shoved into C-47 airplanes and unceremoniously dumped into the heart of Disneyland. Used to cooking rice and fish over wood fires, they were now housed in high-rise apartments with electric stoves. Used to hiking on mountain trails, they now found themselves living by the congested traffic on Interstate 5 along the Los Angeles-San Diego urban sprawl. They had received no pre-departure preparation whatsoever. No English classes; no orientation on American apartment living. They had no clue about American society, culture, or food. The local papers in southern California had a field day with their headlines on the Hmong.

"Laotian tribal women cooking over wood fires in living rooms!"

"Hmong children eating canned dog food!"

"Santa Ana residents up in arms over refugees urinating on lawns!"

The mother and daughter I saw on Balboa Beach had to be part of this disastrous relocation program.

It wasn't long before the public outcry reached the ears of the federal government in Washington, D.C. Only then did the Bureau of Refugee Affairs begin releasing tax dollars for language and cultural orientation programs to prepare the thousands more Hmong still pouring into America. Little did the US government imagine then that the Hmong relocation would open the floodgates for a mass exodus from Laos's neighbors.

The hasty 1975 withdrawal of the remaining American troops had left many South Vietnamese stranded in Saigon. Over the next five years they fled by the thousands, braving ocean currents in leaky boats to reach the shores of Malaysia, Thailand, Singapore, and Indonesia. They came to be known as the "boat people."

Meanwhile, in neighboring Cambodia, Pol Pot's Khmer Rouge decided that genocide was the way forward for the country. Over a million Cambodian refugees poured into Thailand, overwhelming the Thai government, who asked for help from the Americans.

Third-country asylum camps (Refugee Processing Centers; RPCs) were set up all over Southeast Asia—at Phanat Nikhom in Thailand, Galang in Indonesia, and Bataan in the Philippines—to relieve Thailand of the burden. Refugees from Laos, Cambodia, and Vietnam, huddled in makeshift Thai camps, were airlifted to these RPCs, to study English and learn about American culture before being resettled in the States. American refugee agencies, funded by the State Department in Washington, desperately sought American teachers and educators to go and work in these camps.

I saw my chance.

When I became a refugee from Uganda, no one had prepared me for England and the British culture. Most of us Asians who were kicked out were educated and spoke some English, but we suffered nevertheless. I feared that these Southeast Asians, most with no English or even basic education, would suffer much more than we did.

This was my chance to return to Asia. Here was my opportunity to help refugees, like myself, from making the mistakes I did. A chance to help Asian people who had suffered the same fate as me at the hands of their own Idi Amins. A way to find my own path among other chameleons forced into exile. A way to get back to the country I loved: Thailand.

I fired off résumés to refugee agencies and landed a job with one, an organization based in Vermont.

A few weeks later, on the plane to Bangkok, I marveled at my luck. I was to be an "American culture orientation specialist" at the Phanat Nikhom refugee camp, two hours southeast of Bangkok; an Indian refugee from Africa teaching Asian refugees how to adapt to American culture. This would be interesting, to say the least. It was time for me to add new skills to my repertoire. More new names to adapt to: 'refugee worker'; 'American culture specialist.'

My six years in America had been a collage of university life in the Midwest and on the West Coast, and temporary jobs in New York as teacher's aide and salesman in Gimbel's department store. During two summers, I hitchhiked across America, first from New York to Seattle via the north, and then from New York to Los Angeles via the deep south. Was this enough experience for me to be effective as an American culture specialist?

I couldn't wait to find out.

ଓ

Phanat Nikhom, the town where I was housed with eighty other educators, is in Chonburi province. It was only slightly bigger than Nakhon Nayok, boasting ten traffic lights, twenty mom-and-pop restaurants, but no movie theater. About ten kilometers from town, along a tarmac road lined with tapioca farms, the Thai government had put up bamboo huts to house 17,000 refugees. Most of them were Vietnamese and Cambodians bound eventually for America. The place was built on fifty *rai* of land fenced off with barbed wire, and was cramped and overcrowded. A few dirt roads ran through the camp, providing the only open space for kids to play. Food, water, and other rations, donated by the US Department of State, controlled by the Thai army, and distributed by one of the dozen refugee agencies, were hauled in every week from the capital. A medical center with basic supplies took care of health issues.

To save costs and accommodate the Thai government, the American Department of State agreed to hire Thai English-speaking teachers, trained by American supervisors, to deliver English-language and American culture knowledge to refugees during four-month cycles. Since most of the refugees knew no English, we recruited translators from the few that did among the camp's population. Their job was to interpret Thai English into the appropriate language for the refugee students in class. This multicultural hodgepodge in the classrooms had even more layers piled on by the policy makers in the camp.

Thai regulations stipulated that refugees, whether Vietnamese, Lao, or Cambodian, were allowed to work only as volunteers with no salary. The rationale was that if they were allowed to make money, it would only serve as an incentive for them to stay longer in Thailand. They were also prohibited from leaving the camp except in the case of medical emergencies, or for resettlement. Those bound for America had to graduate from the training cycle as a pre-requisite to resettlement. Thereafter, US Immigration and Naturalization agents interviewed each refugee (with their own interpreters) to determine their eligibility for resettlement.

Those approved as political refugees—people who had collaborated with the Americans during the war and whose lives would be in danger if they returned home—would be transported to Bangkok to board the C-47s managed by the International Committee for Migration, a Geneva-based refugee transport agency. The UNHCR was given the task of protecting the refugees from any human rights abuses, although the Thai army had the final say on any complaints. All economic refugees were rejected.

People of ten different nationalities, all with their own cultural biases and personal and political agendas, worked every day in this camp. Sometimes, powerful people like American congressmen, Thai army generals, and Hollywood movie stars, all with their own motives, came to visit for photo opportunities.

I fitted right in. There were too many categorical boxes for anyone to care who I was or how I got there. Unlike my Peace Corps experience, here, the Thai teachers never dared called me *khaek*, the derogatory term for Thais of Indian descent (or south Asians generally). Having been hired by an American agency, the Americans on site—both Immigration agents and teacher supervisors—just assumed I was one of them. One staff member from a European refugee agency even mistook me for a camp inmate. The refugees themselves, though baffled that I didn't look American or Thai, were only too happy to seek help from anybody, including me. No one cared whether I was an authentic American or not.

'Chameleon College' was my nickname for the RPC at Phanat Nikhom. I had arrived at another home.

∞

Nguyen was the first Amerasian child I ever met. Mother: Vietnamese, whereabouts unknown. Father: definitely American, had disappeared back to America when his war tour of duty was over, never to be heard from again. This twelve-year-old boy, dark skinned with curly black hair, dressed in rags but with cool sunglasses and a fake Rolex, was trying to pickpocket me when I caught him in the act. That was how we met.

I promised not to hand him over to his zone supervisor if he agreed to have a soft drink with me at the camp's Sunday market. He hesitated, confused that I wasn't angry. As long as I would throw in a bowl of *pho* (Vietnamese noodle soup) with the drink, he was willing.

"Teacher, you okay-man," he said to me in GI English as we walked over to the market.

His English turned out to be surprisingly good, and he boasted that, besides this and Vietnamese, he spoke some Thai and French, too. I tested him in both. To my great surprise, he wasn't making any of it up. He was both smart and street smart. I asked him to tell me about his journey from Vietnam.

Unlike many children in his situation ("unaccompanied minors" as we educators later classified them), Nguyen had miraculously survived the horrific three-week boat journey from Saigon to Songkhla in southern Thailand. In the Gulf of Thailand, a pirate ship—almost certainly an armed Thai trawler—attacked their boat. The raiders stole all the money and gold and raped some of the women on board. Nguyen's sister was one of them. She never recovered, and died two days before a Thai Coast Guard vessel rescued them from near starvation and brought them ashore near Songkhla.

Shuffled from camp to camp over the next few months, Nguyen had landed at Phanat RPC two months before he tried to liberate me of my wallet. A boy chameleon of circumstance, my heart went out to him.

"Why aren't you in English class for minors?" I asked him.

"I went for two weeks," he replied. "Too simple and too boring."

"Who do you live with in camp?" I continued.

He gobbled up the last of the noodles before answering, "With family in Zone C. You have a job for me?"

He didn't miss a beat. I nodded and cajoled him into becoming a translator for a class of unaccompanied minors like himself. I had to bribe him with an agency T-shirt and cap before he agreed.

Over the next few days, I trained him in the job. Once he realized the attention and respect the students gave him in class, helped by the T-shirt and cap, he showed up every day. Evenings, he pored over the lesson plans with me and the Thai teacher, identifying the Vietnamese vocabulary he would have to prepare for the following day. On the weekends, I would treat him to bowls of *pho* and pork baguette sandwiches at the market.

One evening, at his suggestion, we brought food from the market to share with his Vietnamese relatives in Zone C. Only then was I made aware that Nguyen had no real family in the camp. The family he was living with had no blood ties to him, but had simply adopted him. His 'mother's' parting words to me after dinner: "Teacher, you no look American, but you be good American father for Nguyen?"

That's when Nguyen became my 'adopted' chameleon son. We were already nearly inseparable, so his mother's words struck a chord in me.

Within a few months, under my tutelage, he became the head translator, training new interpreters how to manage the students and prepare for class each day. Every morning, he would bring fresh baguettes from the market. Weekends, we would go to the camp's Buddhist temple to pay respects to his dead sister. Once, I even sneaked him out of camp to visit the town to do some shopping for him and his family.

Some nine months later, Nguyen's adopted family passed the interview with US Immigration and was accepted for resettlement in California. Nguyen, claimed by Mama as her biological son, was to go with them. I kept my mouth shut when Immigration wanted to verify with me that Nguyen truly was her legal son.

Would he survive in America, I wondered. Would the California cops and the Wyoming rednecks treat him any better than they did me? Would he embrace America or flee as soon as he had the means to do so? Would I find him again some day?

At the airport in Bangkok, our farewell hugs were a bittersweet mixture of tears and laughter. I gave Nguyen one of the Buddha amulets my Thai 'mother' in Nakhon Nayok had given me. I told him it was a lucky talisman that would help him ward off evil spirits in America. He promised to guard it safely until we met again.

Five long years would pass before I would see my chameleon 'son' and the Buddha amulet again.

∞

Upon completing our first four-month training cycle, all the American supervisors gathered in Bangkok during R 'n' R to brainstorm on the results and lessons learned. Going through bottles of Mekhong whiskey and Kloster beer, we all agreed that the classroom methodology used by the Thai teachers was not sufficiently preparing our refugee students for America. We could do better. But how?

Howie from Vermont came up with the brainwave of simulating an American supermarket in camp. The idea grabbed us all. If refugees actually went through the motions of grocery shopping, they would learn more about the reality involved. That was when the idea was hatched of building our own "Giant," a well-known American supermarket chain, in Phanat Nikhom RPC.

For weeks afterward, any educator who went to Bangkok was commissioned to bring back American products, labels, and wrappers. American dollars were collected from the Monopoly game; American food containers, jars, and bottles were saved for the project. Boxes, tins, cartons, and packets were then meticulously pasted with price tags and expiration dates by classroom aides. Soon we had enough stock for a grand opening.

One of the classrooms was converted into a supermarket, complete with wooden shelves stocked with pretend groceries, four rickety shopping carts (borrowed from a store in Phanat Nikhom), and two home-made cash registers stuffed with Monopoly dollars and made-up American coins and discount coupons. The Thai teachers, American supervisors, and refugee translators transformed into supermarket managers, stock boys, and cashiers who wore

Giant uniforms and spoke only English. Nguyen was one of the stock boys, sporting a Giant apron and hat.

Refugees were invited to go grocery shopping and look for bargain prices and special discounts. Each one was given a budget of Monopoly money and had to make their own grocery list, select necessary goods for a week (after reading labels and checking for expiration dates), calculate the total cost (mentally) to keep within budget, and finally pay at the cash register and count their correct change. All this had to be done in English only and within the 45 minutes of one normal class period. Observers, dressed incognito, graded each shopper's skills.

Petrified at first, each rotating class gained more and more confidence with each week of shopping. Mistakes turned into laughter as the refugees made the mental connection that no one, no matter how slow, would be beaten or killed by the Viet Cong or Pol Pot's boy soldiers or the Pathet Lao's secret police (although that prospect may have lurked at the back of their minds if they failed the orientation tests and were denied relocation to the United States). It then became a fun game for them to see who would win the weekly prize for the best shopping performance in the whole class.

Some of the shoppers' comments, during analysis in class, had us doubled up with laughter.

"Folgers American coffee no good. Vietnam coffee number one."

"McDonald's cheeseburger make me sick. Saigon baguette delicious. Cheap, too!"

Over the next few months, a simulated post office, fast-food restaurant, and job placement center sprang up in camp. Shopping at Giant, mailing letters at the post office, or eating at 'Kentucky Fried Chicken' became a weekly event for Vietnamese mothers dressed up in their Sunday-best *ao dai*—the traditional Vietnamese outfit.

I must admit that there were times during the simulations project that I found myself wishing I had had this kind of help before being dumped in England from Uganda with no clue about British supermarkets or pounds and pence, not to mention the British police harassing old Asian ladies in the streets of London at three in the morning. That was when I resolved to introduce "Racism in America" as one of the lessons in the cultural orientation curriculum, irrespective of whether my counterpart American educators agreed with the idea or not.

ଔ

The Vietnam War had been over for only a few years, and already Hollywood was replaying the conflict on the silver screen. Francis Ford Coppola's *Apocalypse Now* captured the madness of war with bald-headed Marlon Brando as a demi-god commanding his own private army of gooks in the Cambodian jungle. *The Deer Hunter*, with Robert De Niro, dramatized the inhumane treatment of American prisoners in a Viet Cong jail. Other movies like *Coming Home* and *Born On The Fourth Of July* showed a different side of America: the negative reception that war veterans received when they came home. Three of these movies were nominated for and received Oscar awards.

The bootleg copies of Vietnam movies circulating in Thailand always miraculously made their way into our camp. Everyone was talking about them. Nguyen bugged me to let him see the *The Deer Hunter* when it arrived. We didn't know how to handle this Hollywood invasion. As educators, we agonized over how our refugee students would react to these films. Would the movies help to heal the pain of their horrific journeys just to make it to Thailand? Or would they scare the hell out of the refugees about America, their future home? Would the films release demons (like mine still are whenever I see crocodiles and guava trees), or would the tears invoked by some scenes banish the demons forever? I wasn't sure.

Many of my American colleagues were vehemently against showing the films. The Thai teachers thought we Americans were making too big a deal and underestimating the mental resilience of our students. I claimed that since the movies were circulating in camp anyway, it would be hypocritical of us to ignore them. The opportunity to discuss these movies in the classroom was here and we should take it. Eventually, the decision was left up to individual educators.

One evening, I decided to show *The Deer Hunter* to one of my Vietnamese advanced English classes. De Niro, Christopher Walken, and Meryl Streep, in the first forty minutes of the movie, acted out working-class lives in Pennsylvania. The refugees were mesmerized. The scenes of the men's farewell party, the night before the long flight to the war, even generated a few laughs. But once the Russian roulette scenes in the Viet Cong prison camp commenced, tears silently dripped down some cheeks in the audience. The pain was evident in their eyes. No one spoke after the movie ended. Everyone made a beeline to their overcrowded huts.

In class the next day, they kept asking questions about factory work and Pennsylvania without once mentioning the Russian roulette scenes. When I probed delicately about those scenes, most of them agreed on a comment made by one student: "VC soldiers very bad people. Vietnamese people don't play Russian roulette."

The next evening, to show a contrasting viewpoint, I let the same class watch *Coming Home*, starring Jane Fonda, Jon Voight, and Bruce Dern, an anti-war movie depicting conflicting views on the war's effect in the US. The movie generated much discussion in class. They all wanted to talk at once. They fired questions at me, one after another. Why did America hate its own soldiers? Why were American war veterans treated worse than the rats plaguing our camp? Why did America leave Vietnam without finishing off the Viet Cong? Even young Nguyen demanded, "Why does America hate Vietnam?" I just shook my head. I had no answers to any of their questions.

That night, unable to sleep, I kept looking at my blue American passport, admiring the insignia of the eagle clasping the olive branch in its right talons and the bunch of arrows in the left. "Who am I?" I kept asking myself over and over till I fell asleep.

Meanwhile, movies that depicted this war from a Vietnamese perspective didn't get much attention. The well-researched documentary *Hearts And Minds*, made while the war was still going on, was the first real exposé of the horrors caused by Agent Orange on the rice paddies of Vietnam and the Machiavellian power broking inside the White House and the US Congress. Oliver Stone, who won best-director Oscars for *Platoon* and *Born On The Fourth Of July*, was not considered by the Academy for depicting the consequences of war on Vietnamese farmers in *Heaven And Earth* (his later Vietnam film, made in 1993). Neither *Hearts And Minds* nor *Heaven And Earth* were distributed in major cinemas in America; neither of them became a box office hit; neither of them won any Oscar awards.

∽

Through the refugees, the Vietnam War had left its mark on me, but it wasn't until years after my time at Phanat Nikhom camp that I had a chance to visit the country. In 1998, I went on a month-long journey from Saigon (now called Ho Chi Minh City) to Hanoi. By this time, the United States had re-opened diplomatic relations with Vietnam, and the Vietnamese government, now starved of Soviet funds after the fall of communism, had opened its doors to the outside world. I was excited to take a trip to Nguyen's homeland to see for myself how the country, isolated from most of the world for over twenty years after the war, had coped.

In Ho Chi Minh City, during the hustle and bustle of the morning rush hour, thousands of fair-skinned girls in colorful *ao dais* rode off to work or school on motorcycles. Clad in white gloves up to their elbows and with bandanas tied across their faces to cut out the dust and pollution, they looked like bandits escaping with the loot from a robbery. Good morning Viet*naaaam*!

The war museum in the city was housed in what was once the USIS (United States Information Services) building. Perfect irony. A broken-down tank languished in the gardens. Inside, an array of American weapons was displayed—rocket launchers, rifles, napalm canisters, flame throwers—all speaking for themselves, no descriptive plaques needed or provided. On one shelf stood jars containing deformed babies, preserved in formaldehyde, mangled from the effects of Agent Orange. I shuddered at the sight. On the walls, black and white pictures showed throngs of people protesting the war on the streets of Paris, Buenos Aires, Lagos, Beijing, Kent State University in Ohio.

As I was leaving the museum, I spotted an older American man wearing a New York Yankees cap. He was talking in a low voice to his teenage son, who sported a New York Knicks T-shirt. Eavesdropping as I passed them by, I heard the old man recounting his war memories to his son, tears streaming down his cheeks. I left the museum and the city quickly after that, angry again with the American government.

The four-dollar entry fee to the Cu Chi Tunnels, forty kilometers from Saigon, was well worth the price. Escorted by Thanh, a former South Vietnamese soldier turned tour guide, our group of eight backpackers piled out of the minibus to a marvelous scene of jade-green rice fields stretching to the horizon. Two rosy cheeked girls, clad in orange and purple sarongs and wearing conical straw hats, looked up from their harvesting chores to wave to us. Descending into a small entrance nearby, we crawled into a dark, two-kilometer-long tunnel, reconstructed for tourists to represent the 200 kilometers of tunnels used by the North Vietnamese and Viet Cong to attack, infiltrate, and spy on American forces stationed in and around Saigon. Thanh, eager in his well-rehearsed, non-stop commentary of what took place in these tunnels, explained how a circle of North Vietnamese generals had studied plans for the final attack on Saigon at the very same rickety wooden table we were now standing beside.

"How did the Viet Cong get in and out of these tunnels into Saigon?" asked a skeptical backpacker.

Thanh grinned and pointed to one of the many foot-wide rectangular holes in the tunnel ceiling that we saw along the way. "Holes wide enough for Vietnam infantry to escape, but too small for fat American soldiers to pursue," he replied, and then broke into a laugh.

True or not, I couldn't help but admire his turncoat confidence. His khaki uniform proudly displayed the tour agency name: "Kim's Café Vietnam War Tours."

I made my way north to the cooler weather of Da Lat, where I slept in the honeymoon suite of a fifteen-room guesthouse built inside and around a huge banyan tree. The wall facing my bed was part of the huge trunk. Birds kept me company all night long.

In Nha Trang, now a beachside party town for backpackers, I went on Mama Han's seven-dollar boat trip into Cam Ranh Bay, a huge Soviet naval base only two decades before. On board, thirty foreign backpackers danced to blaring rock 'n' roll and reggae, guzzled mulberry wine from plastic cups and smoked Vietnamese *gancha* on the way to a snorkeling site. At the snorkel site, in the waters where Russian submarines once lurked, the boat crew served up more mulberry wine on floating wooden crates while we swam and dived. The ride back to Nha Trang remains fuzzy in my mind. One kind backpacker helped me find my guesthouse when we got off the boat. Months later, I heard from friends that Mama Han, known to be a motorcyle drug queen of sorts, was put behind bars, charges undisclosed.

By the time I got to the romantic port town of Hoi An, halfway between Ho Chi Minh City and Hanoi, I was ready to rest for a while. Renting a bicycle for one dollar a day, I rode the few kilometers to Cua Dai Beach—and was increasingly pestered by young boys and girls to buy their wares the closer I got to the ocean.

"You buy! You buy!" one boy pleaded with me. "You no buy, my mother beat me, na! You please buy, na!"

"What's your name and why aren't you in school?" I asked.

"Tranh is my name, selling my after-school game," he rhymed back perfectly with a smile. Just one of the many lines these savvy young entrepreneurs came up with to make tourists part with their cash.

I was fascinated by his broken-English ploys and his persistence. I cycled on without buying anything, but he reminded me of Nguyen back at Phanat Nikhom. The last I had heard from the family in California, Nguyen was a computer whiz in high school and also managed the account books for the family grocery store in Santa Ana.

Children were everywhere on the streets of Vietnam. Mothers carrying babies made it a point to encourage them to greet every foreigner they saw. Come three o' clock when school was over, children would spill out onto the streets with their home-made wooden trays, and scatter across the villages, towns, or cities to sell, sell, sell. In the cities they hawked postcards, cigarettes, and bootleg photocopies of the Lonely Planet guidebooks. In the villages they sold straw hats and local souvenirs.

On the sandy beach, a group of five cornered me: two boys with Chiclets and imported cigarettes, and three girls with fresh pineapples, oranges, and dragon fruit, all in season. Tranh, who had followed me to the beach, was their leader. On a whim, I decided to try an experiment with him and his gang of entrepreneurs.

"If I promise to buy two things from each of you, you must agree to play on the beach for the next two hours. Okay?"

They all looked at me suspiciously at first. The questions were endless. What was I up to? How could they be sure I would keep my promise at the end of the two hours? What if their mothers caught them playing on the beach and not selling their quota for the day?

They must leave before five o' clock for Hoi An City Hall to sell to the workers on their way home.

Once assured that I was sincere in my offer, they had a private meeting among themselves. When they came back, Tranh made me specify the two things I would buy from each of them, the price I would pay for each item, and when the playing time would be over. Finally, after twenty minutes, we concluded our negotiations.

Twenty minutes. Smiles all around. Back in 1973, it took Henry Kissinger and Le Duc Tho twenty days—while the killing continued on both sides—to agree on which directions the tables they sat at would face during the peace treaty in Paris. Later that year, both men were awarded the Nobel Peace Prize for negotiating the end of the war. Kissenger accepted the award; Le Duc Tho did not.

Once the deal was made, instant change came over the children. The wooden trays were put aside, the day's money tucked away in a safe place. Now the group morphed from business-minded entrepreneurs with daily goals and net profit to children wanting to play. Let the games begin.

The piggyback tug of war, two per team in the lukewarm water, was an instant success. Even with strong Tranh on my back, we got toppled into the water by one other boy-and-girl team. We rotated partners till all five of them had a turn on my back. Nothing but laughter. Their reminders of my promise to buy their goods were soon forgotten. Burying the strange-looking American from neck to toe in sand induced more peals of laughter. Even the old lady vendor sitting alone on the beach with her tray of Vietnamese sweet treats broke into a howl.

Next we started a race to build sandcastle replicas of Uncle Ho's Mausoleum. The sacred monument created by the girls—with the Vietnamese flag on top, borrowed from a nearby shop—was done and dusted before we boys were even halfway finished. The hours passed and no one noticed until Tranh looked up at the sun and said something in Vietnamese. Instant change again. They morphed back into entrepreneurs and demanded their dues. I kept my promise and bought everything I said I would and gave them more dong notes for each item than what we had agreed. At first they refused the extra money politely. Then, Tranh, always the leader, came up with a bright idea. Running over to the old lady, he used up all the extra dong to buy bags of sweet desserts. The old lady, quite taken aback by this sudden surge in business, beamed him the widest smile, exposing her teeth, rotten and blood-red from betel nut juice. Half the sweets Tranh distributed among the gang, and the other half he gave to me. When it was time to leave, Tranh hugged me, the girls waved in unison, and the other boy gave me a thumbs-up sign before they all sped off to City Hall.

Only when they were out of sight did I realize that my rubber sandals next to my locked-up bicycle were missing. I looked all over but they were nowhere in sight. Had the kids really taken them? Had I been duped, after all? Minutes later, the old lady hobbled over to me, led me by the arm to a spot in the sand, and motioned for me to dig. As I unearthed my sandals, she cackled and pointed in the direction the children had gone.

On the ride back to town, one thought kept recurring: this old lady, the child entrepreneurs of Hoi An, Mama Han—all were budding capitalists. Where were the communist hordes that had threatened America's free enterprise so frightfully that we had to destroy their country with bombs and napalm?

⋈

In Hanoi, Ho Chi Minh's Mausoleum is in Ba Dinh Square, near one of the many lakes in the city. Inside the massive edifice, his embalmed body—in traditional dress with both hands placed across his chest—lies encased in a glass sarcophagus. Pilgrims wishing to pay homage to the father of the nation line up for hours to get inside, and uniformed guards patrol the site to ensure that all visitors are properly attired and behaved: no hats, no shorts, no hands in pockets. Hoi, a cute 22-year-old Vietnamese returnee from Switzerland, and a member of our tour group, was clad in shorts. She was forbidden entry until she went back to our minibus to change into long pants.

In his glass resting place, Uncle Ho exuded serenity. His gray goatee spiraled from his chin. Here was the man who masterminded the defeat of the American war machine, the self-educated villager who had left his homeland in 1911 for the United States and Europe, become a founding member of the French Communist Party, and returned home thirty years later to fight a guerrilla war for his country's freedom. I clasped my hands together in a traditional *wai* to the great chameleon who had changed the course of modern history in Asia. Next to me, I noticed Hoi whispering to Uncle Ho as if at confession, as if atoning for her sins.

Back on the minibus, I started up a conversation with Hoi, curious to find out what she had 'confessed' to the nation's father. She replied that she had prayed to him in the hope that the country would one day live up to his expectations. As we talked, her inner pain at being ostracized by her fellow countrymen—in the country she once called home—revealed itself. At the age of nine, she had fled on one of the boats. Luckily she survived the journey, spent two years in Thai refugee camps, and was resettled in Basel, Switzerland. Thirteen years later, with a degree in sociology and fluent in English and French, she had finally managed to save enough money to make the trip back to Vietnam. But the long-awaited return to the motherland had been a disappointment. Relatives in the village where she was born were more interested in her Swiss presents than her life there. People on the streets of Saigon and Hanoi had scorned her publicly as "traitor." The tears brimmed in her eyes.

Earlier, I had noticed that both the minibus driver and the tour guide had repeatedly ignored her questions during the day's sightseeing. Now I knew why. She was yet another chameleon caught between two worlds and belonging to neither. Just like Nguyen. Just like Uncle Ho. I felt like hugging her tight to make that feeling go away. Instead, I offered her some of my dragon fruit and smiled as we got off the bus to visit the next tourist site.

Hoi's pain lingered with me all day and forced me to think of my own. Idi Amin had been ousted two decades before, content to live out his last years in luxurious exile in Saudi Arabia with his numerous wives and 45 children. Should I thank him again for kicking me out of Uganda so I could explore the rest of the world? Or should I still curse him again and again for taking away the one thing I could never replace?

On the plane leaving Hanoi Airport, I thought back to the time when, after five years in the refugee camps of Southeast Asia, I had gone back to Balboa Beach in California for a friend's wedding. Passing through Santa Ana, on the way there, I saw a mall that had a pagoda entrance. My curiosity aroused, I stopped and went in. Could this be the place where Nguyen's family had a grocery store? The mall had every service and retail outlet imaginable: supermarkets, specialty stores, travel agents, restaurants, real estate agents, dentists, tailors, barbers. All Vietnamese. I found Nguyen working on the accounts for his family's Vietnamese grocery store. He jumped up and held me close for a long time. No words were needed.

Over dinner that evening, he told me about his life in California since leaving the camp. The scrawny pickpocket dressed in rags had turned into a flashy high-school kid with Ray-Bans, Levis, and an all-American attitude. He had been awarded a scholarship to start freshman year in computer studies at the University of California in Long Beach. When we parted, he showed me the Buddha amulet I had given him in Bangkok to ward off evil spirits, and asked if he could still keep it. I said yes, of course, it was his. Then, from his pocket, he fished out another: a Vietnamese one to protect me wherever I was going next. That same amulet, now hanging on a string around my neck, felt warm against my chest. I twirled it fondly as the plane from Hanoi began its descent into Bangkok.

 beginning

Back in Phanat Nikhom, there was a plague of rats in the camp during the rainy season. All the aid agencies complained bitterly to the Thai authorities, pleading with them to do something about it. The Thai army commander, the man with absolute power in camp, decided the best way to handle this problem was to give the refugees an incentive. Side-stepping the official Thai policy of no income activity for refugees, he offered every resident one Thai baht for every rat caught dead or alive. The plan seemed to work as, every day, a representative from each zone hauled in a sack of dead rats to collect the reward, sometimes as much as 25 baht (at that time, one American dollar). Everyone was happy with this arrangement except the rats.

The rat-hunting spree went on for two months and then petered out mysteriously. The Thai authorities happily assumed that the rat plague was over. A few weeks later, to their horror, the invasion started all over again, this time with more rats than before, though much smaller in size. The 'one rat, one baht' project had to be reactivated. Puzzled as to why the rats were now much smaller, the Thai health authorities began an investigation in each of the refugee zones. It turned out that many of the refugees realized that the rat program, though not especially lucrative, was nevertheless a good way to make some money—and they had cannily taken to breeding the rats in secret to ensure more long-term income.

The army commander was not amused. After that incident, all incentive projects promoted by the aid agencies were brought to an abrupt halt. Poor Nguyen was distraught that his weekly pocket money from rats had disappeared overnight. I couldn't help but admire the ingenuity of our budding refugee entrepreneurs. They would do well in America, I thought to myself at the time.

ᥖ

It wasn't too long after the rat episode that I was asked by my agency to transfer to another refugee camp, this one in Indonesia, to work with Muslim teachers preparing Cambodian and Vietnamese refugees for America. I would be there for a year and was promised that I could return to Thailand when the year was over. Why not, I said to myself. An opportunity to re-acquaint myself with my Muslim roots.

3. Islam And Me

Where would the world be today if they had
decided to build a mosque and synagogue here?
Anonymous visitor to 9/11
"Ground Zero," New York.

Islam and I had a love-hate relationship all through my childhood.

Ramadan, the Muslim month of fasting, bothered me every year as a young boy. No parent or sibling sat me down to explain why I had to go without food after sunrise till sunset. "Tradition"; "The will of Allah"; "Builds character." These were the answers to my questions. None helped quell the hunger during the daylight hours.

One Ramadan, around noon, at a market in Kampala, an African vendor offered me a meter-long sugar cane stalk for a measly few shillings, normally priced five times higher. Saliva dripped down my lower lip as I imagined tearing away the skin with my teeth to chew the inside, with the sweet juice sliding down my throat.

"Hey, Muslim, *muhindi*, will your God let you eat this *kikajo* today?"

I deliberated. Was my Muslim background that obvious? He laughed at my dilemma, baiting me to break the fast by holding out the stalk. I fled to a mosque nearby, sat in front of it with my head in my hands. For an hour, I debated with Allah the pros and cons of breaking his will. Would I go to hell if I broke the fast? Why was he so cruel as to deny me food throughout the day? What did fasting have to do with being a good boy? How could chewing on one sugar cane stalk damn me to purgatory? Surely, omnipotent God, you are more compassionate than that.

Allah lost. Before I could change my mind, I got up and bolted back to the market, praying that the vendor hadn't sold my cane already. I bought it and chewed off the whole stalk within twenty minutes, in hiding of course. My secret and guilt were safe with me.

Idd-el-Fitr, celebrating the end of Ramadan, however, was pure heaven for me. Those mornings—as long as I attended the *Namaaz* prayer, recited in Arabic, and kissed the ground in mosque while proclaiming "Allah O Akbar" a few times in unison with all present—my relatives would give me gifts of money. All I had to say to each of them afterwards was "*Idd mubarak*" and they would flick out their wallets. Some of the older, forgetful ones, I hit on two times. In a good year, I collected three times more cash than my monthly allowance and received other gifts like clothes.

One year, my parents bought me a Van Heusen shirt, a silk tie, and a brand-new Italian-cut suit and shoes for the mosque events. Some of my male relatives dressed in white *kurtas* for prayers, while others wore Western clothes. I wore my *kurta* for prayers and Western clothes for the night celebrations, to impress the girls at both events. The celebrations at night included a feast of barbecued goat and marinated lamb. At the music party later, all the girls pranced around in new saris, and singers sang lots of *gazaal* ballads accompanied by tablas and accordions. As they were sung in Urdu, I didn't understand most of them, but the food was plentiful and delicious.

At times, Islam and I also had a confusing relationship. I could never understand why the *mukhi* at mosque requested donations in return for sprinkling holy water, *niaz*, all over my face. Deemed blessed, this water in Uganda had supposedly been touched by the Aga Khan, our spiritual leader, who lived in Paris and spoke French as his native language. Pressured by my family, I usually donated twenty shillings from my allowance. When I didn't have the right coins and had to use notes, the *mukhi* even gave me change from the stacks of money on his sacred table before he blessed me in Gujarati. I assumed he must be a banker in his day job.

Eating pork is forbidden for Muslims. Half of the siblings in my family ate pork and the other half, including my parents, didn't. The mixed signals only increased my confusion. When I was twelve, I ate my first ham sandwich. It tasted great, and yet I threw up immediately. Having been told by Bahadur—my older, unorthodox brother— that this prohibition of pork was institutionalized by the Prophet Mohammed nearly 1,500 years ago, to keep his people from gluttony and to prevent stomach parasites, I was upset with myself for both throwing up and succumbing to this psychological brainwashing. So I ordered another ham sandwich—and forced myself to keep it down this time. Since then, pork and I have been good friends.

All three of my brothers believed that the Koran, just like the Bible or the Bhagavad-Gita, was written to help us tell right from wrong. Two of my five sisters believed that it was the word of God passed onto the Prophet Mohammed. Yet my father, who meditated at mosque every morning at four a.m., narrated bedtime stories to us younger siblings not from the Koran but from the Bhagavad-Gita. Me? I thought that all the religious books I read in the English versions—the Koran, the Bible, the Bhagavad-Gita—were great literature.

At home, my mother and father recited the holy *Dua* twice a day in Arabic. Some of my sisters joined them occasionally to keep them company. I didn't take part. At Aga Khan Secondary School, during religious-studies periods, we had to memorize the *Dua* in Arabic. I was suspended for three days for refusing to say my prayers in Arabic, a language I did not know or understand, although I knew them verse for verse in English.

Though I had a confusing relationship with Islam, it taught me many good things as a child. I learned to be a good volunteer by helping the elderly to chairs and by serving food to them at religious festivals. I also learned Islamic compassion from my parents. One day, after school sports, I was too hungry to wait for dinner, and dipped into a delicious dish reserved for mosque. Ma gave me such a verbal thrashing, which was followed by a harsher physical one from Bapuji, my father, the same night. Only then did I realize that the best dishes were not to be touched. These *had* to be taken to mosque, so the poorer families could buy them cheaply at the after-prayer food auction. (More often than not, the rich outbid the poor anyway.)

My father taught me how to meditate so that I could seek peace of mind—a practice I've found useful throughout my life to seek solutions to difficult situations. My meditation mantra—'*ayinga*'—has been a faithful partner in my head, ever since. From reading the Koran with Bapuji, I also learned that the sacred book praises prophets from other faiths, too.

I learned many bad things about Islam when I got older, though. I learned that some of my Muslim brothers in other countries mutilated the female clitoris to promote chastity; chopped off the hands of thieves caught in the act of robbery; made their women wear black curtains from head to toe in the hot sun; and stoned them to death for adultery.

Then, politicians, in the name of religion, went to war and confused me even more.

After the Second World War, the Middle East conflict began. Israel, through the help of the war victors, became a nation in the middle of an Arabian desert. On television, I saw Palestinian refugees living in barbed-wire camps in their own land. Later, I read about Arabs like Yasser Arafat and Anwar Sadat, and Jews like Moshe Dayan and Ariel Sharon transformed into heroes for perpetrating death in the name of Allah and Yahweh. Mosques and synagogues were burned down, and later, a wall, just like that in Berlin, was erected to keep people separated. The stakes? Desert land where, supposedly, Moses and Jesus and Mohammed once lived. And of course, oil—the lifeblood of modern industrial nations.

My confusion was now beyond tolerance. Wasn't religion supposed to teach us how to live peacefully alongside our neighbors?

But the conflict only escalated. People with power, from many countries, took sides and gave money and guns to all of the combatants to support the hostilities. Soon, Arab children became suicide bombers. Israeli girls brandished Uzi submachine guns at border towns. The conflict spilled over into the countries with people of power.

Peace negotiations hosted by America, European countries, and the UN fell apart over and over again. Then came "9/11," followed by American retaliation, followed by more suicide bombers, until 'Muslim' became a dirty word in many circles.

Me? I hid from all this madness by plunging into my books

Somehow, amidst all the confusion and the good and the bad, I learned to distinguish right from wrong for myself, and realized that God was within me and within Nature, and not in some mosque, temple, church, or synagogue.

During my youth, on one of the seven hills of Kampala I found a beautiful Bahá'i temple, with pictures of all the world's religions around its circular walls. I began to meditate there, like my father had taught me: to look for a god within myself, a god with no name and no color. I prayed that this same god would engender in me the will to do good deeds.

As time passed, I prayed that this god would find and help all the crazy people killing each other in the name of religion, using code names like 'democracy' and "*Intifada*."

೦೩

After Phanat Nikhom, I was a little apprehensive about the upcoming year in Muslim Indonesia. My real name was the first giveaway. I was named Mohezin after 'muezzin,' the man who calls the faithful to morning prayers all over the Muslim world. I was doomed from the start. The other inspiration for my name, according to my father, was a fusing of Mohammed Ali Zinnah, the first prime minister of independent Pakistan. This was equally foreboding. No wonder then that I was apprehensive about being slung into another box by my Muslim brothers. In Indonesia, I decided I would stick with my self-given nickname, Mo—short and simple, and much harder to pin down the origins.

The flight from Bangkok to Singapore was short and sweet. At Singapore's Changi Airport, I was amazed with the efficiency and sophistication. Used to signs in foreign languages and slow service in Asian airports, I was surprised by all the English spoken around me; the comfortable sofas, movie channels, free showers, and nap rooms; and the punctuality and organization of the helpful staff. I stood in the Immigration queue next to a sign that warned of a fine for hailing a taxi on the street. I felt like I was back in a Western country.

I made my way to the ferry port in a taxi. The Indian driver complained to me in Hindi about how the Singaporeans focused more and more on making lots of money and how their various family values were rapidly being eroded. He said that both of his own children, now in college, showed little respect for their parents' wishes. He made me wonder if my parents, now living in Vancouver, Canada, thought the same of me. We made it to the port just in time for the ferry to Tanjung Pinang on the Indonesian island of Bintan.

Tanjung Pinang, a border town that thrived on contraband goods smuggled in from Singapore, was our staging post before we moved on to the nearby island of Galang, where refugees from Vietnam and Cambodia, and a small number from Laos, were temporarily accommodated.

During the first three days in Tanjung Pinang, while waiting for the agency's local staff to process my Indonesian P3V military intelligence visa to gain access to Galang RPC, I soaked up the basic survival vocabulary of Bahasa Indonesia, wandering in and out of mosques during the day, and lapping up chilli crabs and *nasi goreng* at the night market. It must have been at least ten years since I'd last visited a mosque—a weekly event during my youth in Uganda. In Tanjung Pinang, real Muslim food—goat and lamb curries—that I hadn't eaten since my mother's home cooking in Kampala, was now available at every corner.

"*Selamat pagi! Kamu, dari mana? Pergi dimana?*" people asked me on the streets. 'Morning. You, from where? Going where?'

"*Jalan, jalan,*" I replied. 'Walking, walking.'

Bahasa Indonesia was going to be much easier to parrot than Thai. No speech tones to remember, and easy tenses.

Only when the P3V visa was finally approved, was I made aware that only six Westerners—five male Americans and one Canadian female—were allowed this multiple-entry, year-long special visa to live and work on the island. We were to start up the English-language and American culture program for the 30,000 or so refugees already housed in barracks. Agency bosses visiting from America or Bangkok to monitor the program would have to meet with the six of us in Singapore. We were on our own.

The muezzin's wake up call—"Allah O Akbar!"—echoed over the pier as I stepped into the speedboat with two other Americans, Steve and Fred, for the hour-long ride to Galang Island. Besides our luggage, each of us carried a case of Heineken tightly wrapped in plastic bags with the Pepsi logo. Alcohol, smuggled into Tanjung Pinang from Singapore, was prohibited on Galang, so we devised our own ways of getting it over. The agency staff warned us to drink our beer only in Pepsi cans and only in the privacy of our dorm rooms.

I pondered over how this coming year would be for me. New place, new name, new language, new categorical box. Muslim brother? Shia believer? Was I one of them?

Indonesia both scared and excited me. Spread out over an archipelago of some 13,700 islands, about 6,000 of them inhabited, it was home to 180 million people at that time. Ninety percent of them were Muslim, making it the country with the world's largest Islamic population. What if the Indonesian teachers on Galang wanted me to face Mecca to pray with them to a God I had forsaken while eating juicy sugar cane during Ramadan? Would they view Idi Amin as a Muslim hero? Would they ostracize me for being a pork-eating, beer-guzzling pagan who hadn't recited the holy *Dua* in ten years, let alone five times a day? Would they understand what it means to have a chameleon body with Muslim spots peppered here and there? I decided that my Muslim roots would remain a secret on Galang until I was sure that the thirty Indonesian teachers had accepted me for my work contribution rather than my heritage.

The sun, as yet a pale orange ball, shimmered off the churning water as our boat bounced over the waves. To our left, breakfast smoke rose from houses on Penyengat Island, once the home of the sultans of the Riau Archipelago.

The pier at Galang was buzzing with activity. A decrepit trawler was unloading a large group of sea-weary refugees; Cambodian I presumed, from the style of their sarongs. Indonesian soldiers in fatigues shouted into megaphones as they herded the new arrivals towards the registration center. I wondered what horrors these people had been through to get here. Had they braved the seas like the boat people of Vietnam, or had they been shipped out of Thai refugee camps after having survived Pol Pot's genocidal army of child soldiers? The faces looked resigned, weather-beaten, especially the children.

The waves lapped gently on the beach as we docked.

At Site 1, lush green hills edged right up to the one-lane dirt road —the island's only infrastructure. Block upon block of wooden barracks, built into the hills like rice terraces, housed Cambodians and Vietnamese, in separate quarters. Clothes dried on makeshift poles, people 'showered' from water-filled drum barrels, children played in the dirt, a barber cut hair for a client sitting on a metal folding chair under a tree. I read the signs on the two-story wooden buildings: "UNHCR Office" said one; "Joint Voluntary Agency-JVA/USA Office" said another.

The Site 2 dormitory house, where all the Indonesian teachers and us six foreigners would live, had been completed only days before, and still smelled of fresh paint. U-shaped with a large courtyard in the middle, the concrete dorm contained forty tiny rooms. Inside each room were two single beds with mattresses, two tables and chairs, and one drum barrel to collect rainwater for bathing.

Next to the dorm was a mess hall with long wooden tables and folding chairs, where *Ibu* Hati was cooking up *nasi goreng* and vegetable *soto* for the first shift of teachers breaking up classes for an early lunch.

Fred, my roommate, and I took the room nearest to the mess hall and began unpacking our duffel bags.

"*Selamat pagi. Makan dulu?* Good morning. Have you eaten yet?" said a teacher returning from his class.

"*Belum. Kamu?*" I replied. 'Not yet. And you?'

As we followed him to the mess hall, I thought to myself, welcome to 'Chameleon College Number Two.'

❧

Days later, I was interviewing Sayeed Sary, a seventeen-year-old Cambodian, for a volunteer job as class interpreter. He was one of only a dozen or so Muslim refugees in camp.

"Many of the students in your class will be old enough to be your grandparents," I said to him. Cambodians—indeed all Asians—always show respect for their elders, and I was concerned how he, as class interpreter, would get the older refugees to follow the Indonesian teacher's instructions. It was a problem that somehow I hadn't worried about with Nguyen at Phanat.

Sayeed paused for a while, then replied, "Teacher, in Cambodia I saw Pol Pot's soldiers beat up and kill their own parents with shovels. I can do anything you ask me to."

I asked him to recount his story, which he did, in a matter-of-fact tone.

Born in the city of Kâmpóng Cham in eastern Cambodia, Sayeed was one of an estimated 200,000 Cambodian Cham Muslims. The Chams had been converted to Islam by early Arab traders, seafaring merchants who traveled down the coast of Africa and across the Indian Ocean in search of Oriental spices and silks. As a child, Sayeed learned to recite the *Dua* in Arabic, since the written Cham language had fallen into disuse. He spoke his native Cham dialect, but there was no alphabet for him to master.

I thought of my own linguistic background and realized how similar I was to Sayeed. I never did learn the *Dua* in Arabic, despite the school suspension. I too, had never learned how to read or write my mother tongue, Gujarati, spoken in Gujarat State in central India. In Uganda, no one in my family or community or school thought it important enough to teach me.

Sayeed could, however, read and write English and Khmer, having had good language teachers in the *madrasah* school he attended. He didn't touch pork, ate only halal food, and fasted during Ramadan. Dressed in a multicolored sarong, he had never worn a traditional fez and had no beard. I smiled. Another chameleon, but with many more Muslim spots on his body than mine. "Tell me how you got here to Galang?" I asked, and he told me his story.

When the Khmer Rouge got to Kâmpóng Cham, they first destroyed all the mosques and forbade his people to speak Cham. The women were ordered to discard their *chador* headscarves, cut their hair short, and work in the rice fields. Any elderly men who resisted the order to stop practicing Islam were shot in the town's square as an example to the others. Men who wore spectacles— suspected intellectuals or clerics—were carted away to be tortured, killed, and then buried in mass graves. Sayeed's father, a cleric and mosque guardian, was one of them.

Idi Amin's madness came rushing back to me as Sayeed went on. Only a decade before in Uganda, Amin's soldiers had rounded up academics at Makerere University, dragged them to Makindye Prison for torture, and then dumped their bodies in Lake Victoria for the crocodiles to feed on. Mad dictators seemed to follow me from Africa to Asia.

The mass graves that Sayeed referred to became known as the "Killing Fields." In the Hollywood movie of the same name, Cambodian Haing Ngor—a real-life survivor of the Khmer Rouge— would win an Oscar for his performance as a Western journalist's assistant. Ngor's Hollywood fame was short lived, and a few years later he was mugged and murdered in California. The suspects, believed to be a local Asian gang, were never apprehended.

Sayeed went on in his matter-of-fact tone: Male teenagers were torn from their parents and dragged off to re-education camps and forced to become soldiers in Pol Pot's army. Sayeed was sent to Battambang near the Thai border to plant rice, even though he had never been on a farm in his life. He never saw his mother and three sisters again. Along with hundreds of other men from his city, he was forced onto an overcrowded trawler, which took them on the

Mekong River, past Odong, and northwest across the great Tonle Sap Lake. At the end of the Tonle Sap, they made the fifty-kilometer journey to Battambang on foot. They were fed rice gruel once a day. Along the river, Sayeed saw many villages destroyed, thousands of fellow Cambodians on the move. Khmer Rouge militia, in their black pajama uniforms and red headbands, barked orders and flogged and beat the straggling captives. On the forced march, with no food, Sayeed teamed up with some other villagers to surreptitiously scavenge from papaya and banana trees wherever they could.

At Battambang, for the next eighteen months, he slogged in the burning sun, digging irrigation canals and harvesting rice that he never got to eat. At the compulsory re-education classes each night, where Sayeed often fell asleep through exhaustion, indoctrination sermons on the new Cambodia explained why April 17th, 1975—the day the Khmer Rouge entered Phnom Penh—was now defined as "Day One, Year Zero"; why Sayeed's parents were exploiters and had to be punished; why the mobile brigade he now lived with was his only family; why rice, the lifeblood of the country, was to be harvested collectively to free the nation from its past reliance on foreign aid.

Sayeed realized that he was doomed to die if he stayed in this hellhole. His ribs, once protected behind strong muscles, now jutted out from malnutrition. Malaria and dengue fever were rampant in his quarters. Escape was the only way out. Death by torture or a shovel blade would be quicker than death by starvation or sickness.

One night, Sayeed and three other escapees stole a cooking pot and as much rice as they could stuff in their pockets. They would brave the jungle escape route to the Thai border. For eleven days and nights they crept through the forest, heading west by day and sleeping in trees by night. When the rice ran out, they foraged for insects and jungle plants. Sarun, the youngest of the four, was too weak to continue and had to be left behind.

"Maybe Sarun died. Maybe Allah saved him. He was only twelve years old," Sayeed said. His eyes welled up with tears and he could not continue for a few minutes. "The three of us arrived at Khao I Dang camp. I stayed there before they sent me here."

The tears came back, stronger now. I held his head in my chest until he stopped heaving from the sobs. Then he looked up at me and said, "You see? I can do anything."

I nodded, then gave him the agency T-shirt and cap and told him to meet me at Classroom 14 in the Cambodian section the next morning.

Don't get attached to him like you did with Nguyen in Phanat, I reminded myself. You will suffer again when he's gone in a few months to some Western country.

Sayeed left seven months later for a small town in Norway. Seeing him off at the pier, I wondered if he would shed his sarong and forget halal food among the blond-haired, blue-eyed Norwegians.

☙

It was a long time before I got to visit Cambodia, but in 1998 I finally did get a chance to explore Sayeed's homeland when I was invited to a conference on refugees at Siem Reap, the city next door to the ancient ruins of Angkor Wat. Pol Pot, overthrown by the Vietnamese in 1979, had escaped into the mountains. The dreaded Khmer Rouge had been disbanded, its cadres left on their own to blend back into Cambodian life. The country was struggling to rebuild itself from the ravages of a decades-long civil war. Over a million Cambodian refugees had been resettled in America.

After the conference, I spent three days wandering through the temples. Each morning, I cycled to Angkor at the crack of dawn to avoid the throngs of Japanese tourists being unloaded from tour buses. I strolled among the stone *apsaras* and soldiers. Buddhist monks chanted from the towers of the Bayon, their mantras echoing around the ruins in the eerie, mystical ambience of the morning mist. A serene peace reigned, shattered only by the sight of patrolling temple guards dressed in green fatigues.

On the fourth day, I met a local guide, Ok Mory, and we took a windy, hour-long motorbike ride to Kbal Spean to explore the "river of a thousand *lingas*." Here, carved into rock after rock, in and beside the river, appeared the magical *lingas*: dancers, temples, and mythical figures. Most were surprisingly intact, despite the flow of water washing over them for centuries. With no other people in sight, to cool off from the hot midday sun, Ok Mory and I took a dip under a small waterfall in the same river. Just us bathing with the thousand *lingas*.

Once again, just like during my trip to Vietnam, I couldn't help but wonder why such a peaceful country inhabited by such humble people had been made to suffer such horrors.

The next day, at the mouth of the Tonle Sap, I hopped on a ferry that took me to the capital, Phnom Penh. In the city, a tourist guide tried to talk me into going to a popular site where one could fire off guns and grenades for sport. For a special price, I could kill a cow—tethered to a post—with a bazooka or rocket launcher. I declined and instead made my own way to Tuol Sleng, the infamous prison that had once been a school. Approximately 17,000 people had been tortured within its walls and then murdered in the killing fields by the Khmer Rouge.

The place looked like any ordinary secondary school in any Asian city. There were no memorial statues, no entrance fees, just black and white photos of prisoners and rusty chains tied to broken beds. Handwritten signs told of what tortures took place here. In one room, behind a glass case, was a collage map of Cambodia made of human skulls—all victims of the slaughter. In front of the glass case stood a bust of Pol Pot. I shuddered involuntarily at this sight and left shortly after.

For the rest of that day, I thought of Sayeed's sobbing head on my chest, and the fate of his father in a prison like this. The following day, I looked for Cham Muslims all over the city. I never met one.

ೞ

In Galang, to reduce costs, the agency recruited Indonesian teachers, just as they had done at Phanat Nikhom with Thai teachers. Though some of them were of Chinese, Batak, and Malay-Christian descent, they had the responsibility for delivering all curricula and lesson plans about America for the four-month training cycles. Cambodian and Vietnamese translators like Sayeed would deliver the content in the classrooms. This time, I insisted on including lesson plans on racism and the breakdown of Asian child-parent relationships in America.

Every morning, we wrote the lesson plans on a typewriter. These were then mimeographed on stencil paper in the afternoon, and taught to the Indonesian teachers in the evening. They, in turn, discussed them with their translators at night before class the next morning. This went on for the first four months—six days a week, twelve hours a day—until the first cycle of students graduated. Only then did we enjoy our first week of recreational leave in the comfort of Singapore. By then, the stress from working day and night and living with the same forty people, all cooped into the same overcrowded dorm, had taken its toll. In the privacy of our tiny rooms, the Americans drank Heineken in Pepsi cans to put themselves to sleep, while the Muslims prayed on straw mats facing Mecca. I indulged in the former but was curiously tempted at times to watch the latter.

During the break between cycles, I convinced the agency to approve the building of an outdoor badminton court in the dorm courtyard, for the staff to unwind after work. This had been my favorite sport back in Uganda. I asked the Indonesian staff for their help. Very proud of the fact that their country had won the world badminton championships that year, they all jumped at the idea. The court's construction—a welcome distraction from the rigors of Galang life—became an obsession for us all, and it was completed in just two weeks. Our home-made dirt court had wooden poles to hold up the net, chalk-powder lines for boundaries, duck-feather shuttlecocks, and cheap rackets. Needless to say, it became a big hit in the camp. Staff and refugees alike took part in the competitions. The game brought me much closer to my Muslim brothers.

⋅⋅⋅ ⊛ ⋅⋅⋅

One evening, while relaxing around the dorm courtyard, I confessed to my badminton friends that I was a bona fide Muslim. They didn't believe me and laughed in my face. I had to recite whatever parts of the holy *Dua* I could remember before they were convinced. Some were astonished.

"Why didn't you tell us from the beginning?" Yuli asked, incredulous.

"Because I wanted all of you to accept me for my work, not my religion," I replied, hesitating. This rationale confused them even more. Then all the questions came. Did I believe in Allah? Did I pray facing Mecca in America? Did I have any black American Muslim friends back home? Had I met the basketball star, Kareem Abdul Jabbar? Was I circumcised?

I told them my story. All about Idi Amin, the Kakwa Muslim from southern Sudan, who kicked me out of my Uganda.

Yanto, the in-house activist, had heard about him. "Was he as mad as the newspapers make him out to be?" he asked.

"Madder. Human heads in his refrigerator," I replied. "Then there was the time he tricked all the British in Uganda to come to an important press conference and then made them carry him, at gunpoint, on a palanquin through the streets of the capital."

"Rajah Idi Amin!" chimed in Suranto.

Everyone broke out into a laugh. Me, too.

"That's not all," I added. "One time, he declared himself king of Scotland. His new title was 'His Excellency President for Life, Field Marshal Al Hadji Doctor Idi Amin, VC, DSO, MC, Lord of all the Beasts of the Earth and Fishes of the Sea, and the Conqueror of the British Empire in General and Uganda in Particular.'"

Now everyone was howling. So I continued: "Then there was the time when he offered six hundred pounds to Queen Elizabeth to help with Britain's ailing economy, and then asked 'Mrs. Queen' for an apology for not inviting him to her birthday celebrations."

"Our Java generals should ask Suharto to send six million rupiah to Ronald Reagan's economic recession," piped in Nacho, to more laughter.

"Not a bad idea. He'd probably use it for an invasion of Russia," I added.

"But wasn't it Amin who built a great mosque in the capital with funds from Gaddafi?" queried Yanto.

"Right. At this very moment he's probably drinking more Scotch whisky in Saudi Arabia than all the Commonwealth put together," I responded. "Amin is as real a Muslim as I am," I added.

Everyone went quiet all of a sudden. You could have heard a pin drop. So I continued quickly about my life in Idi Amin's Uganda, and why I punched a British bobby in London at three in the morning. Why Wyoming rednecks took rifle shots at me. Why some Thais always took me for a Thai-Indian tailor. Why I had to leave all those countries. Why God was within me and not in some mosque.

They listened patiently, then Didi, my favorite badminton doubles partner, broke the ice: "From now on, we'll call you our Galang *Gado-Gado*." There were smiles, but no laughter. (*Gado-gado* is a popular Indonesian salad, with everything mixed together—vegetables, eggs, boiled potatoes, fruit, and sometimes meat—and topped by a peanut sauce.) A *gado-gado* chameleon, I thought to myself.

Darkness came over the dorm courtyard as the cicadas began their evening songs. Time for bed. Tomorrow was departure day for another 200 refugee graduates bound for America from the pier at Galang.

From that evening onwards, a few of the Indonesians, just a few, kept their distance from me in the camp.

It made me recall a similar encounter to this, when I'd first landed in New York from England back in 1974.

I arrived in the United States on July 4th, Independence Day, and brother Amir, who was supposed to pick me up at JFK Airport, never showed. I was lost in the city and ended up getting off the airport bus in Harlem. Outside a grocery store, I asked a black man for directions to Brooklyn, where my brother lived. Hakeem laughed and, on learning that I was from Africa and quite lost, invited me in to the family barbecue going on in their backyard. Once I had settled down on a wooden bench and been given some juicy spare ribs and cold, tangy lemonade, the questions began.

"So, man, where is it you's from?" Hakeem asked again. "Zanzibar or Zaire. . . ?"

"No, I'm from Uganda, next door to Zaire."

They still looked a little baffled, until one of the daughters fetched her school atlas.

"What's it like over there? Do they dig brother Marcus Garvey?" asked another man.

"I do," I replied, "but he's not very well known over there."

"What do Muslims in Africa think of Elijah Muhammad? asked Hakeem's son, who had a small red fez on his head.

All I knew of Elijah Muhammad was that he was the leader of the Black Muslims and the Nation Of Islam in America.

"East Africans love Muhammad Ali and Kareem Abdul Jabbar and the LA Lakers, but they don't know much about the black Muslim movement over here," I replied.

Though I was a little uncomfortable with the questions, I could sense that their curiosity was genuine. They seldom met anyone who came from Africa, and certainly not a brown Indian man. It felt odd being placed in the position of being an Africa expert just because I was born there, and an authority on Muslims just because I grew up as one. The people around the bench had heard of Idi Amin, but certainly had no clue about East African Asians.

That afternoon, I learned a lot from my newfound friends. I learned that Central Park, the great green space in the concrete jungle, was not safe at night, but was *the* place for free music concerts and Shakespeare plays every summer; that Toni Morrison was a new and popular black female writer from New York; that Detroit, Michigan, the home of Motown soul music, was only 25 miles from where I would be going to college. I learned that many black folks believed that President Nixon was a crook who had sent more black people than white to the Vietnam War and then rigged peace with Vietnam just to win the presidential election. I settled in even more, and ended up staying with Hakeem's family in Harlem for my first two days in America. On the third day, Hakeem personally escorted me to Brooklyn to find my brother.

CB

At Galang, nightmares that had first started in Uganda returned with greater intensity, now jumbling up people and places from different portions of my life. They hadn't recurred for years until now. One seemed to go on forever. . . .

I was playing badminton on Kilimanjaro with my friend Monk Marut. Pol Pot's soldiers were killing Ugandans from the north at the Aga Khan Gym near my home to feed to the crocodiles in the moat at Angkor Wat. Ho Chi Minh was at the White House asking for more napalm for the Khmer Rouge. Sayeed's blonde-haired daughter, with dark-brown beady eyes, was born in Gaza, Palestine with the Koran in one hand and a Molotov cocktail in the other.

Nguyen, now sporting an oily ponytail covered in blood, was climbing my guava tree in Kampala looking for a chameleon made of gado-gado ingredients.

Mumbling in my sleep, I woke up my roommate Fred twice that night.

ભ

During a week off in Singapore, I spotted a hardcover copy of V. S. Naipaul's *Among The Believers* in a bookstore. It was about his travels and perceptions of Muslims in four countries: Iran, Pakistan, Malaysia, and Indonesia. It would make a perfect conversation piece with some of my more open-minded Indonesian friends back in Galang. I bought it and read it that week.

I wished I had met Naipaul—a Trinidad-born Indian (and later, in 2001, a Nobel Prize laureate)—when he was teaching at Makerere University in Kampala. But I was only a young boy at that time. My writer brother, Bahadur, did in fact meet him—and came away with the impression that he was both arrogant and pompous. Little did I know that, many years later, I too would have my chance to meet him, in a stalking sort of way.

Over the years, I had read some of Naipaul's other books. His first one, on life in a Trinidadian family, *A House For Mr. Biswas*, I loved, but the rest, especially *A Bend In The River*, about East African Asians like me, I disliked. His cynical contempt for people in Third World countries—based on superficial, short-term travels to those places—bothered me. Far more dangerous, the Western literary community, having found a perfect Indian spokesman, idolized him as their incisive cultural expert on the Third World; their Indian Anglophile; their 'Uncle Tom,' to borrow an American insult.

I wondered if Naipaul realized how duped he was. My travels in Africa, England, North and South America, had forced me to look within and to understand my own duping, by the media, on how the world really was. My Peace Corps and refugee work experiences in

Asia were two concrete examples of how America acted outside its borders. Surely, as a prolific writer with a supposed mastery of his craft, Naipaul could see his Uncle Tom shadow? After all, he *was* being proclaimed as the great cultural chameleon of our time. Was he a literary genius or a ripe coconut: brown on the outside but white on the inside?

One evening, while discussing the Indonesia section of *Among The Believers*, I asked my Muslim friends in Galang what they thought of the *gado-gado*-ness of Indonesian Islam that Naipaul exposes, citing the ancient temples of Buddhist Borabadur and Hindu Prambanam as examples. Their responses, though varied, were thought provoking.

"What does this Hindu from Trinidad know about Islam from talking to a few people for a few days?" said Yanto.

"Indonesian Islam is a fusion of various religions and also of animism," said David, the historian. "So what? So are all the others: Christianity, Buddhism, Judaism. Does that make Islam any less real?"

"Mo, seems to me that this Naipaul is ten times more *gado-gado* than you are," jumped in Didi, always ready with a tactful joke.

"Trouble is, people in the West think that this fake cultural expert speaks the truth," I replied.

The gong for evening prayer rang at our dorm and dispersed the group. We never did get a chance to finish the discussion.

ఴ

Nearly a quarter of a century later, in 2004, in Thailand, I would finally have my chance to meet this controversial writer. The International Peace Foundation, a Norwegian institution, invited Naipaul to speak at the annual book fair in Bangkok, three years after 9/11. Naipaul, by now a Nobel laureate and knighted by Queen Elizabeth, showed up with his Muslim wife, Nadra, for a book signing of his latest novel, *Half A Life*.

Like Naipaul, I am an Indian who has never lived in India. Both of us studied in England—him at Oxford, me at East Anglia. Like Naipaul, I have traveled extensively in tropical countries, and I have read most of the books that he wrote about those countries. Thrilled that he was coming to Bangkok to talk about Muslims in non-Arab countries (of which I am one), I sent my credentials and asked the organizers for a personal interview. The first obstacle was that Sir V. S. Naipaul doesn't give interviews (except, on this occasion, to the *Bangkok Post* and *The Nation*, the two English-language dailies); the second was that he demanded all questions from the audience be sent in advance and in writing for approval. So I dutifully wrote up detailed questions and requested an audience again, only to be told that this was impossible. Given no other choice, I decided instead to attend all three of the author's appearances in Bangkok (at the book fair, the Foreign Correspondents' Club, and Chulalongkorn University) and tape the audience questions and Naipaul's answers.

At the book fair, youngsters dressed in traditional Thai theater costumes amidst life-sized posters of the author, frantically danced and waved Thai versions of *Half A Life* to visitors. I asked one of the Thai 'fans' in attendance, a student, if she had read any of Naipaul's books. She said she had never heard of him but was attracted to the publisher's booth by the dancing troupe.

The dinner event at the Foreign Correspondents' Club was rather more sensible, but it meant that Naipaul might have to compete with the clanking of knives and forks—which he adamantly refused to do. When dinner and then Naipaul's reading was over, I turned my mini tape recorder on. An audience member started off the questions by asking, "What are your views on the separation of religion and state, both politically and legally, in the context of Islam?"

Naipaul replied: "Islam is aiming at nothing less than world conquest, world domination. We are involved in the middle of a religious war and we have to accept that."

A British man went up to the microphone. "You recently supported publicly the Indian Hindu nationalists. Would you kindly give us the reasoning behind this?"

"I didn't actually support them," the author replied. "They asked me to come and see them and I said yes, I'd like to come and hear what you have to say about various things. I'm actually quite interested in their movement. I'm interested in all movements."

Seconds later, perhaps realizing that his reply might be misconstrued or misquoted, he turned to his journalist wife, Nadra, sitting next to him, to help him elaborate. She said, "I am a Muslim, this is very personal to me and *not* something I can talk about." But then she went on for fifteen minutes proclaiming that Muslims were very regressive in India. Most of them were illiterate and therefore in the hands of the *madrasahs*, whose money comes from Saudi Arabia. These were people whose minds had gone. They were blank. You could only bring Muslims into the mainstream of Indian society if you got rid of Islamic law. Unless you stopped the money coming from Saudi Arabia for the *madrasahs*, you would never stop the communal riots in India.

A perturbed Indian woman (of unknown religious background) followed up with the query: "How do you respond to the fact that the president of India is a Muslim?"

Nadra cut her down by yelling back, "Big deal, baby!"

A Thai gentleman, in polished English, then asked about the US invasion of Iraq: "What do you see as the outcome of the American occupation in Iraq. What will the ending be?"

"Well, actually I don't know," Naipaul replied. "I hope the Americans keep their nerve, but I don't think they will. I'd like them to stay there as an occupying force for a good long time—a couple of generations at least, to re-educate the people. They have a very good history of occupying and re-educating the people—like in the Philippines."

This brought much laughter from the audience.

"On the issue of religion, a well-known scholar, Edward W. Said, in his book *Orientalism*, makes a nasty attack on you for your views in *Among The Believers*. How do you respond to that?" asked a well-informed Naipaul reader.

"I write certain books to get the squeal of pain from people who are affronted," Naipaul responded. "Because usually they are all scoundrels. The idea that the Western world has been against Islam for all these centuries is certainly false. There is no greater champion of Islam than the eighteenth-century writer Edward Gibbon. Anyone who talks about the persecution of Islam is dealing with half truths."

Then I took to the floor to ask the question that nobody had yet dared to ask: "Because of the nature and content of many of your books, some critics have chastised you as catering predominantly to a Western audience, and that you portray Third World countries in a demeaning and negative manner. What are your views on this?"

"I think perhaps you haven't been at this meeting which we are now attending," he said. "You heard me talking about the Indian situation, one of the largest countries in the world and certainly not a Western country. It's an idle question actually."

Quickly aware that her husband hadn't fully understood the question, Nadra, the watchdog wife, jumped in: "Yes, people do criticize my husband about this. But these critics did not risk their lives and go out to Africa twenty years ago and predict what was going to happen to Africa—which has now come true. I think they should read his books first."

When a concerned Thai parent mustered up the courage to seek advice on how, in the age of the Internet and computer games, she could get her children to appreciate or even start reading, Naipaul replied, "It may be impossible, madam. We had a period of literature. Now we have a period of non-literature and non-reading."

There was applause at this.

One traveler, obviously inspired by Naipaul's journeys to so many countries and his insights into various cultures, asked the innocent question on the minds of many backpackers: "In today's mongrel world, is it possible for cultural nomads like us to be global citizens instead of rootless wanderers?"

Naipaul was scathing in his response: "I distrust people who talk about global citizens and global souls. When you press them, you see that they are thinking about people taking aeroplanes or shopping in malls or driving motor cars. They think [that] using these tools creates a global citizen. That's a concept of nonsense.

"People used to phone me and ask me, was I searching for an identity, was I part of any movement? I never thought of myself as part of a movement. Writers who think they are part of a movement are probably writers who are running out of things to say and clinging to productive people to give themselves an illusion of activity, of strength."

Then, in perhaps in his most ironic statement of the whole visit, he went on to conclude: "When I say that I wish to know places and people, I meant that I wish, all the time, to look at the world through other people's eyes, to see what they see. It has always been my practice."

I wondered how many of his readers—whether Muslim or of any other religious persuasion, whether Western or Asian or African—would actually agree with this last comment.

Frustrated and obviously taken aback with the lack of praise coming from the floor, the husband and wife team decided that all questions at the third event at Chulalongkorn University would be selected by and asked by Nadra and no one else. The audience was thus treated to boring anecdotes about Naipaul's fascination with cats, and how all his literary works were really one big book, and how he was too old now to write about Thailand.

The Chula reading was followed by a reception, at which the audience was invited to meet the author and his wife. It was supposed to be an intellectual dialogue, but ended up being a self-congratulatory gathering of the mutual admiration society. Saddest of all was the painful look on the author's face when one Thai audience member kept badgering him about where exactly in India he was from, even though Naipaul had told him thrice that he was an overseas Indian who had never actually lived in India. I came to the rescue, whereupon Nadra, though busy talking to someone else, immediately joined us and questioned me: "Are you following us?"

I smiled and congratulated them on their visit without bothering to reply to her accusation. I left soon after.

Invited to Thailand by the International Peace Foundation, along with other personalities from varied professions, to create "bridges and dialogues towards a culture of peace," I wondered how much actual dialogue and peace Naipaul generated or bridged during his visit. I was puzzled why someone of such obvious high intellect would be so paranoid about questions from the floor, or from a fellow Indian genuinely interested in knowing the man behind the books.

So, is Naipaul a genius or a ripe coconut? I asked myself in the taxi home. Is he a visionary with a global perspective or just an ex-colonial yearning to climb up the British aristocratic ladder? Or maybe just a crafty author posing as a cultural chameleon? Was it mere coincidence that he was awarded the Nobel Prize for Literature just three months after 9/11?

In 1988, six years after the publication of *Among The Believers*, Salman Rushdie, an Indian-born Muslim, half chameleon, half Anglophile, would write a brilliant phantasmagorical spoof on Islam called *The Satanic Verses*, for which—instead of a Nobel Prize—he would earn a death *fatwa* from Iran's Ayatollah Khomeini and have to spend the next ten years in hiding.

The dilemma of freedom of expression versus the intentional or unintentional insult of Allah or the Prophet Mohammed (and, therefore, Islam) would rear its ugly head again in 2006. The cartoon depiction in European magazines of the Prophet with a bomb in his turban would turn into a global war of beliefs. Parts of the Muslim world would erupt into violence, leading to deaths and destruction— even though the same cartoons had been printed in an Egyptian magazine (with hardly any negative reaction) four months before the international headlines.

That Islamaphobia has increased after 9/11 is well documented. That double standards of freedom of expression have been applied to Islamic and non-Islamic writings is becoming an issue. The accountability of the mass media over cultural sensitivities often goes unchecked, and this is also a cause for concern. Once again, moderate Muslims, the majority of followers worldwide, were being undermined by minority factions that grabbed the headlines with their violent behavior. Rushdie's public call, urging the moderates to take back the basic Islamic tenets of peace and hospitality, went unheeded. All at the expense of simple folk like me who abhor violence and war as means to resolve problems.

I thank my stars that other beliefs, like Bahá'i and Buddhist principles, less confrontational and divisive, are there to guide me through this madness.

ఇ

Just before my year in Galang was up, I got a mysterious phone call from the Aga Khan Foundation in Geneva. I knew that the Foundation did charity work in Muslim countries and had an excellent reputation for grass-roots development work in Pakistan and India. But why were they calling me? How did they find me in remote Galang?

It turned out that my father had passed on my résumé to the Foundation's CEO in Vancouver, who in turn had forwarded it to the headquarters in Geneva. They wanted to know if I was willing to work for their education program in northern Pakistan. They wanted me to reform the curricula of the *madrasahs* (to be more progressive) and train teachers in 120 schools all over the Gilgit Valley watershed.

Sayeed and his *madrasah* experiences came to my mind. Would Pakistan, home to 10 million Ismailis, my people, be as accepting as Indonesia was of a renegade Muslim like me? I had no idea.

I asked the Foundation if I could visit Gilgit first, to see for myself what the job entailed and who I'd be working with. They agreed to fly me out there when my Galang contract was over in another month's time. After the Gilgit visit, the plan was that they would interview me for the position, in person, in Geneva. I asked if I could bring my wife, Corazon, at my own expense for the visit. They agreed.

Corazon was a gorgeous 28-year-old Filipina refugee worker that I had been seeing for the last three months in camp. Born Catholic, she grew up in Muslim Mindanao in the southern Philippines before her parents moved the family to Cebu City on the large island of the same name. As a twelve-year-old, during Holy Communion one Sunday, she asked for more wine before being blessed by the priest. At sixteen she ran away to the beach town of Moalboal on the central west coast of Cebu to scuba dive with other young rebels.

In Galang, Corazon and I would hike up to the Buddhist temple at night and make love in the dark. Though she was a fellow chameleon, she was certainly not my wife. Her contract finished the same week as mine, and we had made plans to travel together in Asia. Marriage was certainly never discussed. Not yet anyway. But I knew better than to let the people in Geneva know that. Besides, I hadn't even asked her yet if she would travel to Pakistan as my pretend wife.

After the call, I wandered over to the camp's market to ponder what I had agreed to. Pakistan. Birthplace of Zinnah, my namesake.

Ancient homeland of the Ismailis. K2 and the Himalayas; the roof of the world. I recalled the Foundation's work in Uganda.

When Idi Amin expelled my community from Uganda, it was the Aga Khan Foundation that helped finance my university studies in England. They had been good to me. Here was an opportunity to pay them back for their generosity. Yet, how would the Pakistani Ismailis react to me? Would they expect me to attend mosque? Would they want me to pray to Allah facing Mecca? And Corazon? How would they react to her? Would she even agree to go? If she did, she might give up her shorts worn in Galang, but would she wear the *chador* around her head at all times in Pakistan?

I thought more. My knowledge of Hindi, close to the Urdu spoken in Pakistan, would help us there. After the interview, maybe we could trek in the Himalayas or backpack through India. She loved travel just as much as I did. Mayon Volcano in the Philippines was her triumph, and snow-clad Kilimanjaro was mine. What did we have to lose? After all, neither of us had been to south Asia before.

Corazon and I left Galang three weeks later. The farewell was bittersweet. My American colleagues got us drunk on Heineken. Cambodian refugees gave me a hand-carved wooden replica of Angkor to remember them by. A Vietnamese translator gave me a painting of boat people stranded at sea. The Indonesians and I played our last badminton games together. At the party, they presented me with a cake made of *gado-gado* ingredients. The inscription, made of mixed vegetables, said "*Selamat Jalan Kakak.*" 'Happy Trails Wanderer.' And at the bottom, in smaller letters: "*Kembali chapat, chapat.*" 'Come Back Soon.' In return, I gave them two books: *Among The Believers* and Salman Rushdie's *Midnight's Children.*

ଓ

Before the flight from Singapore landed in Islamabad, the capital of Pakistan, Corazon switched from rubber sandals, shorts, and a tank top, to long beige pants, a long-sleeved batik shirt, and formal brown shoes. The headscarf she bought at Changi Airport was stuffed in her pocket in case of police spot checks.

In Islamabad we stayed overnight with Bob, an old colleague from Phanat who was now managing the JVA American immigration program for Afghan refugees fleeing the Soviet occupation of their country. The house he lived in had six bedrooms, a huge garden, three servants, one cook, and a gardener. All for himself and his Malaysian wife, Yasmin.

During the jeep ride into the city, we had passed a day market swarming with Afghans selling hand-woven Persian carpets. Worth a fortune in the West, they were priced for next to nothing. Cash only. American dollars or British pounds. No rupees please. Bob had four thick carpets in his house, the one in the living room as big as three dorm rooms in Galang. Working for the American government came with its perks.

That evening, Bob and Yasmin invited us to the Country Club, once a bastion of British colonialism, and now the only watering hole for guests and invited members to drink alcohol outside their homes. The place was full of white people drinking up a storm. Bob ordered a round of four gin and tonics from the Punjabi bartender. He served only three. When asked why, he politely insisted that I would have to prove my foreign identity before he could serve me, since locals could not be served. Yasmin, he knew as a regular, and Corazon certainly didn't look Muslim. House rules made by the British, conveniently picked up by the Americans, now imposed by Punjabi Pakistanis. Though passports were preferred, my California driver's license would suffice this one time. One more new identity for me: Islamabadi.

Upset at this affront, I drank more than usual. At the bar, I sat next to Mike, a blond-haired construction engineer from Toledo, Ohio who was watching an NBA basketball game on television.

Since we were both rooting for the Los Angeles Lakers, he became my buddy for the night and kept buying me drinks. On the ride back to Bob's place, Yasmin told me that Mike was actually an arms dealer for an American company supplying ammunition to the Mujahadin for the war against the Soviets.

The next morning, good weather permitted us to take off on the once-a-day flight to Gilgit. The ride on the twenty-seat Cessna was frightening and bumpy, but the views of the mighty Karakoram Range from the window were superb. On the runway in Gilgit, the October air at 4,900 meters altitude was bitterly cold, biting through our thick wool sweaters and jackets. Snow-capped mountains were everywhere we looked.

Inside the terminal, while waiting for our baggage, Corazon pointed out the waiting-room signs in English and Urdu. "Women Only" said one. "Man" said the other.

Dadu Khan from the Aga Khan Foundation had a minibus waiting for us outside. Corazon had to sit up front with two other girls. I sat in the back with the men. Male-female contact was not permitted, even in a private vehicle.

The hotel in Gilgit, despite its spectacular sunset views of Rakaposhi and K2, was deserted, with no guests braving the winter. The room heater, fueled with kerosene, gave off fumes, making sleep difficult. Corazon and I clasped together, freezing through the night, till the sun crept over the mountains and into our room. Outside, the pink and purple slivers of dawn sky over the majestic, snowy peaks took me back to Kilimanjaro.

Next day, our jeep bumped through huge potholes on dirt roads only inches wider than the vehicle itself, as we visited one village school after another. In each classroom, a gold-framed picture of the Aga Khan—with the Ismaili insignia in red and green (just like the ones in the mosque and school in Kampala)—hung proudly above the old blackboards facing the rickety tables and chairs. Teenage boys and girls, many of them blue-eyed and fair-haired, stood to attention and sang in unison, "Good moooorrning, sir." Descendants of Alexander the Great and his Macedonian armies.

Corazon taught one of the classes the English words to the song "Ten Green Bottles" while I sat with Dadu Khan on a wooden bench outside to learn more about my potential job. Mastering the song rapidly, the students sang their hearts out, "Ten Green Bottles" echoing in the hills and valleys below the mountains. As we were leaving, I saw one of the girls take out a small tin charcoal heater from under her skirt and replenish it with fresh coals from her school bag.

There was a lot of work to be done here, and I spent the next two cold and rainy days talking to teachers and Foundation staff in Gilgit. On the third day, the weather cleared, so we had to fly back to Islamabad while we could. Dadu Khan saw us off at the hotel.

At the airport, the plane was delayed for a few hours, so Corazon was hustled off to the women's waiting room with two other female passengers, their headscarves revealing only their beady blue eyes. The only other male passenger with me in the "Man" section was a dark-skinned Muslim with a bushy black beard. He wore a fine-bladed scimitar that stuck out from his long woolen coat. Bored at the delay, I looked for my book of poems by the well-known Pakistani author, Iqbal, only to realize that it wasn't in my bag. It must be with Corazon, I thought, and wandered over to the women's section to get it from her.

Corazon was happily chatting away in sign language with one of the women who, by now, had taken off her headscarf. She had beautiful rosy cheeks and a fair complexion. Upon seeing me, Corazon screamed with a look of complete terror on her face. Her eyes were focused behind me. I turned, just in time to see the man with the bushy black beard, two feet behind me, scimitar raised in the air, about to slash my head off.

I swerved to avoid the blade, but it cut through to the skin on my elbow, and blood trickled out slowly. Petrified, I screamed "Help!" as loud as I could. A crowd, including airport staff, appeared at the women's waiting room. Some of them pulled off the black-bearded man, who had now grappled me to the floor. It took two solid hours of animated persuasion in Urdu before an airline staffer could get it through to the man that I had not purposefully walked into the women's waiting room to see his wife's unveiled face, that the only reason I had gone there was to get my book from Corazon. When she produced the book from her handbag, this was of no consequence to him. He only backed off when it was time to board the plane to Islamabad. He forbade his wife to get on the flight—I had already seen her face, and that was more than enough for him.

During the flight, I was shaking all over, imagining all the worst-case scenarios if the blade had caught me on the head.

In Islamabad, I was supposed to get on a flight to Karachi and then board a later return flight to Geneva for my interview. I never got on either flight. Instead, I mailed the tickets back to the Foundation in Geneva with my apologies and regrets.

4. African Days

I am the hero of Africa.
Idi Amin *Dada.*

Only when you have suddenly lost the everyday world you live in, do you truly appreciate what you loved about it so much. Once gone forever, memories come back in sudden flashes or fragments that haunt you. So it was with Uganda and me. Like, for instance, the patch of red ground in Madras Gardens where my childhood friends—Hindus, Sikhs, Muslims, Bagandans—and I played marbles till our mothers' calls for dinner turned to threats.

Over time, our gang of brown and black boys—the "Kampala Kudus"—became organized, daring, and resourceful. During raids on neighborhood fruit trees—guavas, mangoes, custard apples for the taking—we had sentries posted to help us avoid capture and subsequent whippings. The spoils were divided equally, and we got an early introduction to cross-cultural management, African style.

When independence came in 1962, we welcomed Prime Minister Obote's call for nation building (*Uhuru na kazi*, 'Freedom and work') by joining voluntary work projects all over the city. After all, we were the new generation of free Ugandans.

Four years later, during inter-tribal political turf wars, the government declared martial law and a curfew. One evening, from the balcony of my home, I saw patrolling soldiers kill Luwanga, one of my African gang mates. Caught on the street after the curfew, they shot him in cold blood as he tried to escape into the bushes. They laughed like hyenas as their jeep sped off into the eerie twilight. That's when '*Uhuru na kazi*' became '*Uhuru o kufa*,' 'Freedom or death,' for the Bagandan people.

Aga Khan Secondary School was a mixture of brown and black students, with the browns being the majority. Mr. McCourt, a defrocked Irish priest, was the headmaster chosen by the Ismaili board of governors to be our role model and disciplinarian. As long as the school notched up the best graduation scores in the country, the board ignored his penchant for caning pupils in his office with the black curtains drawn. Being one of the more frequent recipients of McCourt's 'Monday morning maulings,' I learned quickly that two pairs of underpants and socks stuffed in my back pockets provided good insulation against the dreaded bamboo cane.

But it wasn't all beatings and grades mania. Winning the Sportsman of the Year trophy and the badminton and tennis junior championships made up for the regular Monday doldrums. Girls, both at school and Friday mosque, took much more notice of the sports star.

Then came Kilimanjaro. In 1970, I was chosen to be my school's representative on a three-week Outward Bound course—with 28 other students from all over East Africa—to the continent's highest peak. It would be the highlight of my life in Africa.

ങ

Sunrise on the mountain, and I was the lone climber high above the clouds. At this altitude of over 18,000 feet, the temperature was below zero. In the pre-dawn light, I could make out hills stretching for miles across Tanzania, into neighboring Kenya and Uganda, and even reaching far into the Republic of Congo. As it crept over the horizon, the rising sun brought warmth to my freezing back. I wiggled my toes to keep the blood circulation flowing. I dug the ice ax into hard-packed snow and planted my feet firmly into my own footprints before taking off my backpack. Then I turned to bask in the sun's rays.

It was the first time I'd ever been in snow, and here I was plodding through it, ice castles and glistening glaciers all around me. Uhuru Peak, the very summit, was in sight and within reach, less than a thousand feet to go. The rocky summit of neighboring Mount Mawenzi poked its snow-capped nose above the clouds like some fantastic white pyramid floating on a carpet of cotton. I remembered the legendary carcass of the dead leopard supposed to be frozen on the cliffs of Mawenzi.

By now, pink, yellow, red, and purple streaks shot across the crystal blue sky, contrasting with the snow all around and the dark-brown, scraggy rocks. The raw power of Nature humbled me to my knees, and with hands clasped together as if in prayer, I thanked Allah, the Creator, God, whatever his name was, for the amazing sight facing me. I dragged myself up to the very summit. The view made me gasp. Raising my arms to the sky, I let out a shout of joy as loud as my lungs would allow in the thin, crisp air. *Ayinga!* I was on top of my Africa.

I signed my name in the ironclad book chained to the Kenyan flag (on this side of the ascent), and took 360-degree pictures. I didn't have long to savor the moment. Just minutes later, the wind picked up, kicking up swirls of snow that brought back the icy cold and forced me to start the descent.

Aware that I was one of only two Indian boys among the Africans, most of them hardened to the bush from their village childhoods, I was overjoyed to be one of the nine who actually got to the summit. Besides Daniel Moyale, I was the only other climber in our seven-man team to make it. I reflected on the two hellish weeks of training at Loitokitok base camp before the actual week-long climb.

During the first week, each morning before sunrise, we began with a dreaded dip in the outdoor swimming pool. At about 6,000 feet, the camp was high enough for a layer of thin ice to form on top of the water. "I don't care if you swim or not," Okello, our team instructor would laugh in our faces. "Every hair on your head must be wet before you come out."

The second week of trekking, with fifty-pound packs on our backs, through the wild plains of Amboseli National Park, was the hardest for our team of seven. The park was teeming with wildebeest, zebras, kudus, gazelles, and impalas. One morning, we came upon a family of giraffes munching their breakfast from tall, thorny trees. On another occasion, we tiptoed past a female white rhino with two calves grazing along our route. But wildlife spotting was easy. The hard part was finding our way through the park in the burning sun.

Using a compass to guide us, we climbed specified hills to look for metal cylinders left by our instructors. Only by finding those cylinders would we get directions to the next hill and the next clue. If our team navigated correctly, the fifth and last instruction of the day, on the fifth hill, would guide us to the campsite. If we got lost, we had to find our own food and shelter for the night. Our team did get lost one day, and ended up spending the night in a Masai village. The Masai, who hunt game with spears and paint their faces in caked mud, had a reputation as fierce warriors who shunned strangers. We had no idea how they would react when we stumbled into their village as dusk approached. Daniel, our team leader, spoke to the elders in Swahili, explaining who we were and why we needed help.

One of the elders translated in the Masai language to a group of his men, and suddenly they all burst out laughing. Then they talked among themselves, pointing to certain huts in the village. By now, the seven of us had bunched up together. We had no idea what we would do if they decided to hold us hostage. But we had nothing to worry about. One of the men led us to two red adobe huts, which would be our sleeping quarters, and later that night the village women brought us tasty skewered beef and boiled cassava for dinner.

So much for the myth of Masai ferocity and our stupid fears of being kidnapped. Next morning, outside our hut, girls with multiple earrings giggled as the elders invited us to drink fresh cow's blood for breakfast. After one of the Masai had poked an arrow into a vein in the cow's neck, each one of us had to squat on the ground to catch the stream of spurting blood. Daniel went first and gulped down a mouthful. Dixon and I were the only ones who vomited immediately after our turns. The Masai girls howled at this, their small breasts jiggling as they reveled in our discomfort. Dixon and I felt foolish, but we joined in the laughter to hide our embarrassment.

Kilimanjaro was my first time for many new things. My first time with so many Africans for a long period of time—eating, sleeping, and suffering together at base camp. Daniel was the first African I had become such close friends with. We shared the same love of the wilderness—the climb to Uhuru Peak, the long treks in Amboseli—and both of us wanted to teach in schools, him in Kenya and me in Uganda. We both loved and appreciated our East African heritage. Back at base camp, when I twisted my ankle and agonized that I wouldn't be allowed to make the climb, Daniel was there to console me. I wondered how my close Asian friends back home would take to Daniel. Would they see him in the same light as I did? Most Asians in Uganda thought of Africans as just servants or employees.

It was my first time to make friends with an American, too. Scott, from Flagstaff, Arizona, was one of only two white instructors at the

Outward Bound mountain school. Sure, I had been taught by white teachers before, mainly British, at school in Kampala, but for some reason this bearded white guy in his twenties seemed very different. He was a seasoned traveler and Peace Corps volunteer who had come to Kenya to teach science at a school in the bush. It intrigued me as to why someone from the land of the Kennedys and moonwalker Neil Armstrong would leave such a country to come and live in the African boondocks. His advice and guidance on important life decisions was invaluable, making me realize for the first time what questions I should be asking myself about the direction I would take. It was the first time that any foreigner had been interested in me or my life. Scott and I enjoyed many campfire chats, during which he told me about college life in America and the many places he had been to—places that I now yearned to go to. Someday in the future, I thought, I might visit him in Arizona and hike down the mighty Grand Canyon.

ଔ

As I descended, down, down, down, the snow, tundra, and scree gave way to green ferns and thick undergrowth, but I still had to dodge rocks and avoid slippery spots on the trail. Meeting up with the rest of my team at Kibo Hut, the highest camp, we spent one more night on Kili before the final descent to Loitokitok camp. The rainforest vegetation re-appeared the next day, and a group of Colobus monkeys darting from branch to branch on a large tree by a mountain stream made me realize that we were getting close to the cave which was used as the ascending climbers' second camp-site.

Just three days before, I had sat by this same stream in the middle of the night after getting out of my toasty sleeping bag in the cave to urinate. That night had been so serene. With a full moon high in the sky, I could see raindrops shimmering on leaves all around me. 'Moondrops' I had called them. The air was moist and pure. The forest insects were so quiet, all I could hear was the trickling of the stream. *Ayinga* and *shantih*.

At Loitokitok, on our final night, we enjoyed a huge campfire barbecue: a banquet of charcoal grilled beef and plenty of the local brew—which hadn't been allowed during training. After the badge awards ceremony, group photos, and team hugs, the party continued with dancing around the flames and a marathon of songs about our trials and tribulations over the three weeks.

The bus ride back to Nairobi from Kilimanjaro was uneventful. From the camp, we descended through coffee plantations where girls, dark as charcoal, in flowery dresses and straw hats, picked beans with their sisal baskets tied snugly around their waists. Children playing by the roadside chased the bus and waved and screamed before going back to their games.

We slowed at the main tarmac road with two forks, one leading to Nairobi and the other to Tanzania. One signboard proclaimed "Nairobi" with "Masai Mara National Reserve" written underneath it. The other said "Tanzania" and "Serengeti National Park." Seeing the latter, I recalled a family trip to the Serengeti when I was still a young boy, and a jeep ride into the adjoining Ngorongoro Crater. It was during the rainy season and the switchback road had become a carpet of mud, the jeep's wheels sliding left and right in the mire. Most of the road was a 45-degree slope, with the crater wall forming cliffs on one side and steep drop-offs on the other. Brother Amir had resorted to narrating stories from the *Ramayana* to keep us young ones entertained and oblivious to the danger. In the crater itself, nature had gone wild. Hundreds of thousands of wildebeest, on their annual migration from the Masai Mara in search of water and pasture, formed huge lines, one after another, almost as if they were queuing for tickets to a big event. Gazelles and kudus grazed the grassy knolls. Elephants and giraffes strode off in the distance. Lions slept in the hot sun. Later, I remember complaining to Huseini, our Tanzanian park guide, that I still hadn't seen any cheetahs yet. Then, one early morning, Huseini woke me up before anyone else, forefinger on his lips to assure my silence, and pointed up to a flame tree near where our jeep was parked for the night. Lying there on a big branch, with all four feet dangling down, was a full-grown cheetah, sound asleep. Its belly was heaving and the long bushy tail was curled up around the branch. I was mesmerized. Huseini and I crept over to admire this fastest of all animals. Moments later, noise from the camp woke the big cat and, after a quick stretch and yawn, he nimbly darted down the tree trunk and sped off into the plains.

The outskirts of Nairobi were approaching now, and soon we were passing through Kagera, East Africa's largest slum, with mile after mile of corrugated tin roofs on decrepit dwellings, open sewers and garbage, and naked children. The afternoon scene at the train station in Nairobi was chaotic, with touts, pickpockets, and hawkers everywhere. I dodged them all and got a lower-berth ticket for the next train to Kampala, which left in two hours and would arrive at six the next morning. Looking around for a food kiosk, I saw an Arab vendor with the black *chador* around her head. She was probably from Mombasa, down on the coast. I ordered samosas, a plate of mutton biryani, a chicken *murtaba*, and a cold Coke.

"Two slices of lemon with the food please, mama."

She gave me four, and I ate silently and quickly. It wasn't Ma's home cooking, but after three weeks of barbecued meat and boiled eggs every night, I wasn't complaining. From a fruit stand further up, I bought a ripe mango and sucked the sweet juice dry around the big seed. For the trip, I bought *mogo*, cassava roasted on a charcoal grill—a favorite snack of mine since childhood.

The train from Mombasa was late, but took off again within fifteen minutes after the passengers got on and off. In the dining car, I ordered a large bottle of Tusker, the local beer, and shelled peanuts from the white-gloved waiter. He was obviously perturbed that I had brought my own food and wasn't going to order any from him. Still grubby and disheveled from the mountain, I observed the white linen table cloth, the silver cutlery wrapped neatly in a spotless white napkin, the waiter's starched white uniform, his ridiculous red hat with tassels, and those stupid white gloves, all remnants from the days when Kenya was a British colony. Built by African and Indian sweat to transport cotton, coffee, and tea to the vast reaches of the Empire, the British rulers had insisted that the East African Railway maintain certain standards. Years after independence, those standards were maintained with vigor.

I drank my beer and looked out the window as a lone farmer headed home from another hot day of slaving on his small piece of land. The African sun was setting among the green pastures, a rainbow of colors painted across the sky. Unfortunate, I thought, that darkness would be upon us before we reached the more spectacular views of the Great Rift Valley. This ancient geographic cataclasm that cleaves through East Africa, a hundred kilometers wide in places, is full of hot springs and alkaline lakes where shoals of tilapia fish attract flamingoes throughout the year. The sight of hundreds of pink flamingoes flying off into the sunset at Lake Naivasha was one of so many childhood memories that I cherished. I stared out the window until darkness fell, finished the last few gulps of beer, and straggled back to my berth for sleep, sweet sleep.

The dawn light was creeping in as the train pulled into familiar Kampala Station. Refreshed from a deep sleep, I decided to walk home to take in the morning sights and sounds of my city.

"*Jugu, bwana?*" called a peanut vendor, hoping for his first sale of the day.

I bought some roasted peanuts from him and walked down the street where my father worked as an accountant for an import-export firm called African Products Limited. Some of the *askaris*, the night-watchmen, were still asleep on the job while others huddled around their small fire, drawing warmth from the last of the embers. The sun was coming up over Kibuli Mosque on one of the seven hills surrounding the city. The minarets and crescents shone in the first of the morning light. On another hill stood Rubaga Cathedral, the oldest Christian church in the country, where only a year before, Pope Paul VI, or "Papa Paulo" as his African followers knew him, had canonized sixteen martyrs from the Ugandan Church. On yet another hill stood the circular Bahá'i temple with its dome, arched doors, and stained-glass windows. At times when I wanted to be alone with my thoughts, or to escape the repressive dogma of Islam, I had gone there to meditate and think about my future. Inside, surrounded by icons and symbols from all of the world's religions, I always felt a sense of serenity that, unknown to me then, would take on greater meaning in the years to come.

As I approached my neighborhood of Old Kampala, I looked at the familiar signs of Madras, Bombay, and Delhi Gardens—the triangular residential complex where some of the Asian community lived—and wondered for the first time in my life what these names meant to Africans. And, more importantly, why this thought had never occurred to me before now.

As I climbed the steps to the front door of my house, I heard a voice shouting out. I turned to see a black man staggering on the road, obviously still drunk from the previous night's excesses. He was pushing along a cart full of empty bottles.

He pointed a finger at me and yelled in Swahili, "*Wewe! Shenzi muhindi. Rudi jumbani kwah India!*" 'You! Fuckin' Indian. Go back to India, where you came from!'

He kept repeating it, goading me into a response. I yelled back in Swahili, "I'm a Ugandan Muslim, you fool!"

Toppling the cart as he staggered along, he fell over by the side of the road and passed out.

ᴄ᯾

One evening in January 1971, at Kristos, a popular Greek restaurant on Kampala Road, I was sitting on a sofa facing the street, sipping a cold chocolate shake and chatting with two of my best friends, Nizar and Ashok. All three of us wore bell-bottomed jeans, but I had on a *kitenge* shirt while the other two sported flowery Hawaiians. The Doors' "Light My Fire" was blasting from the speakers as Elena, the owner's daughter, entered the place with her friends, and all heads turned as one. This Helen of Kampala with long legs, wholesome thighs, and a black suede miniskirt, strode past without as much as a glance to anyone. She was followed by her two blonde friends, also sporting scandalously short skirts. Jim Morrison cranked it up as we leered at the three beauties and wondered what it would be like to date one of these white girls. The white boys in Kampala were just as protective of their girls as we brown boys were of our own. However, the black boys never interfered with brown or white men dating black girls. I guessed it was the natural order of things in all African cities.

Ashok snapped us out of our fantasies, asking if we wanted to join him for the new Shashi Kapoor film. Making faces of boredom, Nizar and I declined—we had seen it just a couple of days before— so he left us to go watch the film with his family. Across the street, an African vendor was handing roasted peanuts to a small Indian girl. Her long hair, braided in a ponytail, smothered in coconut oil, swished back and forth on the back of her Punjabi dress.

Nizar and I began chatting about what American movie we might see that evening. He and I were childhood friends, having been in the same classes in the same schools for over ten years. From our marble playing days in Old Kampala, onto muddling through our first sexual encounters with girls, and now through our love of sports and mountain climbing, we had looked out for each other even when competing for the same prizes. Suddenly, there was the sound of rapid gunfire down the street and we saw people fleeing. We ran out of Kristos and followed the sound. A convoy of tanks and jeeps, full of Ugandan soldiers, was rumbling its way along Kampala Road. The soldiers yelled out to people in the crowded street, "*Jumbani, jumbani! Haraka, haraka!*" 'Back to your homes! Right now, hurry!'

People ran about in confusion looking for their loved ones as rifle shots rang in the air. Children screamed as parents hugged them tight. Unable to find her parents among the panic, the girl with the oily ponytail in the Punjabi dress dashed across the road and got run over by a tank. The convoy didn't stop, but kept heading in the direction of Parliament House, where most of the government buildings stood.

"What the hell's going on?" Nizar said as we walked quickly away from the convoy, looking for a side street to escape to.

"I don't know. Did you see that poor girl crushed under the tank?

"I know. The fuckers just kept going."

"Something big is happening."

"We'd better get home."

Neither of us had a car that evening. Around us, people huddled together and drove off home to warn their friends and relatives. Restaurateurs ushered out customers, closed down their venues, and summoned their night-watchmen to keep watch from inside. Vendors packed up their wares and hurried off as the rumble of tanks replaced the chatter of voices and laughter.

Nizar and I walked swiftly, keeping to the side roads till we came to the only main road that led to the old part of the city where both of us lived. We dreaded going down this hill and over the bridge, the underside of which was known as a thief's paradise. Just a few months before, at this same bridge, walking back from a late-night movie, the two of us had been mugged. The thieves, one with a machete and the other with a scythe, had pointed to our necks and forced us to empty our pockets. We gave them everything we had, whereupon they hurled furious insults in Swahili because we had so little money on us. They then demanded all our clothes. It was sheer luck that I was able to plead with them to allow us to keep our underpants on, and we ran home in fear and embarrassment. Tonight, we ran across that bridge as fast as we could.

Nizar's father was watching "The Fugitive" on television when we told him the news. He hurried off to mosque to get the rest of his family. From Nizar's place, I called home to alert my parents. Bapuji answered, and I told him what I'd seen. He insisted that I stay put till one of my siblings picked me up. Before he hung up, he said that there was nothing but military music on Radio Uganda. The last time that had happened was five years before, when Milton Obote's militia, made up of loyalists from his northern provinces, had laid siege to the city and deposed the *kabaka*, the king of the Baganda tribe and president of the country, forcing him to flee to England. Martial music meant that a coup was likely in progress, since the radio station was the only way that politicians and the army had to communicate with the eight million people in the villages of the country.

Just before midnight, my brother Phiroz picked me up after collecting two of my sisters, Shamim and Sultan. (One of my three elder brothers and all my five sisters were married and lived in their own houses in the city.) My other brother, Bahadur, at Makerere University, was still unaccounted for. At home, Ma, relieved to see four of her nine children, wrapped herself around each of us. *Kuku paka*, chicken in coconut-milk sauce, and *Peshawari* rice was still on the dinner table for anyone who was hungry. Bapuji's ear was tuned to the radio. The BBC, more reliable in giving the facts of what was going on in our own country, was going on about racial tensions between West Indians and white youths in London. At midnight, Bapuji demanded silence as we all huddled around for the hourly international news.

There had indeed been a coup. The army had taken control of the government, Radio Uganda, and the one national television station. Gunfire at Entebbe Airport had resulted in the death of two Catholic priests. Prime Minister Milton Obote, in Singapore at the Commonwealth Conference, had been advised not to return to Uganda. Coup leader, Major Idi Amin, accused Obote of greed and corruption. He had the support of the army and had promised a caretaker government until the situation was stable again.

Bapuji turned the radio off. "Ya, Allah! We're in for curfews and martial law again."

"Idi Amin? Isn't he that boxer? The fat idiot with the big mouth?" Phiroz said.

"I saw him once, during a football game at Nakivubo Stadium, clowning around with tribal dancers at half time," I said.

"He's a Muslim, isn't he? Maybe he'll be better than Obote," Sultan said.

"Forget about that. Where's Bahadur, why hasn't he called?" Ma said.

Bahadur was the family night owl. The rest of the family was safe in their homes.

"Probably out with his friends. He's sensible enough not to risk the roads when there's trouble," Bapuji replied. After four or five phone calls, Sultan finally managed to track him down. He'd been out drinking with his friends and didn't have a clue about the coup.

Sleep didn't come easily that night. I lay in bed wondering if my friends were safe at home. What if Zainab, my girlfriend, hadn't managed to escape from the tanks?

ೞ

News trickled in over the next few days, some from the BBC, some at mosque, some from acquaintances in the government, some from the city grapevine. Obote, unable to return home, went to neighboring

Tanzania, hoping to raise an opposition army with support from his friend and ally, Mwalimu Julius Nyerere, the socialist president there. Word from Indian merchants in the north claimed that Acholi and Langi troops, loyal to Obote, were being slaughtered in large numbers to consolidate Amin's hold on power. The British were glad to be rid of Obote, with his socialist leanings. He had centralized the banks and was threatening to take over British-owned companies. The Brits, instrumental in Amin's rise through the military, publicly applauded the loyal soldier who had fought for them during the Mau Mau rebellion in Kenya.

Within days of the coup, the British Conservative government, almost too quickly, officially recognized Amin's new regime. The United States and Israel followed shortly thereafter. Sure that they could manipulate Amin, all three countries promised military aid to Uganda, despite objections by most African governments in the continental body, the Organization of African Unity. Kenneth Kaunda, the chairman of that organization and president of Zambia, pleaded with the international community to reconsider this recognition and aid, but his pleas fell on deaf ears.

In Kampala, the Baganda, whose king had been deposed by Obote, rejoiced in the streets and lauded Amin when he ordered the body of the deceased monarch, Kabaka Mutesa II, back from England for a royal burial. Relieved that Obote's intentions of nationalizing Asian-owned businesses were no longer a threat, the Asians also welcomed Amin's initial promises of economic reform and a quick return to civilian rule. Stores and factories opened for business within days, and Entebbe Airport once again welcomed international flights. Most people went about their daily routines and ignored the ridiculous new decrees that were being announced periodically on Radio Uganda:

"Today, in Kampala, General Idi Amin declared that the new name of Government House will be the 'Command Post.'"

"In future, all Ugandan currency will carry the picture of General Idi Amin. Currency with pictures of Milton Apollo Obote will no longer be accepted. Citizens are advised to exchange their old currency at the Bank of Uganda."

"This afternoon, President Amin commissioned the construction of a great mosque to be built in the city of Kampala in honor of the Muslim heritage of our country. Funds for the construction are to be donated by Colonel Mu'ammer Gaddafi, president of Libya."

People in the city laughed at Amin and went about their business as usual.

When schools re-opened, I got my first real job—as an English teacher at Oxford Secondary School, a private school for African students who had failed to get into the prestigious Kampala schools because of low grades and lack of money. Owned by Mr. Dastur, a philanthropic Indian businessman who was also the part-time headmaster, the school offered poor, not-so-smart Africans an opportunity to still finish their education.

My first struggle with the well meaning but conservative Mr. Dastur was over which books to teach in literature classes. I argued that Shakespeare and Yeats, the traditional texts preferred in most schools, had little relevance here. I wanted to teach the new African writers, Chinua Achebe from Nigeria and James Ngugi from Kenya, and certainly the Ugandan oral poet, Okot p'Bitek. These authors told stories about life in African cities and villages, and the effects of the social and political problems facing many African countries after independence. What relevance did the English classics have for my country? I recalled my high-school history exams, having to memorize and regurgitate pages and pages of events from the reigns of English kings and queens. I probably knew more about Tudor and Stuart history than most British students. Why? To ask why was to be insolent, and would have led to more of Mr. McCourt's dreaded canings.

After days of argument, we eventually compromised on Shakespeare's *Merchant Of Venice* and Achebe's *Things Fall Apart*. Okot p'Bitek's *Song Of Lawino*, a poetic lament about a village prostitute, was acceptable to Mr. Dastur (though he had no idea what the book was about) as long as I took on the personal responsibility of ensuring the availability of the books and getting bulk prices at the bookstore.

Soon, I got back into my routine in the city. In top physical shape after Kilimanjaro, I resumed my sports activities with renewed vigor. Nizar and I teamed up for doubles in badminton at the Aga Khan Sports Center on Kampala Hill, where we were still the unbeatable pair. Before the coup, we had been practicing almost daily in anticipation of an inter-city tournament coming up in two months' time. The short rainy season had come and gone, cooling the red soil and nourishing the greenery all over the land.

As the months wore on, Amin's actions became more and more outrageous, soon affecting all ethnic groups in the country. One day, I went to Makerere University to see Bahadur about some literary materials. At the Livingstone Dormitory, I walked into an informal political discussion going on among the students and their professors. Ba put his forefinger to his lips, indicating that I should listen carefully. It became a lesson in people's loyalties as I heard these intellectuals discuss our new leader.

Some of the Bagandan students were very concerned. "It's not funny that Bagandan soldiers are being harassed and killed by Amin's troops," said one. "Fishermen at Lake Victoria say the crocodiles are getting fat from dead bodies dumped in the water every day."

"Have you heard about what happened to High Court Chief Justice Benedicto Kiwanuka? He was dragged from his courtroom in broad daylight by Amin's soldiers, forced to take off his shoes, and shoved into the trunk of a car. Nobody has heard from him since. Makindye Prison has become a torture center."

Then the Catholic students jumped in:

"The coffers have run dry. So what does Amin do? He's found his long-lost Muslim heritage and got funds from Libya and Saudi Arabia."

"We know this, but the Libyan money for the mosque has disappeared. Israeli military advisers are being expelled, and overnight our *Dada* is a champion of the anti-Zionists."

A student who had relatives and friends in the Ugandan army added, "Mind you, he's not stupid. He knows that the loyalty of his troops depends entirely on his bribes. My brother-in-law is a soldier and he says that Amin has promoted telephone operators and night-watchmen to army officers. Every week he orders whisky runs by Ugandan planes to Britain to keep the *pombe* flowing for his men."

"At least a dog with a bone in his mouth can't bite you," said another. "And our self-appointed general's uniform is made by some Indian tailor on Nambirembe Road."

Reactions to Amin were mixed. Some of the more radical students thought of him as an African hero. Most agreed that he was a political buffoon, but a dangerous one.

The group dispersed after a while and Bahadur and I drove home, shocked and confused by what we had heard. As we drove past "Bat Valley," the sky was full of bats making their evening foray to hunt for insects in the forest.

What was happening to my country? Would we survive this madman? I shared my concerns with Bahadur that Makerere University, where I might still go the next year, may become a place of protest and death. He kept shaking his head and mumbled something about making sure that Bapuji knew about what we had heard.

ପଞ

More than a year had passed since the coup, and people in Uganda went on with their lives. One afternoon in July 1972, I was explaining to my students why Shylock the Jew wanted a pound of flesh from Antonio's heart instead of the borrowed money he had lent him, when the school janitor rushed into my classroom.

"Headmasta Dastoo want see Mista Teacher right away, sah!"

In his office, Mr. Dastur looked very somber. He quickly closed the door behind me and told me to listen to the radio. Idi Amin was speaking to the nation about a dream he'd had the night before. . . .

"Asians are the bloodsuckers of Uganda. They have ninety days to leave our country. If they do not leave, they will find themselves sitting on the fire. Africa is for Africans only. They are milking our country of its wealth. Businesses and properties of these bloodsuckers belong to the common man of Uganda."

Mr. Dastur told me to cancel classes for the rest of the day and go home to my family.

ʘ

"*Toka toka! Toka hapa!*" yelled the black policeman with the rifle slung over his khaki shirt. My father almost fell over, his gray hat flying to the ground.

Bapuji had arrived at seven in the morning, but his spot up front in the long line at the Ugandan Immigration office was now gone, after he had left to urinate. A few months before, Bapuji would have slipped some Ugandan currency into the policeman's hand, and that would have been the end of the matter. But since Amin's dream speech that all Asians were bloodsuckers, the police had been much greedier, some even resorting to beating up citizens in public.

Clutching his manila envelope tightly against his chest, Bapuji picked up his hat and quietly walked back to the end of the line, his left eye twitching from nervousness. Like all the other Asians, he was there because, two days after his dream, Idi Amin had come out with another decree: Asians with Ugandan passports had to verify their status with Immigration immediately or risk losing their citizenship.

Amin wanted Britain to take responsibility for all Asians in Uganda who held British passports, because they were "sabotaging the economy of the country."

The mid-morning sun beat down hard on the people waiting in line. All were anxious to get their *kipande*, the little red book that would verify that their families were bona-fide Ugandan citizens. Only Asians who had this *kipande* would be allowed to stay in the country. Bapuji had ten passports in the manila envelope—eight of us nine children, and his own and Ma's; Amir, the eldest son, had already emigrated to the United States the year before. Seven of the passports were Ugandan, with the national emblem of the shield with a deer and spear on either side. Some years before, he had secured British passports for Phiroz and me, knowing that this would make it easier for us to go to university in England. Our expired Ugandan passports had never been renewed. Being a practical man, he had hung on to his own British passport since he left India 44 years before, just in case the political winds in Africa changed.

ఆ

Bapuji was born in 1908 in Gondal, a small town in Gujarat State, India. Because he liked books and numbers, his parents shipped him off to Bombay to finish high school and study English. When he was seventeen, his father died in a train accident, forcing him to drop out of technical college to look for a job to support his aging mother, three younger brothers, and two sisters.

The British were recruiting skilled laborers to help build the East African railway from the Kenyan coast to Uganda. They also needed teachers for their East African colonies. Armed with his good knowledge of English and his half-finished technical degree, Bapuji volunteered. In exchange, he was given a British passport and a passage to East Africa. It was 1928, and he was twenty years old. He first taught in a bush school in Sultanhamud, Kenya, and was then transferred to another school in Singida, Tanganyika (now Tanzania). Singida back then was surrounded by jungle, where Bapuji could hear the roar of lions in the night.

By 1931, Bapuji was already 23 years old, and custom dictated that he should find a wife. Since he was now teaching in Kenya again, he went to Mombasa, where there was a small Indian community, and arranged for a marriage with Fatima, a nineteen-year-old Ismaili girl who was born on the island of Lamu on the Arabian coast of Kenya.

Over the next decade, while traversing East Africa from bush school to bush school and raising a family, my parents spent all their savings on getting Bapuji's mother and three younger brothers out of India and settled in Africa. His mother, Dadima, spent her last years happily with Bapuji and Ma in Singida, and died in Kampala when I was nine or ten years old. His younger brothers came from India and went into business for themselves in Uganda and now had their own families. One of his sisters died in India, but the other sister, Sakina, married a merchant in Bombay and had her own family and home in the Muslim part of the city. In Uganda I knew my uncles, of course, and was very close to my cousins, but I had never even seen a photograph of my surviving aunt in India.

Over 41 years of moving around East Africa, my mother Fatima gave birth to nine children, four in Singida and the rest in Sultanhamud and Kampala. The eldest son, Amir, became a doctor in India, married a Parsi woman, Nergesh, and emigrated with his family to America in 1971.

Bahadur, the second brother, had studied in England before the coup, and Phiroz and I would follow in his footsteps. Of my five sisters, two of them, Gulshan and Sultan, married Ismaili men, while the other three, Shamim, Nisha, and Leila, married non-Ismaili Asians. All now had families, decent jobs, and their own houses in Kampala.

My parents, forced to move home numerous times in India and Africa for more than half their lives, had been relieved to settle in Kampala as our final home for the rest of their lives.

ಐ

When Bapuji got his turn at the Immigration office, an official reviewed all the documents, paying particular attention to the three British passports. He asked if any other family members had British passports. Bapuji tried to explain that Phiroz and I had also held Ugandan passports, but the man cut him off. He informed my father that the three British passport holders would have to leave Uganda within ninety days and should make arrangements with the British High Commission for our departure. The rest of the family could stay in Uganda and would receive their *kipandes* within two weeks. Stunned, Bapuji pleaded with the man, who snarled and flared his nostrils. "Are you being cheeky with me, old man? I can cancel all these Ugandan passports if I want to. You never revoked your British citizenship. And two of your sons are also British, not Ugandan. Now you must go! Next!"

At home that night, I knew there was something wrong because Bapuji was asleep instead of listening to the radio or watching TV. Dinner preparations that night were an unusually quiet affair, punctuated only by the grating sound of cicadas on the tall *pafu* trees. Gulshan had just finished dressing up ten-year-old Shilo, her daughter. From the kitchen, the aroma of *gharum masala*—that blend of cloves, pepper, and cinnamon used in most Muslim curries—being sautéed with onions was wafting into the dining room. Leila rolled up the last of the chapattis for Nisha to bake and serve while hot with the meal. My mother called for Suleimani, our houseboy, to bring the food to the dinner table.

Suleimani held the record for lasting the longest under Ma's supervision. He was from the Chagga tribe, farmers who tilled the volcanic slopes of Kilimanjaro. He had danced with glee when he saw my pictures of the mountain he hadn't seen since childhood, having been brought to Kampala at the age of six by his widowed mother. Over time, he had earned the trust of my mother, who was a natural-born detective when it came to tracking down missing bottles of salt and sugar from the kitchen shelves. Any theft by her houseboys was reason enough for her to get rid of them on the spot. "If they steal sugar when I'm here, who knows what they'll steal when they are alone in the house."

All of us siblings had been asked to come home for the family meeting, and some were staying over for the night. Bahadur told Bapuji about the latest round-up of academics by Amin's goons at the university. I wondered how long before there would be no more Oxford Secondary School. Lately, Mr. Dastur had been too preoccupied with his own family's safety to pay attention to the future of the school.

Normally our dinner table was like a fish market, a cacophony of voices talking in pairs or across the table, like the frenzied haggling of vendors and buyers. But tonight we ate in silence, all pondering the gravity of the decisions that needed to be made after dinner.

"Why is everyone so quiet?" Shilo asked.

Nobody answered, so instead she asked for more fried potatoes and less fish on her plate.

After dinner, Gulshan took Shilo to bed, promising to tell her two *Ramayana* stories instead of the usual one. When everyone had settled down in the living room, Bapuji recounted his day at Immigration in a serious tone. Ma was the first to react when he finished.

"When is this madness going to stop? These Amin *gundas* will stop at nothing." Her brow was furrowed with the news that the family might have to break up.

"It's not safe anymore. We have to go. We have to leave this country." Bapuji sounded definite.

"Go? Go where? Forty years of toil, raising nine children, not knowing what I will feed them from one day to the next. Isn't that enough? I am tired of moving. This is our home." Tears welled up in her eyes.

Bapuji then did something I had never seen him do before. He took Ma's hands in his and looked her in the eye. Showing affection in public, even in family, was simply not done, not in my culture, not in my community, and certainly not by my parents. Even calling each other by their first names in public was taboo.

"I know. I'm tired, too," he said. "I haven't forgotten Singida, with you pregnant with Mohezin and no meat on the table. Kampala's been good to us. But we have no choice, Ma. We have to think of Shilo's future. We'll find a new home. A better home, I promise you."

His words made some of my sisters break into sobs, as well.

"Where will we go? Who will take us?" worried Sultan.

"Britain, India, Pakistan, Congo. Wherever they'll take us," Bapuji replied.

Sultan informed us that our Aga Khan had petitioned Western governments to intervene on our behalf. She joined her hands in prayer, facing the gold-framed photograph of the Aga Khan on the wall.

"Is India or Pakistan really a place where we can live?" Shamim said. "The younger ones can't read or write Hindi or Urdu, or even Gujarati."

"What about all our things? And our jobs? Our furniture, our saris, the patterned china. . . ? How will we take all this with us?" Ma sobbed.

"The boys and I will look for ways to get our money and things out over the next few weeks," Bapuji said. He didn't want to elaborate on how this would be done.

"Will I be able to finish to finish my degree in another country? Phiroz asked. "What about Mo's university applications?"

"You'll have to get academic transcripts and continue wherever we end up."

Woken by all the sobbing and loud discussion, Shilo walked into the living room, half asleep and rubbing her eyes. The discussion broke up soon after, since the BBC news—now a nightly imperative—was about to start. The family had decided that Bapuji would go to the British Embassy to submit our documents, with me to help him with the English. Bapuji asked for silence as the news came on.

The reports were not comforting. In the House of Commons, the debate continued over the plight of us Ugandan Asians. Some MPs argued that we had no connection with Britain and should go back to India. Some argued that, given the racial tensions in Britain and the high level of unemployment, bringing us Asians into the country would not be an economically wise decision.

Bapuji kicked the radio in disgust, and it shattered into pieces on the floor.

ভ

In Kampala, the various embassies greeted the ninety-day ultimatum with mixed responses. At the British Embassy, the lines were even longer than at Uganda Immigration. When an official came out to address the waiting crowd, he announced that all travel applications to Britain had been suspended until further notice. Verification of British nationality for passport holders would have to wait until the embassy received its orders from London. Little did we know at that time that the debate going on in Britain included a suggestion to dump the Asians with British passports on some former colonial island for a nominal price per head—like goats at a market. Some MPs proposed paying off each applicant with 2,000 pounds if they gave up their right to live in Britain. (This information was only revealed publicly after confidential documents were declassified thirty years later.)

The Americans shrouded their response in diplomatic language, insisting that the plight of the Ugandan Asians was an internal matter for the Ugandan government. They reiterated that the United States's immigration policy was based on pre-defined quotas for nationals from each country, as determined by the State Department, but individual cases would be reviewed at the embassy upon submission of all required documents.

The Indian Embassy response was anything but Asian. It issued a bulletin informing us that Ugandan Indians holding British or Ugandan passports were not considered to be Indian citizens since they had willingly given up their citizenship.

We began to feel like shuttlecocks in a game of political badminton as the ninety-day deadline drew nearer. No country was willing to take responsibility for us, so we got caught up in the crossfire of post-colonial posturing. Eighty thousand was the figure touted as the total number of Asians in Uganda, with about a third of that figure holding British passports. These were numbers that scared all the embassies. Japan and Australia refused outright to have anything to do with us.

ଔ

By now, Amin had become a star in the international media. His outrageous statements were front-page news. The press quoted him over and over again when he proclaimed that Hitler was right to have killed the six million Jews. When ousted president Obote called Amin "the greatest brute an African mother has ever brought to life," they chose to emphasize Amin's response instead: "I am not an ambitious man. I am just a soldier who is concerned for my country and my people." *Punch* magazine in the UK started printing a satirical weekly column supposedly written by Amin on current events. The well-known Nigerian musician, Fela, described Amin as a progressive, anti-Western hero, comparing him to African champions like Kwame Nkurumah, leader of the continent's first independent nation, Ghana; Patrice Lumumba in the Belgian Congo; and even Nelson Mandela. Meanwhile, within Uganda, reports from concerned journalists on atrocities committed by Amin's thugs at Makindye Prison fell on deaf editorial ears. The media were more interested to know if the African buffoon had any more crazy one-liners for their front pages.

Kampala is a small city, where the grapevine works faster than the mail or the telephone. Alerted that the Asians were desperate to get their possessions out, Amin planted spies within our communities to find out exactly what was going on. He promised free passage and immunity from confiscation of properties to poorer Indians who had nothing to lose and were willing to be his eyes and ears. Then, one evening, dressed up in his general's uniform with all his fake medals on his huge boxer's chest, Amin appeared on national television and proclaimed yet another decree: the Ugandan borders with Kenya and Tanzania would be closed, to prevent Asians from smuggling out their money and possessions. Asian families leaving the country would be allowed to take out no more than the equivalent of fifty British pounds. Families found with foreign currency and valuables would be detained at Entebbe Airport.

The reaction all over the country was one of celebration. African customers refused to pay their debts and demanded goods for free from Asian stores. Trucks carrying supplies for Asian businesses were diverted to the nearest army barracks, never to be seen again. In towns all over the country, shops were looted and vandalized within hours of their Asian owners departing to the capital. "*Funga safari, muhindi! Salamia* Shashi Kapoor!" 'Pack your bags, Indians. Greetings to Shashi Kapoor!' The taunts were heard all over Uganda.

In Kampala, the reaction was mixed. Bahadur called in to say that, at the university dormitories, many students danced with joy upon hearing the latest Amin decree. Academics and intellectuals cautioned that Asian businesses were the backbone of the country's commerce and that Africans should be trained to take over or else the economy would collapse. Their warnings went unheard and then stopped altogether once Amin sent troops to storm the faculty complex and round up any vocal dissidents. He ordered the university's chancellor to sack all non-Ugandan professors or face execution himself. All classes were cancelled and the campus became deserted.

The city itself soon became a ghost town. Businesses closed down, restaurants and shops didn't replenish their stocks, more and more shop windows were barred by iron grilles. Vendors no longer came to Kampala Road, since their most valued customers had gone. At roadblocks all over town, soldiers harassed the few drivers who ventured out on the streets at night. Life came to a standstill.

As panic set in among the Asian community, each group reverted to cultural norms to cope with the fear of an unknown future. The Ismailis, reciting special prayers and hymns at mosque to invoke Amin's change of heart, appealed to the Aga Khan to ask for divine intervention. Like everyone else, they sought out foreign clients to help get their savings out of the country. The Hindus lit more incense and placed more garlands on their favorite gods at temples around the city. At the same time they sneaked goods into Kenya, where business associates could help get them shipped out from Mombasa. The Sikhs held secret meetings at the *gurdwara*, contemplating ways to protect their possessions and businesses. They even considered arming themselves with weapons to be brought over by their Indian brothers. Meanwhile, they smuggled their sons and daughters— pockets and bags stuffed with dollars or pounds—to neighboring countries where friends and relatives could then get them to safer places.

Then, from the Canadians, came the first good news in weeks.

Sultan came home from mosque one day with the exciting news from our community leaders. The Canadians had opened a temporary consulate in the basement of the main library in Kampala and were accepting applications from all Asians, irrelevant of their background or passport. Aware that most of the Asians were educated, adept in some trade or profession, and spoke good enough English, Canada, in need of skilled immigrants, had opened its doors to our plight.

The consulate staff was very welcoming. They took on volunteers from our Asian communities to help with translations and medical check-ups, and promised updates within a week when we presented our papers. Shamim, now a qualified doctor, volunteered to help their medical staff.

The following week, at the consulate, the official came straight to the point. Except for Phiroz and myself, the whole family including Bapuji, had been accepted for emigration to Vancouver. He said that the Canadian government preferred not to split up the family, but that Phiroz and I, being British passport holders, had been accepted for entry into Britain as special cases. They had been notified by the British Consulate, and they gave us the letter for reference.

The waiting was finally over. Our family had a place—or places—to go. We clustered in the waiting room and digested the bittersweet news. Ma broke into tears, upset that our family would not all be together. Bapuji looked relieved and kept reassuring her that Phiroz and I would rejoin the family after finishing our studies in England. Bahadur hugged Gulshan tight and kissed Shilo's forehead. We all embraced each other in sheer relief.

Thoughts, all muddled together, rushed to my head. England, the colonial motherland. The home of Shakespeare, The Beatles, and The Rolling Stones. London. Rock 'n' roll concerts. Phiroz and I, all alone, separated from the family by that huge Atlantic Ocean. When would we see our parents again? And Nizar and Ashok and Zainab? Would I ever see my friends Daniel or Dixon again?

Meanwhile, in London itself, British prime minister Edward Heath announced: "It is our moral responsibility to help all the Asians in Uganda who have British passports." To ensure an appropriate strategy of repatriation, the Home Office (the UK interior ministry) had established a Ugandan Refugee Board, which would be responsible for organizing resettlement centers throughout Britain, to avoid overcrowding and undue pressures.

Little did we know then, that other alternatives had been seriously considered by the British before this announcement was made? We would only find out thirty years later what actually happened during the chaos of those months.

The scheme to offer each British subject 2,000 pounds (to relinquish their right to citizenship) was dropped when it was realized that Enoch Powell, an overtly racist British politician, might demand the same for immigrants already living in Britain. In addition, places like the Solomons, the Seychelles, the Caymans, Bermuda, British Honduras, Gibraltar, and the Virgin Islands had refused acceptance of the Ugandan Asians.

When the Foreign Office threatened to cut off all aid to Uganda, Amin still refused to revoke his decision. Plans were then drawn up to mount a military operation against Amin, but only if he turned on the 7,000 white British settlers and expatriates in Uganda. Leading the assault would be the Parachute Regiment supported by 25 Hercules aircraft from Oman in the Persian Gulf. Another four battalions were to seize the airport at Entebbe and the 21-mile road to Kampala to ensure that the white community had safe havens to rendezvous at during the attack, and to ensure their evacuation if necessary. These plans didn't come about, only because the military preparations never got off the ground in time for the Amin deadline. Again, this information only became public knowledge, once declassified, thirty years later.

಻

Events moved faster as the departure deadline got closer. Phiroz and I were to leave for London within a week. The rest of the family would leave for Canada two weeks later.

Bapuji visited all his foreign clients to find someone who would help him get money out of the country. Eventually, for a handsome fee, two American clients agreed to accept Ugandan currency in Kampala and then open an overseas account for Bapuji and deposit the equivalent sum in American dollars and British pounds. Bapuji also purchased open-ended plane tickets to Europe and India for the family, so as to use up some of the money left over from the family savings, since Amin had decreed that no Asian could leave Uganda with more than the equivalent of fifty British pounds.

At home, the women in our household agonized over what to pack and what to discard. The plan was to sneak luggage chests into Kenya and have them shipped out to Canada from Mombasa. There were no guarantees that the chests would make it to their destination. The most precious things—money, jewelry, plane tickets, were carefully hidden away in the bags going to the airport. We took our chances, like everyone else.

My goodbyes with friends took place happenstance at mosque or in town, in between last-minute errands. Nizar's family was going to Toronto. We exchanged our Outward Bound badges and promised to give them back to each other in the Western world. Ashok's family had decided to go back to India, and we never got to say goodbye to each other. Zainab and her family were to be resettled in Edmonton, Canada.

On the day of departure, Ma was frantic, hugging Phiroz and me at every opportunity and fussing over the final packing of our cases. Inside each were the symbols that made up nearly twenty years of our life in Uganda: photos of family safaris, birthdays, and funerals; sports trophies; *kitenge* shirts; my "African Kingdom" animals set. As the car pulled away, I took a long last look at my home. The balcony from where I saw Luwanga shot stared back at me. My eyes zoomed in on the guava tree in front of the house, where I played with the Kampala Kudus. I knew all the best spots on the tree—for clipping the fruit, for hiding during tree games, for escaping the neighbor's dog. The lump in my throat stayed all the way to the airport.

The ride through Kampala was eerie. The city was almost deserted. All the tailor shops were closed; the shoe and safari outfitters were all boarded up; money exchange houses and restaurants were barred by iron grilles. In the sky, the bats were on their way to the forest for their nightly hunt.

On the road to Entebbe, no one spoke; everyone was worried about the roadblocks. We were stopped seven times and made to get out of the car on four occasions. Hurled insults and more bribes each time. Shilo, in a pink dress, cried the whole trip; she was terrified when a soldier at the first checkpoint poked his rifle through the front window.

At the airport, the British Embassy officials put stickers on our coats to make sure we got on the right flight. The Ugandans searched us from head to toe, undid all of Ma's packing of our suitcases, and demanded extra money for excess baggage. Bapuji did what he had to do. More baksheesh.

"*Salamia* Queen Elizabeth!" 'Give my regards to Queen Elizabeth!' taunted the last Customs official as we neared the boarding gate. The tears flowed freely on my mother's face as she held me tight. Her kisses were salty. Our sisters kept sobbing and asking if we had all our carry-on bags. Bapuji held both our hands together and said, "Be strong. Help each other. We will all be together again. *Inshallah*." Phiroz and I stepped onto the tarmac and walked to the plane. As we climbed the last rung of the ladder before entering the Boeing 707, we turned to search for family faces on the upper deck of the terminal. All we could see was waving hands. Shilo, in her pink dress, was lost in the crowd.

5. Are You Experienced?

Music is my religion.
Jimi Hendrix.

African music and dance was all around me in the streets of Kampala. Day or night, all over the city, the sensual rhythms blared out of Radio Uganda. As a cocky teenager, I grooved with the best of them at dance contests. Every October 9th, during Independence Day celebrations at Lugogo Stadium, we gyrated till dawn, amid a sea of black bodies in grass skirts, to the beats of deer-hide drums. It became an annual tradition for me.

When the craze for Chubby Checker's "Twist" swept though the city in the sixties, I memorized every move I saw on television till I too was twisting the night away. At the age of eleven, I saw my first ever live concert when American blues guitarist, Buddy Guy, played at the Silver Springs Hotel. By the outdoor swimming pool, under a starlit African sky, a throng of dancers—black, white, brown—

112

rocked till four in the morning. I squeezed my way up to front stage, mesmerized by the new sound.

In 1963, jazz legend Louis Armstrong played with his band at Makerere University to a packed auditorium of students. I cajoled my brother Amir and sister Shamim to take me along. That night, "Satchmo" must have soiled over ten handkerchiefs wiping the sweat off his brow, as he blew his golden trumpet, number after hot number, in the humid non-air-conditioned hall. Weeks later, Shamim was still singing "Mack The Knife" over dinner at Madras Gardens.

One October during the mid sixties, Harry Belafonte and Miriam Makeba, sponsored by Pepsi, crooned calypso songs with South African beats for thousands of revelers ushering in another year of freedom from the British. A stadium full of *kitenge kanzus* singing the choruses to songs like "Matilda" and "Day O." When the two stars broke into "Malaika," a popular Swahili song, the crowd went berserk.

By the time I was sixteen, I had talked my unsuspecting father into buying me a set of drums to play in a pop band. Gone were the Bollywood film songs from my repertoire that my parents had enjoyed so much. Our band, the "African Lions," performed gigs at local parties and dance halls. Influenced by rock 'n' roll stars of the West, Elvis Presley and Cliff Richard, we belted out hits like "Jailhouse Rock" and "The Young Ones" with an African beat. When Jamaican reggae pioneers, Jimmy Cliff and Desmond Decker, came on the scene, we copied them, too. Then, in the late sixties, came the blitz of the rock revolution that shook our music world.

After evening prayers on Friday, in the mosque courtyard, I would rattle off lyrics to the latest Beatles song to impress all the hot Ismaili girls clad in their midriff-baring saris. During the week, band practices took up most of my spare time, as we memorized "Satisfaction" and other Rolling Stones songs. At home, my siblings complained bitterly that I was taking twenty-minute showers, crooning love songs and screaming rock 'n' roll in the only bathroom for nine family members. I was in my own zone.

My poor mosque-at-dawn father was baffled that his youngest son and daughter would almost come to fists over whether "Sergeant Pepper's Lonely Hearts Club Band" was funkier than Aretha Franklin's "Respect"—music so far removed from his generation, language, and culture that he must have felt pangs of fear over what had become of his Indian children.

My whatever-makes-you-happy mother, who had never danced a jig in her entire life, was suddenly forced to jive with me to the wailing guitar of Jimi Hendrix's "Voodoo Chile." Shocked that her son wanted to teach her how to dance, she eventually went along, oblivious to what the sounds and lyrics meant to me. Never questioning this musical metamorphosis in her younger children, she just assumed it was a passing phase for us, since the older ones were not smitten as much.

At university in England, far from any family pressures, I strayed even further from my heritage. With John Lennon glasses and frizzy long hair like Jimmy Page, I became the token Asian hippie of my dorm. Acid trips at Pink Floyd concerts and magic-mushroom space rides to Hendrix on "Third Stone From The Sun" became my cosmos.

In 1975, at graduate school in Ann Arbor, Michigan, I was one of the organizers of the Ann Arbor Blues and Jazz Festival—a week-long party with bands from all over Europe and America. I shook hands with B. B. King and John Lee Hooker, and got backstage after a Miles Davis concert.

A year later, on a hitchhiking trip to the California coast, I caught Bob Marley and the Wailers in Santa Barbara. Stoned on Californian weed and a flask of tequila sunrise, the tears spilled over my face as Rastaman Bob belted out "War," railing against dictatorial regimes in Africa.

It wasn't till I got to Otavalo in Ecuador that I learned to appreciate *indígena* folk music as a way to help revive a lost culture. On a full moon Christmas Night in 1977, wrapped up against the Andean cold in a handwoven alpaca wool poncho and sipping hot cinnamon wine, I danced with Otavalo Indians to the sound of Incan music played on sixty wooden instruments, all hand-made by village artists now long gone.

Music became my escape route to places where chameleons go to lose themselves in crowds, temporarily transformed by melodies and rhythms. I gravitated to places and venues where music chameleons flocked, magical places that gave me a library of music from three continents.

ᘓ

In 1973, Mick, my dorm mate at university, and I made the trip from Norwich to Earls Court in London to see Pink Floyd play a benefit concert for the homeless. With hundreds of other fans that night, we walked in under a large yellow banner with big blue letters that read, "TRIP TO THE DARK SIDE OF THE MOON ON A PINK FLOYD SPACESHIP."

Inside, the house lights were still on as the last of the audience found their seats in the packed auditorium. The "Ummagumma" album was blaring out of the enormous speakers on either side of the stage in quadraphonic sound. The atmosphere was electric as I took in the scene. With stage lights off, the crew was almost finished setting up the mounds of equipment, checking the sound and light system with torches. In the crowd, students were blowing soap bubbles into the air. A couple of girls in Floyd T-shirts and ankle-length skirts were dancing in one aisle, hands waving in the air like a magician's wand at a magic show.

I had dreamed about such a scene many a Saturday night in Kampala, dancing to Floyd albums at some party or another. To be here in England at my first ever Floyd concert was beyond those dreams. I was so psyched up that I plumb forgot to piss before I went into the hall.

"Come on, man, let's find our seats," Mick said, and I followed him, dodging a paper airplane coming straight at me. He led the way. With straight blond hair down to his shoulders, he was working class all the way, with faded dungarees and torn sneakers. The phrase 'English reserve' did not exist in his vocabulary; he was the kind of student who shunned negativity and was friends with everybody. With baby-face cheeks, Mick Jagger lips, and round blue eyes, he was a cuddly teddy bear the girls just loved. Drunk and stoned, Mick and I had danced to Hendrix on the jukebox till closing time at the university bar one night, and had been pals ever since. I liked him because he accepted me as if I were no different than any of his friends back home in Preston.

For the concert, I wore bell-bottomed jeans, a sky-blue Hendrix T-shirt from the Monterey Festival, my African bead necklace, and an elephant-hair bracelet on my right wrist. Just after we took our seats, someone passed around a big fat joint. We both inhaled a few tokes before passing it back. The smell of dope lingered in the air like a strong perfume.

"I'm gettin' a buzz, Woggy." Mick grinned.

Mick was the only one who I let get away with calling me 'wog,' a derogatory term for blacks or Asians in England, that I had changed to mean 'wise oriental gentleman.'

"Sure thing, Mickey Mouse. Bring on the cocktails," I replied, pointing to his knapsack. The thermos full of vodka mixed with orange juice would keep us well lubricated throughout the show.

"Bet you a beer the opening song'll be 'Brain Damage,'" he said.

"You're on. I'm betting my money on 'Money,'" I replied.

The alcohol and ganja were mixing well together. It seemed to me that the Brits always needed the high to let loose. Even Mick. Kill the inhibitions. Trample the taboos. Africa had taught me that music was all I needed to get my butt wiggling, but the booze and weed did indeed take it to another dimension.

The atmosphere became surreal as the weed took hold, my ears now able to distinguish the notes of each different instrument from the speakers. "Set The Controls For The Heart Of The Sun" now floated in. The bass sounded louder now with much more *oomph* as my mind wandered around the sounds and I imagined myself riding in a spacecraft heading into the sun. The warmth inside me, unlike the short-lived tepid heat of an English sun, was a dry scorching heat. I was on top of Kilimanjaro once again. I was an African Icarus piloting a Floyd spaceship headed into the solar system.

Mick lit up one of our joints, rolled up like a Jamaican spliff. More tokes as we gazed all around us. Two thousand fans brimming with anticipation. More girls dancing in the aisles, tie-dye skirts and waist-length hair flowing in the smoke-filled air. Another paper airplane swerved by before swooping down on some reveler. Someone tossed out a beach ball into the crowd; hands kept tossing it back and forth in the air and it floated from group to group. Then the stage lights came on simultaneously with the house lights going off. A huge roar erupted.

"Rock 'n' roooooooll!" Mick shouted at the top of his lungs.

The sound of cash registers and coins filled the hall. *Ka-ching*! *Ka-ching*! The roar was deafening now. Everyone recognized the beginning of "Money," and then the bass came in for a few notes followed by the guitar then the vocals. The crowd settled into the groove. Lights zoomed in on some of the band . . . Gilmour on guitar . . . Mason on drums . . . Waters on bass and vocal. The screens flashed images of cash registers in supermarkets and the London stock exchange, coins flying in the air. . . . Now the saxophone kicked in. Lights flashed on the horn player bobbing up and down. A drum roll swept in and the lights zoomed back onto drummer Mason, hands twirling sticks in the air, and then the whole band took off, the guitar wailing, the sax blowing hard, cash registers clinking away, the bass booming louder than ever. The drums lifted the song to a crescendo and then just as quickly brought it all right back down. Waters' soft vocals for the second verse started the whole cycle all over again.

"You owe me!" I yelled to Mick.

He nodded, snapping his fingers and stomping his feet. I was on my feet playing air guitar. A neighbor passed me a pipe with Afghan hashish, the embers still burning. More tokes of dark chocolate. The band segued into "Time." Hundreds of hands waved in the air, bodies swayed back and forth as they sang along, "Ho-ome. Home again. I like to beee here when I caaaan. . . ." I was one of them, happy as a warrior at a war party, jumping with the throng. One music chameleon among hundreds. Dancers moved into the aisles and we joined them. A roving blue light meandered through the crowd as the revolving strobe made our body movements writhe in slow motion like some ancient t'ai chi meditation ritual.

When the band switched to a section from "Atom Heart Mother," immediately I went into a funk. Wanting to be alone for this one, I rushed back to my seat, closed my eyes, and rocked my head between my legs. I saw images of Uganda, of Ma cooking in the kitchen in Madras Gardens. She was beckoning me to come to her. I touched her warm face smiling at me as she turned over the saffron rice in the big pot. She kissed my forehead and called me 'Sachu,' a pet name she used for me as a boy.

The Moog synthesizer took us on another galactic cruise. The mirage of colors mushroomed on the screen. Cylindrical rays of blue and red from the stage lights streaked out all over the auditorium. Purple smoke poured from the stage floor, lingering between the band members.

"One Of These Days" came next, jolting me out of my funk. I was back in the aisles, dancing like a whirling dervish, my fingers, working the air in sync with the beat. A barefooted girl with long, curly red hair slid beside me, mimicking my movements until she was in sync with the song and me. Her name was Ursula and we wove our way through all the other dancers, in and out, over and around, song after song, like a choreographed rock ballet. Time had no meaning now.

For the encore, the band played "Us And Them" and "Eclipse." At the end, they left the stage to thunderous applause. That night, I felt like I was part of a communal movement, a member of a tribe that thrived on the ecstacy of its collective cohesion.

೦೩

Nearly thirty years later, in 2002, at Impact Arena in Bangkok. Roger Waters, on an Asian tour with a new band, played all the old Floyd hits.

Outside the arena, under yellow Singha Beer umbrellas, I sat eating Thai snacks and smoking dope with new friends, much younger than me: Jewish-Canadian Waxy, another teddy bear like Mick from Preston; Carolla, a Chilean beauty with cascading hair; and Kung, a Thai rocker with buckteeth. Also with me, were friends from my generation: Vancouverite, Al; guitarist Pong, from Isaan, and his lovely wife, Nong; and Roachie from Melbourne.

With short-cropped hair and oval-shaped glasses, I wore a Neil Young T-shirt that proclaimed, "Rock 'n' Roll Will Never Die. Better To Burn Out Than To Fade Away."

Inside, British hippies had been replaced by a crowd of Thai dolls dressed in tight jeans and skimpy tops, hanging onto *farang* boyfriends or long-haired Thai rockers. The oil-lamp projectors from the 1970s were gone, replaced by giant-screen close-ups of the band. Soap bubbles had become laser pointers. The beach ball was now a human body tossed around by outstretched hands. Fans popped Ecstasy and *yaa baa* instead of puffing on hash pipes and joints. On stage, a much older Roger Waters—without Gilmour and Mason and Wright—took us back to the wild 70s.

Throughout the show, I marveled at all the younger chameleons reveling all around me. The stage had moved from London to Bangkok; the hype surrounding the event was more organized, more technically hip, the whole thing more expensive. Yet, the dancing fans had the same glow, the same tribal camaraderie, the same unified abandon that I had felt three decades before.

When the band broke into "Mother," once again I went into another funk, this time grieving for Ma, who had passed away in Vancouver a few years before. She no longer called me Sachu. Instead, she was right beside me at front stage, brushing away the tears, urging me to 'Dance, chameleon, dance.'

∞

The burgundy Mustang that Scott picked me up in just outside Flagstaff had the convertible top down and the eight-track tape player blaring out The Eagles' "Take It Easy." With his Ray-Bans, wavy auburn hair blowing in the summer breeze, and head bopping to the song, he looked like one of the 'rebels' in a James Dean movie.

"*Jambo sana, rafiki, karibuni*," he greeted me with the traditional Kenyan Swahili welcome. His accent still sounded authentic.

"*Muzuri dugu yangu*," I replied, calling him 'brother' in Swahili. We hugged each other and shook hands African style, marveling that we were together again in America.

On the ride back to his parents' house in Flagstaff, we caught up with each other's lives. It was the summer of 1975, my second year in Michigan. I told him all about England, university in Norwich, the Floyd concert, and hitting the cop in London. Scott was back home from Kenya for his sister's wedding and was staying on for another two weeks before heading back to his school in the boondocks. He missed Africa terribly, couldn't stop talking about Kenya. While filling up the car at a Texaco gas station, he even threw in a few Swahili words to the pump attendant, who looked at him completely baffled. We had a good laugh at this.

But all of a sudden, I felt dejected. The Swahili language, the talk of silverback gorillas, the Masai Mara National Reserve . . . they were all taking me back to a place where I didn't want to go. But Scott went on and on with anecdotes of wandering through Kenyan villages where the elders wouldn't give him a glass of water unless he ate with them, even when they didn't have enough to feed their own, and schoolgirls bringing juicy mangoes as gifts for their teacher. I had just spent the last couple of years trying to forget about all that. Thoughts of Africa made me feel helpless. I hated the fact that I couldn't go back. Scott, on the other hand, was swimming in African adventure and dying to return to it. The difference was, despite his two-year African safari, he knew where he came from and where he belonged. I didn't.

We stayed overnight at his parents' house, a luxurious suburban home with sprinklers for the manicured lawns. Over dinner, the family wanted to know all about Africa and how I had got here. I found myself in that depressing situation, yet one more time, of having to explain again why I had to leave.

The next day, we threw our backpacks and sleeping bags into the Mustang and drove to the Grand Canyon to start our hike down the Bright Angel Trail, which winds all the way down to the Colorado River. At the South Rim, we picked up lots of water and a few other supplies for our week-long trip and started off. The views were spectacular.

Now that we were back in the wild outdoors, away from family and city life, we both forgot our woes of feeling like African fish in American waters. The panorama before us demanded our full attention.

"This is God's country," Scott said as we started down.

"Must be much older than Olduvai," I replied, referring to the famous gorge in Tanzania where Louis Leakey discovered *Zinjanthropus* Man, the ancient remains of one of the earliest known hominids.

The Grand Canyon is over 270 miles long, ten miles wide, and over a mile deep. The rock strata revealed the ancient history of the earth: layer upon layer of geological time, deeper than Olduvai. I imagined water gushing through this vast red land millions of years ago, carving its way through the plateau, eroding this stupendous monument, sculpting a zillion shapes and forms that not even a celestial Michelangelo could envision. Every corner turned brought into view a new plethora of wonders. A chasm exposed sculpted castles of red clay as we went around one switchback; pyramids, stacked one upon another, stared back at us around a second; upon reaching a third, gigantic red *mesas* stretched all along the horizon.

We passed spots with exotic names: the Coconino Overlook, which boasted a panorama of red castles under a *mesa* that formed a perfect straight line of red rock; the Supai Tunnel, a rockfall shaped into a cave that we walked through to escape the heat for a while. At Roaring Springs, in front of a ranger's hut, stood a small wooden table where some good soul had left an almost full pitcher of ice-cold lemonade for thirsty hikers on their way up or down. Never had lemonade tasted as deliciously tangy as it did right then, going down our parched throats.

At the bottom, the mighty, cold Colorado River rushed through the rock, shimmering in the sun. We picked a spot to lay out our sleeping bags and, that evening, after dinner and a couple of joints, Scott and I sat around our Coleman stove and talked just like we had done so many times at Kilimanjaro, the beginning of our friendship. We talked about music again and compared notes on concerts we had seen. He turned me onto The Grateful Dead and Fleetwood Mac, whom he'd seen in the States, and I told him about the bands I'd seen in England and America, and then about Buddy Guy and Satchmo and Harry Belafonte in Kampala.

Then, inevitably, the topic turned back to Africa.

"What I miss most are the smiles and '*jambos*' wherever I went in Kenya," Scott said.

"I miss them, too," I replied. "Especially from the children. Don't forget though—as *muzungu* and *muhindi*, we were given privileged status by Africans." More than a decade after independence, Africans still looked upon the white man and the brown trader as saviors of some sort. So I believed.

"That's true. Maybe that's why I miss Africa so much. Over there, people count on me to help them. I'm not just another Social Security number, like I am here."

It seemed like a good time to confront my denials of longing for Africa. Only then might I be at peace with myself. "Scott, do you like Kenya enough to want to call it home?" I asked, antsy to get to the heart of the matter.

Scott paused for a while. "Good question. I guess America will always be my home."

"I hope I can say the same . . . one day."

This was the first time I had actually verbalized the desire to find a new home. My anger towards Amin and my lost Uganda was dissipating with time.

"I can only imagine what you're going through," Scott said softly, seeing the contorted lines on my forehead. "But now that most of your family's here and in Canada, this *is* your home, isn't it?"

"I sure as hell hope so," I replied almost too quickly, as if trying to convince myself.

☙

In 1976, while living at Balboa Beach in southern California, I was wrestling with my book idea on Idi Amin's Uganda, attempting to free myself from his long-reaching chains once and for all. By now he was a notorious figure, a political idiot who had invited Richard Nixon to Uganda's national parks to help him recover from Watergate. Therapy through the pen was my latest idea. Therapy through music was my escape from the ongoing pain of having to re-live the Uganda days in the writing process. At weekends I played my conga with black dudes at the drumming jams at hip Venice Beach.

Danny and Talmadge, my housemates at the beach house, were my mental and musical inspiration. Danny, raised by hippie parents at a commune in Big Sur, looked like a poster Jesus Christ. He was an avid animal lover who fed the lions at Lion Country Safari, just south of Los Angeles. One weekend, during feeding time, I went with him in his jeep full of fresh cow meat. This safari park was a Disney version of the Serengeti. In my youth, I had seen many a pride of lions lurking in the grasslands of Ngorongoro Crater in the Serengeti, but had never got so close that I could gaze into those hypnotic green eyes. Now, only the jeep's iron grille window was between us and the great cats, standing just inches from my face.

Buddhist in his thinking, Danny got upset if you killed a fly in his presence. "Animals are smarter and kinder than people," he would say. Positive thinking and peace were his mottos in life, pills and peyote buttons his short cut to nirvana. He secured all the drugs and other stimulants for our Friday evening jam sessions on Balboa Beach.

Talmadge, from Chicago, was a walking encyclopedia of music who collected recordings and native instruments from all over the world. Working on a doctoral thesis on the influences of music in primitive societies, he would bring Indian flutes, African harps, and Guatemalan marimbas to our jam sessions in the City of Angels.

University mates, Big Bob from Iowa and "Wild Man" Baser from LA, were trekking Nature lovers who could never get enough of the West Coast's scenic parks. They would pile us all into Bob's truck—the "Green Beast" as he dubbed it—for long weekends making music with Nature in the Sierra Nevada Mountains, the Anza-Borrego Desert, the canyon lands of Utah.

One September, on Labor Day weekend, the five of us took off in the Green Beast for Joshua Tree National Park in the California desert, 140 miles east of LA. Armed with Rainier's Ale and California weed, we zoomed east along the Interstate, Traffic's *Low Spark Of High Heeled Boys* booming out of the tape deck. Past Palm Springs, we made a pit stop to munch on roast-beef sandwiches with *jalapeño* bread; then it was into the high, empty desert, cactus and sagebrush for miles in every direction.

The first time I had seen cactus was in the movies in Uganda, as cowboys rode past them, with "Rawhide" playing in the background. In these Westerns, the cacti looked mean and dangerous, but out here in the desert they were bursting with flowers that had me spellbound. Baser, our botanical expert, explained that thunderstorms from two weeks before must have induced the bloom of buds and flowers, producing this plethora of yellow, purple, and red flowers against the ubiquitous green and brown sagebrush. This happened only once a year and lasted no longer than a fortnight. From his desert guidebook, Baser educated us all on the exotic species: beavertail, ocatillo, prickly pear; flowers with names like "blazing star" and "Indian paintbrush"—names that evoked images of cowboy stories by Zane Grey and TV shows like "Bonanza" from my youth.

We drove to Jumbo Rocks within the park and found an isolated spot with a superb view of granite monoliths and rocks that twisted as if they were shaped by heavenly Hopi Indian spirits. Around us, boulders as big as houses peppered the landscape, creating shadows and offering protection from the wind. There was total silence except for the occasional scurrying of lizards or kangaroo rats among the brush.

Flat ground at the foot of a boulder, miles away from park rangers and tourist Winnebagos, would be our sleeping place for the night. As the North Star appeared in the twilight sky, Bob cooked up a spaghetti and beans dinner on his Coleman stove. Danny advised me to skip dinner. Fasting before chewing on peyote buttons the next morning would prevent the normal vomiting induced by the bitter taste. Though it wasn't the month of Ramadan, I went along with his advice. Danny and I drank and smoked some more weed instead.

After dinner, Baser made a small campfire from wood he had brought along. Tal started up a soft melody on a Peruvian flute that invoked, for me, an image of a fakir on a bed of nails playing to a cobra. Bob, with an empty Rainier's bottle on his lower lip, chimed into the melody. Danny blew on a kazoo while I picked up a beat on Tal's wooden marimbas. Baser, clad in a Mexican poncho, mimed a dance in slow motion around the fire. *Baila chameleon, baila!* It was like a one-night-only show for the nocturnal creatures of Jumbo Rocks, attracted by the sparks spiraling up from the fire and the music bouncing off the boulders. Above us, the sky was splattered with stars, Old Milky Way arching across the black dome. The band played on till the last embers died out and the last pair of coyote eyes disappeared back into the dark.

Mescalito (as the Yaqui Indian sorcerer, Don Juan Matus, nicknamed peyote in the books by Carlos Castaneda) has the ability to alter the way you look at the world, to bring forth feelings from within that you never knew existed. It induces both demonic fears and ecstatic visions. The user's thoughts and environment determine which of the two will dominate. The time had come for me to take this voyage of self-discovery.

The peyote, washed down with more Rainier's for breakfast, was foul, but I managed not to throw up. Danny and I took off for a hike among the boulders, just as the first tingling sensations ran through my body. The peyote was already working its magic.

The hallucinations began. The boulders in front of me started moving, ever so slightly. The sagebrush all around waved to me like long lost friends. Even the red grains of dirt at my feet moved on the ground as I walked. I felt like everything was talking to me. Our slow hike was filled with distractions. We peered inside flowers, blew cotton-ball dandelions into the wind, and stroked the sagebrush. We were jammin' with Nature.

Two hours later, the trail headed east past ocotillo bushes with blood-red pulsating flowers. We came upon a semi-circle of boulders. "American Stonehenge," I whispered to Danny. We climbed up a fifteen-foot boulder and perched at the top to admire the view before us. The bright morning sun reflected off the moving boulders and threw eerie conical shadows on the ground. White puffy clouds in the crystal blue sky melded with each other, creating weird animal shapes.

"See the dog with a human face," said Danny, pointing to a cloud. A few minutes later, it had turned into a manta ray, the elongated tail out of place. Suddenly, with his forefinger to his lips, Danny pointed to a crevice in the boulder we sat on, just a few feet away. There, motionless, with head cocked upward, was a half-meter-long lizard staring back at us. It had gray scales with a black collar and patches of white and yellow along its vertebrae. The sun shone on the top half of its body, leaving the bottom half in shadow. It moved forward a few inches to get more of the sun on its tail. For a few seconds, just when it moved, I thought I saw large, bluish-green oval spots around its belly. Chameleon! I marveled. I looked for the blue-green spots again, but they were gone. Minutes later, with its tongue flicking in and out of its mouth, the lizard turned and disappeared deeper into the crevice.

"Did you see it change colors when it moved?" I asked Danny.

"Don't know. Sure was beautiful though," he replied.

My thoughts wandered. A real chameleon or just the peyote playing tricks on me? A gift omen from Don Juan or just wishful thinking? I wasn't sure. Were the blue-green spots really there? Africa had many chameleons, though I'd never seen one. Did they wander this far, all the way to Jumbo Rocks? If ever I got back to Africa, I would find one of my own, I promised myself.

A CHAMELEON'S TALE

The afternoon walk back to camp revealed a small oasis, an oval swimming hole not much bigger than a Jacuzzi, shaded by two palm trees. We stripped naked and dove in to cool off. I felt hot and cold flushes all over my body as we splashed each other. Later, we found two rocks to stretch out on to let the sun dry us. Brown African Mojo and blond Jesus Christ Superstar basking naked in the desert sun of Jumbo Rocks. Just like the lizard in the crevice.

That night, as the music by the campfire echoed once again off the boulders, I improvised a dance with Baser. Together, we made reptilian movements as if we were two lizards chasing each other in a mating ritual. When I fell asleep by the fire, my peyote dreams brought back the chameleon I thought I'd seen earlier in the day.

The next morning, the Green Beast sped us back west to the City of Angels. When I recounted our weekend trip to my Balboa Beach neighbors—four girls, all studying jazz ballet at Costa Mesa College—they came up with the idea that I help them choreograph a jazz dance depicting lizard visions in the desert. I jumped at the idea. The song I chose was "The Low Spark Of High Heeled Boys." The girls designed the lizard costumes from their wardrobes. I worked with French Claudine, the head chameleon for the ballet, on the choreography.

Three weeks later, on a Friday night, the four girls performed at Balboa Beach to an audience of desert rats and beachcombers. It was a great hit. The chameleon dance was born.

Years later, while spending a summer with my family in Vancouver, I found other music chameleons at the Seattle Folk Life Festival and the Vancouver Jazz Festival to participate in that same lizard dance jazz ballet.

ભ

The following January, I was invited to spend an exchange semester in a writers group at the Instituto Allende in Mexico, with the intention of finishing my book on Uganda. Big Bob drove me down in the Green Beast from Balboa Beach to the town of San Miguel de Allende, in the state of Guanajuato.

After living in "Beach Blanket Bingo" southern California for over a year, being in tropical Mexico was a revelation of images long forgotten. Brown people everywhere, with only the occasional gringo standing out. Men in sombreros kept offering me drinks in *cantinas* wondering why I was traveling with a white man. They took me to be one of their own. *Compañero, comprade, hermano, maestro*—new names to make my own. *Indígena* women served up tortillas from round hot plates just like Ma used to with chapattis at home in Kampala. I felt a sense of exhilaration in this New World, unable as yet to understand the cause. At one pit stop south of Mazatlán, thrilled to find a woman selling roasted cassava sprinkled with chilli powder and lime, I broke into a spontaneous jig around her grill, eliciting a "*gringo loco*" from her. 'Crazy foreigner': a precursor to *farang baa* in Thailand. When she eventually realized it was the cassava that I was so ecstatic about, she broke into a wide grin and wrapped up three big pieces in a sheet of newspaper. "*Gratis, para ti, bailero!*" 'Free for you, dancer.'

We took a southern detour, bypassing San Miguel and Mexico City, in order to climb Mount Popocatépetl, the great volcano southeast of the polluted capital. There was a paved road leading up the mountain, and the Green Beast lumbered up to 11,000 feet till the tarmac disappeared. After that, we climbed for four hours through mud and volcanic ash. At the snow line, the ashen terrain turned to cold alpine tundra, and the view stretched for miles all the way to the Bahía de Campeche coast.

The volcanic summit was up ahead, a mound of snow just like Kilimanjaro. A wisp of smoke came out of the cone. The crisp tundra air and the mountain flowers took me back to my Outward Bound expedition to the top of Africa. I wanted to keep going up to the summit, but it was not to be. The final hike to the peak required crampons and ice axes, which we certainly weren't equipped with. So we had to head back down. To compensate for the disappointment, we bounded and somersaulted over the volcanic ash like gazelles on the Serengeti, two *gringo locos*. We were back at the Green Beast just in time for the sunset light show: pink and purple arrows shooting across a pale orange sky. The next morning, after a *huevos rancheros* and tortillas breakfast, we retraced our journey northward to our final destination.

San Miguel de Allende, three hours north of the capital, in the Guanajuato desert, is known as a colony for artists and writers. It boasts cobblestone streets, colonial Spanish churches and haciendas, two food markets, and a host of small Tex-Mex restaurants catering to retired gringos, resident artists, and weekend tourists from the capital.

We parked in the *zocalo*, the town square, and slept the night in the Green Beast. Bob left for California the next day, to get back to his classes at UCI. I wandered across the square in search of a room to rent, and came across a group of boys playing marbles in the red dirt. I froze, thinking back to the strip of red dirt in Madras Gardens where I, the marble king, ruled over my peers every day after primary school. Same scene, different language. I just had to see what game they were playing. Sure enough, it was a Mexican version of a game I had loved as a kid in Kampala. The exhilaration I had felt earlier was now overwhelming. In broken Spanish, drawing from four years of French in secondary school, I convinced the boys that I had to play with them. The search for a roof over my head could wait a while.

An hour into the game, which I lost more times than I won, the realization finally hit me. Brown people everywhere who looked a lot like me, the roasted cassava just the way I liked it, the climb up a Mexican Kilimanjaro, and now playing marbles with brown boys like I did as a kid—I had arrived at a new home.

೦೮

Four months later, I had a good grasp of the language, thanks to Don Crucito, a Spanish teacher at the Instituto Allende, who looked very much like my older brother, Amir, with his salt-and-pepper beard and black mustache. Realizing that I could rely on my knowledge of French grammar and that I had no inhibitions about being corrected in public, Don Crucito took me everywhere he went in town—post office, restaurants, Sunday food market, movies, art galleries, poetry readings. There was only one rule: all communication had to be in Spanish. English was forbidden. Every night, armed with my grammar book, *501 Verbs*, and my trusty notebook, I would dutifully record all the new vocabulary to be practiced the next day.

My language immersion continued at La Cucaracha, a local drinking hole where I played my conga drum with musicians on *ranchero* songs. One evening, I met up with Peter—one of the eight Nigerians studying at the Instituto—for a few drinks. We had met before at parties and hit it off as African brothers united in a foreign land—especially when it came to the pretty girls in pairs, both Latino and gringo, looking for a good time. We started off with tequila shots and moved on to Negra Modelo beers over domino games. When the *ranchero* band finished up, Peter went to the jukebox, selecting every Western rock hit he could find. We got dancing, downing more tequila shots between songs, oblivious to the stares of brown men in white sombreros, who were shocked to see two men dancing so intimately. The more Jose Cuervo danced in our heads, the more Peter and I pantomimed our way around the bar, like two tigers prowling around each other. We made quite the sight, this Jimmy Page-looking brown Mojo from Uganda and the Fulani herdsman from Kano dancing to Western hits in a Mexican *cantina* full of macho men.

Aware that I wanted to make an overland trek to South America, Don Crucito urged me to travel to Oaxaca on my own for *Semana Santa*, Easter week. Instructions for the trip? I was to pretend to be a Mexican who didn't speak a word of English, and was forbidden to hook up with any gringo travelers. I passed the test, making my way to the beaches of Puerto Ángel, where I slept in a hammock to the sound of crashing waves. I came back fully confident that I was ready for my trek, three weeks away, when the semester was over. When I tried to pay my mentor for being my mouth, eyes, and ears in San Miguel, he responded, "Bring me back a gorgeous señorita from Cali"—reputed to be home to the most beautiful women in South America.

As a farewell gift, Don Crucito gave me two books in Spanish: one on the Mayan ruins and culture of Central America, and the other on the Incan Empire of South America. In return, I gave him my elephant-hair bracelet and a *kitenge* shirt from Uganda.

My unfinished book on Idi Amin would have to wait for another time. The new desire to master the Spanish language and explore the Latin world would be therapy enough. With a backpack and my conga drum, I set off on a trip that would eventually conclude at the 1978 soccer World Cup in Argentina.

ಸಿ

On the road, there were numerous occasions when I got to play spontaneous music with people from many countries. Each brought together a unique blend of fellow nomads yearning to create sounds and melodies that brought joy to whoever happened to be passing by.

In the Mayan ruins of Palenque in Chiapas, I met Maya, a self-named ponytailed Huichol Indian from Tepic. Stranded in a downpour, he was playing his Bolivian flute in a room of the temple ruins, facing the jungle. I struck up an African beat on my drum to his Mayan-Incan melody. The thrashing rain and monkeys howling in the trees completed the ensemble. We jammed for over an hour, synchronizing beats to melodies. When the rain finally stopped, he took me over to a backpacker campsite to meet up with Texan hippie guitarist, Carlton, who was driving his VW van around Mexico with a group of traveler musicians he had picked up on the road. Besides Maya and Carlton, there was Japanese Masaki, crew-cut hair dyed blond, who jammed on his portable Hammond organ; German brunette, Uta, on summer break from university in Tübingen, who carried the beat with her maracas and hand cymbals; and red-haired Duffy from Winnipeg, Canada, piping in with his alto saxophone. Carlton invited me to join the ragtag band for a few days. They were heading north into Yucatan, and so was I.

We became a United Nations motley crew of musicians touring the plazas of Palenque, Champotón, and Mérida, entertaining the city folk passing by. Often, after the jam sessions, people invited us into their homes for beef tacos or chicken enchiladas. In Mérida, a family cooked up a large pot of *sopa Azteca* spiced up with avocados and *chiltepe* chillies and served with fresh, hot tortillas from the grill. In smaller villages, people offered Negra Modelo beer or tequila shots with limes. At the ruins of Uxmal, after the nightly laser show, we played for the ancient Mayan gods. Before heading to Tulum, where the ruins face the Caribbean Sea, we came upon Dzitnup *cenote*, a sacred Mayan water well, about seven kilometers west of Valladolid. Inside the *cenote's* subterranean cave, we struck up a jam, the magical sounds echoing off the stalactites, enchanting the blind fish in the sacred water. *Aurale amigos!*

A few weeks later, when Carlton had to go back to Austin, Texas to continue university studies, the band, spontaneously born, died just as quickly. Uta and I continued south to San Cristóbal de las Casas in Chiapas, to explore the jungles leading to the Bonampak ruins on the Guatemalan border.

"Why did you leave Germany and why choose Mexico?" I asked her on the way down.

"Germany is one big hospital," she replied. "Too clean, too organized, too boring. I love the dirt of Mexico, the people surviving on the street, friendlier than most Germans." In her own way, she too was searching for another place to call home. Her Spanish was excellent. No wonder we became travel partners.

Uta liked to go 'native' wherever she landed. Usually clad in huaraches, Mexican sandals, and a long Guatemalan skirt with a matching handwoven blouse, she sought out places well off the beaten path, the more remote the better. In San Cristóbal, to prepare for the supposed three-day jungle hike, we left our backpacks and my conga drum at a guesthouse, switching to smaller knapsacks with a few clothes, a medicine kit, hammocks, fruit, and money.

On the bumpy "chicken bus" ride out of San Cristóbal, Uta struck up a conversation with Julio, a pig farmer, who was heading into the jungle. By the time the bus arrived at the last stop, she had convinced him to be our jungle guide for a week.

On the first day, on a trail a two feet wide with nothing but jungle on both sides, we hiked about ten kilometers with Don Julio and his ten piglets. Julio talked to his pigs in sounds I'd never heard before, to ensure that they never wandered too far from the trail while foraging for food. For our own food, Julio gave us maza, the dough from which Mexicans make tortillas. He pointed out lemon trees near the trail, and we squeezed the fruit into our bottled water to make fresh lemonade.

That night, at the village we came to, Julio negotiated a fair price for some of his piglets, and then led us to the village casa de viajeros. This was a dirt-floor hut furnished with a blackened pot over a charcoal fire: a 'hotel' for jungle travelers. A barrel full of rainwater outside the hut served well as a shower. For dinner, Uta cooked up some chicken, acquired in the village, in a leafy vegetable broth. It wasn't long before we fell asleep in each other's arms through sheer exhaustion.

For three more days, we hiked with Don Julio during the day and slept at a different 'hotels' each night. The distance from village to village ranged from five to ten kilometers. On the fourth day, Julio, realizing that we weren't able to keep up with him and his pigs, apologized that he had to go ahead to keep to his schedule. But he assured us that at every village he passed on the same trail, he would alert the people to take care of us and let us use the travelers' hut. I was apprehensive without Julio as our guide, but Uta, ever the optimist, talked me into it. Julio kept his promise. At each village, the welcome shouts from villagers relieved us every evening. "*Pasa adelante viajeros.*" 'Welcome travelers. Come in.'

By the end of the first week, we became comfortable with jungle hiking, assured that we would have somewhere to sleep come nightfall, with the humid heat of the day washed off by a barrel bath. At each village, before setting off in the morning, we would stock up on fruits—oranges, guavas, avocados—and clean water. One day on the trail, in the middle of nowhere, Uta's *huaraches* broke beyond repair. I suggested we turn back, offering my hiking boots, even though they were too big for her. She wouldn't hear of it, and continued barefoot for the next two days till one villager, taking pity on her torn-up feet, insisted she take his flip-flops. No hospitals for my Uta.

On another day, realizing that my birthday was coming up in a few days, I said to her, "I wanna celebrate my birthday dancing with you in the square at San Cristóbal."

"*Tranquilo, hombre.* We'll make it back by then."

By the time we got to the village of San Quentin, near the Guatemalan border, some fifteen days into our adventure, our bodies couldn't take any more. So we rented another hut by a small creek, to rest up for a few days. Hammocks for beds, charcoal pit and basic cutlery for a kitchen, we turned the hut into our home. Buying food from small villages nearby—a pineapple here, a few eggs there, some meat if we were lucky—became the main daily chore. At night, sitting on our hammocks, strung up on the porch, Uta, with her maracas and hand cymbals, would sing and dance while I drummed up beats on an old fire-blackened tin can. Under starlit skies, jungle creatures joined in with their own nightly orchestra. We lost count of the days, free of time and space.

One morning, Uta demanded that I go out looking for *guaro*, the local strong brew. I was not to come back until I found some. After trekking from village to village, I finally found a bottle in one hamlet and got back to the hut just as daylight was fading. Thrilled, she kissed me and led me inside. I couldn't believe my eyes. On the dirt floor was a candle-lit dinner, set for two. My Bob Marley towel served as the tablecloth. A plate of mouth-watering small river crabs, placed in the center, was the main course. Next to it, in a wooden bowl, was the side dish: one sweet potato and a squash. Uta, looking like a native queen in her flowing skirt and a wild flower in her hair, poured the *guaro* into two tin cups, handed me one, and said softly, "Happy birthday, my Mojo-man. Dinner is served!"

She felt it was important that I receive a blowjob on my birthday, and dessert continued with love making in the hammock on the porch. We made different musical sounds that night.

Although we never made it to the Bonampak ruins, we did eventually get back to San Cristóbal by hitching a ride—for a negotiated price—on a 'flying doctor' plane. The six-seater aircraft was picking up a patient in San Quentin. But I never did get to dance with Uta in San Cristóbal. Running out of time, she had to zip back to Mexico City to catch a flight back to Germany for autumn semester at Tübingen. Weeks later, my *huarache* chameleon wrote, saying the German hospital staff were appalled at the state of her torn-up feet.

❧

After Uta left, I backtracked up to Chetumal and crossed into Belize, keen to explore the music of the Garifuna people, who, from 1797 onwards, had been forcibly expelled by the British from the island of St. Vincent. These black Carib slaves and their mixed descendants became scattered along parts of the Caribbean coast, but most had ended up in Belize by 1832. In America, I'd learned how music had become a force of hope for black slaves, and how gospel music and the blues had developed from African roots. I was curious to find out what sounds the Garifuna, with their West African heritage, had developed in music, and to experience their lifestyle now. Bob Marley, whom I saw perform with the Wailers in California, had shown me how deeply reggae was creating awareness of social issues. Maybe Garifuna music would add another dimension to the search for music being used as a weapon of change for the poor and the underprivileged.

But Belize, formerly British Honduras, thrust me back into speaking English. Remembering Don Crucito's advice to keep up with the language, I sought out Spanish speakers in Orange Walk. The country still retained a colonial hangover. Black Creole families still had adopted British names likes Jones and Smith. I wondered why. British soldiers roamed the cities in trucks, in case neighboring Guatemala—where maps of that country included Belize as a Caribbean province—decided to attack. Belmopan, planned as the country's new capital upon eventual independence (still a few years away), was still just one big construction site. Supermarkets full of baked beans and jars of Marmite and English butter showed that the British would be here for a while yet.

My expectations of finding a small piece of Africa were dashed. I found only ugly reminders of the struggle for independence, much like those from my Ugandan youth. The country's forests, the main resource, had already been raped clean by the British. As a result, there was even a local movement to stop the independence negotiations with Britain: what would be the point if there was nothing left to build a new country upon, and if the Guatemalans were massing on the border?

A thought crossed my mind: When the freedom celebrations were over, would the Belizeans prosper, or would they create their own Idi Amins? If downtown Belize City, a den of drug pushers, thieves, and scam artists, was anything to go by, the future did not look good. A souvenir T-shirt I bought asked the question on the front: "Are you in heaven?" The answer on the back read: "You better Belize it!"

I escaped by boat to the islands, where a few weeks of snorkeling with nurse sharks and lionfish off the reefs of Cay Caulker were a welcome respite after the jungles of Chiapas. Fresh lobsters in butter sauce, deep fried conch fritters, and shark's fin soup replaced the raw *maza* and lemonade of our jungle hikes; clean linen sheets over a soft bed, the stringy hammocks. At Martin's Bar, where the gringos gathered on the beach to watch the sunset, and the locals gathered on benches outside the bar to watch the gringos, I enjoyed evening drinks and ganja, and floated from one group to the other.

One day, I was at dinner with a Garifuna family, when Edith, who cooked up the best conch fritters on the island, told me that Dangriga and Punta Gorda, on the southern Caribbean coast, would soon be celebrating the annual Garifuna Settlement Day. These were the places to be on November 19th, just days away. She told me that there I would find my piece of Africa, with non-stop dancing till dawn to Garifuna music.

I got on the move, stopping in Belize City only long enough to catch the bus south to Dangriga. The trip was a ten-hour nightmare of potholes and bumps. The deserted town, with a few mangy settlements, held no appeal, so I kept moving the following day. The bus ride to Punta Gorda was even more horrendous, only made bearable when I struck up a friendship with Kent, a Garifuna social worker in Belize City, who was going home for the celebrations.

At the bus station, a group of drummers beating on big, hand-carved goatskin drums provided a raucous welcome. People danced everywhere in the streets as Kent led me to a Garifuna family he knew, where I could rent a room. By the next afternoon, I was drinking pineapple wine with the owners and learning how to 'punta rock' with sensuous, ebony skinned Rose, who had buttocks bigger than some of the Ugandan women. The dancing involved gyrating your hips while shuffling your feet, with hands flying in the air to the drumbeats. Not too different from the *din ding* bird dance performed by the Acholi people in northern Uganda. Plucking up courage, I joined the drummers with my conga, desperately trying to keep up with the changing beats. Left in the dust a few times, I went back to the dancing with Rose.

On November 19th, hundreds of canoes filled with celebrating Garifunas re-enacted the historic resettling of their people in a new home. Later that evening, the party moved to the sandy floor of a huge community hall, where drummers formed a circle and played to a huge crowd of swaying, charcoal bodies. I felt like I was back in Lugogo Stadium with my Ugandan friends. Same beats, same struggle for freedom, different country.

Huge black mamas, some older than my mother, pounded the floor. They wore tie-dyed Belizean dresses like the *basutis* worn by Ugandan women. A group of them, spotting the brown-skinned stranger with Rose, formed a semi-circle around me, egging me on. Rose decided to disappear, leaving me all alone in the middle of this braying mob. Closing the circle, they took turns to grab me by the hips and lift me high up in the air, ululating in unison when I staggered to regain my balance after the fall on the sandy floor. I was a human toy, smothered by the bouncing bosoms of big black mamas. Rose reappeared with more drinks, and one of the mamas hugged me tight before the circle moved on to another victim in the crowd.

For two more days and nights, the dancing continued all over Punta Gorda. Drunks and dancers, exhausted from the revelry, fell asleep where they were—on the streets, in chairs, at café tables, and inside toilets. When awoken by more drums or a nudging elbow, they resumed what they were doing as if a short nap had been a full night's sleep, or vice versa.

On the last night, when Kent and his friends hooked up with me and Rose at another gathering on the black-sand beach, I drank too much pineapple wine on an empty stomach. That night and the next morning remain a hazy blur. If I had dreamed that night on the black sand, as a falling star raced across the sky, I must have been pantomiming my own dance, first as a *din ding* bird, then as a punta-rocking big black mama, before finally turning into a lizard that slithered across the sand into the sea.

∞

The next time I would witness as good a drum session would be in 2002 at Sanam Luang, the big *maidan* in front of the Grand Palace in Bangkok. On a bright Sunday afternoon, hundreds of Thais, sitting on straw mats on the open green space, were tucking into their picnic foods. Kids were flying yellow and purple kites against the backdrop of the palace's golden spires. At the far end of the *maidan*, a crowd was cheering two teams playing *takraw*, the acrobatic Asian version of volleyball that is played with feet, not hands, and a small rattan ball. The agility of the players was incredible. The crowd erupted every time one launched himself high enough in the air, in a backward somersault, to slam the ball over the net with the sole of his foot. Compared to these guys, Michael Jordan was a flat-footed water buffalo.

At the other end of the *maidan*, a stage with a giant drum attracted my attention. As I got closer, I read the banner proclaiming, "THAILAND DRUM FESTIVAL. WORLDWIDE. ASIA FIRST." On stage, a group of bare-chested Sri Lankan drummers furiously pounded their odd-shaped drums, building the beat up to a frenzy as sweat poured from their faces. A Moroccan team, all decked out in kaftans and chequered headbands, followed the Sri Lankans, hammering out North African beats. Then, to my surprise, the master of ceremonies, Todd Thongdee, a young American gone Thai native, asked two players from the two countries to switch drums before the two bands played together for the first time. Buddhist Sri Lankans and Muslim Moroccans jamming to a Bangkok sunset at Sanam Luang. Only in amazing Thailand. This international, inter-religious jam session, though awkward at first, built up momentum, and ended with the Indians and the Thais, the biggest contingents, drumming up a foot-stomping climax that had the normally reserved Thai crowd up and dancing.

For a finale, MC Todd talked some of the drummers from all ten countries into stepping off the stage and playing amongst the crowd. Thai families, at first taken aback by this sudden intrusion into their Sunday outing, soon joined our growing train of drummers and dancers snaking around the vendors' stalls. For thirty minutes that Sunday, Sanam Luang became a world stage of drumming, dancing chameleons, before the night dispersed the crowds and brought out the ladyboys and the hookers with their greasy make-up.

ॐ

Back in 1979, while going through Peace Corps training in Nakhon Nayok, I was eating lunch at a restaurant with Ajaan Uthai when I noticed a picture on the wall of Thailand's King Bhumibol playing alto saxophone. I asked Ajaan Uthai about it, and this is what he said to me: "'Nai Luang' is both a musician and a composer. When studying overseas, he wrote many songs that are often played at concert halls in Bangkok."

It fascinated me that the king, the most revered figure in Thai society, was also a musician who was largely responsible for the introduction of jazz to Thailand. We got to talking about how Western music became popular in Thailand.

During the Vietnam War, American GIs, stationed in or enjoying R 'n' R in Thailand, helped popularize rock 'n' roll and blues. Hotels brought in Filipino bands to entertain their Western guests, and in local bars and backpacker hangouts, Thai bands, often with very little knowledge of English, memorized the lyrics to songs by Creedence Clearwater Revival, The Beatles, and The Rolling Stones. Those were the kinds of places where I hung out.

Over the next two decades, music festivals sprang up in Hua Hin, Pattaya, Koh Samui, and Phuket—places where tourists flocked for the white sand beaches and the sumptuous Thai seafood. In Bangkok, venues big enough to draw international bands and singers opened up to host Western stars like Santana, Whitney Houston, and many others. The music explosion was well on its way.

The annual jazz festival held at Hua Hin on Thailand's Gulf coast became a coming together of jazz musicians from all over the world. The festival boasted four stages, including one at the famous railway station. In 2002, I took the five-hour train ride from Bangkok to Hua Hin to see for myself. Jazz notes from the stage next to the station greeted me as I walked off the platform. On stage was a Filipino Louis Armstrong singing "Wonderful World" accompanied by a quartet. With a thick, gutteral voice, amazingly similar to "Satchmo," he followed up with "Mack The Knife," making me homesick for Uganda and my sister Shamim. On the beach stage, Thai saxophonist, Mr. Saxman, was blowing his horn to a backdrop of crashing waves from the Gulf of Thailand.

In Bangkok, blues and rock venues are found all over the city. The best one I ever found is a hole-in-the-wall blues bar named "Adhere The 13th" on Samsen Road in Banglamphu, a five-minute walk from where I lived. That's where I got to know Georgia, a rotund, beady-eyed Thai Janis Joplin from Chiang Rai, and the three amazing guitarists in the house band—Pong from Isaan, music teacher Phet from Samut Prakan, and Hanz from Holland. Every night they made the genius of my hero, Jimi Hendrix, come alive again, taking me back to when I used to make my mother dance with me to "Voodoo Chile." Jimi has always sat next to me wherever I've been: at Madras Gardens; at university in Norwich; and in Michigan, where friends would take bets on which Hendrix song was the anthem for the crazy Ugandan hippie—making me realize that Hendrix was much more than an amazing musician for me. He was a liberator, and still the epitome of a free spirit.

No one ever guessed that the song was "Little Wing."

The musicians and regulars at Adhere became my comrades. During the time I lived in Banglamphu, new friends would show up to play with Pong till midnight. More often than not, an all-night party would follow at the "Alamo Sports Bar"—the giggle factory—till a morning breakfast of *khao tom muu*, rice soup with pork, sobered us enough to sleep off the day.

ॐ

Some music and dance moments in my head will never be forgotten. Like the time when Maya and I played to the monkeys of Palenque; druid dances with Ursula at Stonehenge, or the lizard dances with Claudine at Balboa Beach; hammock aerobics with Uta in San Quentin; and Rose in Punta Gorda. There have been many moments of sheer joy when music has made me jump out of all the categorical boxes and just dance. Like the night at Adhere when Pong, teeth picking his guitar strings, fused in traditional Thai *mor lam* melodies during a solo on "Purple Haze." Or at Tokyo Joe's, also in Bangkok, when Hanz and Jeff, from The Soi Dogs blues band, battled it out on lead guitars for ten minutes on "Sunshine Of Your Love." Or one Saturday night at The Brasserie in Chiang Mai, when local guitar hero, Took, picked up an almost empty Singha beer from a guest's table and used it as a bottleneck in an everlasting medley of Hendrix songs. And the maestro, Phet, accompanied by a violinist and a piano

143

player in his new band at The Brick Barn on Bangkok's Khao San Road, dazzling the crowd with the most amazing version of "Little Wing" I have ever heard.

I danced through them all with that lizard from Jumbo Rocks skittering away in my head.

6. Robbing The Poor

We discuss malnutrition over steaks
And plan hunger talks during coffee breaks
Whether Asian floods or African drought
We face each issue with an open mouth.
Ross Coggins, "The Development Set."

The first time I ever stayed up all night was while engrossed in a novel, *Cry, The Beloved Country*, which lamented the misery of black people in apartheid South Africa. The book provoked me to tears, so much so that I had to get up and wash my face twice that night to be able to finish it. That Alan Paton, a white South African, had brought the horrors of racial discrimination to my consciousness moved me even more.

I now understood why my Ugandan passport had an official stamp on the last page proclaiming, "Travel to South Africa prohibited by Ugandan law."

From then on, books became my window to the world. I buried myself in travel literature, devouring journals by Paul Theroux, and novels by Gabriel Garcia Márquez. I read books on Gandhi and

Nelson Mandela, so my travel and social consciences were blooming every year, like an ocatillo cactus during the desert rains.

Justice and equality soon became issues I obsessed about. In 1968, at the peak of the Black Power movement in the United States, when I saw my first black American parading the Kampala streets with a placard that read "Black Is beautiful," furtively I trailed behind him, carrying a cardboard sign, written in ball-point pen, that naïvely boasted "Brown Is Better."

So it came as no surprise to my family that I chose social studies for my major at East Anglia University. In England, the education minister, Maggie Thatcher—the "milk snatcher"—had recently abolished free milk for school children. Many of my fellow students were politically active. I was one of the organizers during the student boycott of Barclays Bank, a major investor in apartheid South Africa. With the Vietnam War still going on, students all over the world were protesting in the streets for peace. During a trip to London one Sunday, I stood up on a soapbox at Hyde Park Corner and publicly thanked Idi Amin for deporting me, and thus enhancing my political awareness.

Two years later, in New York City, while working at Gimbel's department store over the Christmas holidays, I distributed socialist pamphlets in the street during my lunch break. When one of my colleagues went sick for a week, I took over his Santa Claus job outside the main entrance, dressed up in red with a white beard, ringing my bell, *ho ho ho*. I must have been a sight for sore eyes: a Ugandan Indian dressed up as Kris Kringle pushing Karl Marx to Christmas shoppers. But the New Yorkers had seen it all before. No one blinked an eyelid.

On the trek to Buenos Aires, I recall getting a real-world lesson on the global economy from a Peruvian street vendor in Cusco when she screamed out loud, "*El dollar esta siempre jodiandome!*" 'The dollar is always fucking me over!' She explained that because the Peruvian peso was pegged to the American dollar, every time the dollar took a dip, the value of the peso dipped much more, ensuring that her nine children would eat even less that week. When I asked why the Peruvian peso was pegged to the dollar, she threw her hands up in the air and replied that only God and the World Bank knew the answer to that.

In the refugee camps in Phanat and Galang, where boys like Nguyen and Sayeed pierced my chameleon heart with their life stories, I became aware of how madmen like Idi Amin and Pol Pot, through fear and terrorization, can easily turn frightened people into a cruel, hysterical mob.

Relief efforts from richer countries to the poor often came because of a separate economic agenda. Like the time America, with 20,000 tons of surplus cheese to get rid of to maintain market prices, sent the whole lot to Thailand for Vietnamese refugees. All of it went to rot because no one bothered to check that the Vietnamese don't usually eat dairy products.

By 1984, I had come to the conclusion that if I wanted to make a long-term difference with the poor, I had to be working in villages, not air-conditioned suites; in projects that respected and enhanced cultural traditions instead of destroying them; in agencies that valued and built on traditional skills. The challenge was to find an aid agency that actually practiced these principles in its daily work rather than just promoted them in glossy brochures to secure funds and donations.

ဆ

In the autumn of 1984, I went back to America on a scholarship to do an interdisciplinary Masters in International Studies, at Ohio University in Athens. This university town with 14,000 students, a quarter of them from overseas, was a liberal oasis in the middle of a conservative desert. I concentrated on my studies, fully aware that within a year or two I would be back at work in the developing world, where the basic human needs of food, shelter, education, and health were the greatest. Having returned to America twice before, once from Thailand and the other from South America, this transition was made easier by two circumstances. First, I took a part-time job at the International Center as the Peace Corps recruiter on campus, which gave me an opportunity to convince others to give up two years to travel and work—a schooling on life that would change their perspective on America and the rest of the world for ever. The job developed into a cause when I realized how little most American students knew of what their government was doing outside its borders (a tragic situation that, though improved somewhat with access to the Internet, is still apparent today). Second, since many of the graduate students in international studies were either former Peace Corps volunteers or had traveled abroad extensively, the classroom seminars on the North-South dialogue were often a raucous but productive debate. We students loved challenging our professors—especially those with self-aggrandising labels like "Philippinist," "Nicaraguanist," or "Africanist."

In my work—hosting slide shows by returned volunteers eager to show off their achievements—I became the 'advocate of travel.' In class—drawing heavily from insights gained from the Peace Corps and the refugee camps—I became the 'advocate of culture,' debating my lecturers on the best strategies for working with the world's poor. The year went by quickly. My academic papers ranged from Tanzanian socialism for the poor to media manipulation and American foreign policy in Allende's Chile to grass-roots education projects in Thailand. The thesis committee challenged most of my arguments, but in the interests of academic free thought, approved my thesis for graduation. After all, I did my homework and was prepared to back up my conclusions with extensive reading and research. I couldn't wait to return to the non-academic, dog-eat-dog world to make my mark.

After graduation, in 1985, my job hunting focused on working with children for a non-profit, non-governmental organization (NGO), preferably in Asia. Nguyen and Sayeed had steered me to this decision. Having worked in refugee emergency relief, I was now keen to make a difference in some long-term development programs for underprivileged children.

The NGO I ended up with (let's call it Children Incorporated, or CI) worked in 45 countries, accepted no more than fifteen percent of its total budget from USAID—the 'Midas' of grants and funds for most American NGOs—and had its headquarters in Rhode Island. Using children's success stories from the Third World in promotional videos and annual reports, CI raised program and staffing funds through mass-media appeals, requesting a 22-dollar-a-month donation from private citizens in America and other Western countries. In return, each donor ('foster parent') would receive three progress letters annually from their 'sponsored child,' translated into English by local staff in country. The agency looked sound on paper, and I joined as an assistant country director, to be trained on the job as a country director for another posting within two years. The only decision pending was what country I would be sent to.

CI told me to choose between Kongoussi, and Khon Kaen, both small cities in the poorest regions of two countries where CI had vacancies. The first, in Burkina Faso, West Africa, would be an opportunity to help impoverished people with Islamic roots, similar to my own, in the continent where I grew up but hadn't set foot in for over two decades. The second, the more familiar capital of northeastern Thailand, was the center of an ancient Lao Buddhist culture. Though nostalgic for Africa, I chose Khon Kaen, since I knew the language—the key to understanding any culture. In October 1985, within a month of signing the two-year contract, I was on a plane to Asia.

ଽ

Khon Kaen in 1985 boasted one three-star hotel, three massage parlors, and a well-known university with a huge campus. Within a week, with Jeem, the procurement manager, pretending to be my Thai wife (to secure a Thai rental rate instead of a *farang* rate) we managed to find a small but decent house for me to live in.

At CI, I teamed up with two other Americans: Steve, the country director; and Ray, the other assistant director. Both were proficient in the Thai language and both were married to Thai women. The three of us were responsible for managing a 1.5-million dollar budget with projects in health, education, agriculture, and community infrastructure for 25,000 rural people in four districts of two provinces.

I refreshed my knowledge of the the Isaan dialect with a local tutor, and lived in different villages, two to three weeks at a time, to better understand the needs of Isaan farmers. Quite soon, I was happy with the progress I was making in the language and in understanding the inner workings of communal village structure. And CI seemed genuine in deferring to field staff on how to run its country programs. So it seemed. The 13,000-dollar annual salary, along with a decent house, was more than enough for me, given my hippie backpacker mentality.

At the end of the first year, with invaluable help from our 45 Thai staff, village headmen, and district community leaders, we were proud of the progress made on the comprehensive five-year plan of programs we had developed for the drought-stricken region.

The plan focused on providing training and vocational skills based on the Buddhist proverb: "Give a man a fish and he eats for a day. Teach him how to fish and he eats for life." Included in the strategic plan for the second year—for Rhode Island to assess and decide upon—was a new proposal to assist the Hmong refugees at Ban Vinai camp on the Thai-Lao border. By 1985, a decade after the end of the Vietnam War and the spillover conflict in Laos, there were still 10,000 Hmong languishing in Ban Vinai, with nowhere to go. Many of them were children, born and raised in the camp.

Because working with refugee children was a new direction for CI, the vice president of programs, Bill, with ten years experience at headquarters, made a special trip to Khon Kaen. I set all the preparations for his visit in motion, and guided him through Ban Vinai camp. The Hmong, dejected from repeated rejection of their resettlement in any country—and terrified of returning to communist Laos, now run by their former foes—looked resigned to remaining in this dusty, run-down place. Bill and I toured the camp for two days, talking to the Hmong leaders and people, aid workers, and Thai government officials. Bill was shocked to see hundreds of children and youths living in filthy, overcrowded huts with no schooling or vocational prospects. A throng of children who followed us everywhere in camp, hanging on to his Armani suit, moved him.

During the ride back to Khon Kaen, Bill got down to business with his vision on how to proceed with the project. He asked me if I was familiar with how McDonald's drew children to their burger restaurants through creative marketing.

I shook my head, bewildered by the question.

"Back home, the reason why kids always bug parents to eat or have birthday parties at Mickey Dee's is because of marketing enticers: Ronald the clown, the free toys, the playground. Not just the food."

"Okay," I said, still not clear where he was going with this analogy.

"I'll send a media team to take videos of all these destitute kids. You guys should write up a few tragic stories about their plight. With all this promo material, we can raise major funds in the US, Canada, and Europe. You see where I'm goin' with this? We can cover schools and playgrounds in the camp for at least five years."

I couldn't believe my ears. McDonald's marketing strategies for Hmong children in Ban Vinai? Surely there must be a better way.

The more Bill went on, the more I realized that his primary objective was to exploit the Hmong's situation to raise funds. He couldn't care less about project details and the impact they would have on the kids' lives. A five-year campaign! These kids had known nothing but the camp. Our goal was to get them *out*, not keep them in it for another five years.

I kept silent the rest of the way home and, when we parted, asked him to keep me updated on the response at head office. The next morning, at the airport, just before boarding the plane back to Bangkok, he said to Steve and me, "I think we've got a winner here in this refugee project."

I had just got my first good taste of management realities in humanitarian work.

A month later, we got a telex from headquarters advising us that the CI board of directors had determined that the Hmong project was not viable because of the political overtones with the Thai and Lao governments. CI was nevertheless keen to send a media team to take footage in Ban Vinai for fund raising. I wondered if the directors ever got to see the project document we had outlined in our plan, or whether Bill bamboozled them with a slick marketing presentation. The upshot was that CI would not support our project, but were still happy to exploit the Hmong's misery to generate more funds for themselves.

๕

In December 1986, CI invited me to a leadership development training seminar in Miami, Florida. Why Miami and why the week before Christmas? asked many participants, especially those who would have to fly for two days just to get there. The official reason was that Miami was the most central point that CI could come up with for the 45 participants from Africa, Asia, and Latin America. The real reason was that the new head of CI—a Dutchman hired a few weeks before from Shell Petroleum—had already arrived in Rhode Island and wanted to meet all the directors in the country programs, all in one shot. What we found out later was that he had already set plans to spend his Christmas holidays in the sunny Caribbean, and Miami was a perfect stopover for his half day with us before going on to his well-earned rest by a turquoise sea. The 200,000-dollar bill for this seminar—for air fares, five-star hotel accommodations, and nightly seafood buffets—was rationalized in CI's monthly newsletter as a sound investment in skills building that would generate long-term returns. It was roughly 25 percent more than our training budget for 4,800 farmers in Thailand for a whole year.

The seminar was held in the conference suite of a five-star hotel. The two professional trainers, hired from a reputable training agency in Washington, D.C., started us off with some ice-breaking activities to generate team spirit. Aware that there were multiple nationalities in our group of 45, they pinned up the names of all five continents on the walls. A flip chart on an easel begged the question, "Which continent are you from?" When they asked us to walk over and stand next to the continent we came from, I was immediately in a dilemma. Should I choose Africa, where I was born, or America, whose passport I carried, or Asia, which was my ethnic origin? I saw a few others struggling with the same dilemma.

"Just choose the one you believe you belong to the most," said one trainer, insisting that we choose. Andreas, a vocal veteran country director of Honduran descent with a Swiss passport, working in Zimbabwe, pinned up his own self-made sign that read "Earth Human" and stood under it. I followed suit, happy to find another chameleon. Within minutes we had almost half the group under his sign.

The poor American trainer was at a loss for the rest of the week on how to deal with the rebellious participants who constantly questioned his cultural bias in discussing concepts such as leadership techniques and methods of giving constructive feedback to local staff.

Later in the week, we were asked to fill out a two-hour multiple question survey for the Myers-Briggs Type Indicator Test, supposedly renowned for its capability to determine character and temperament types for cross-cultural managers like ourselves. Our replies to the questions—designed to include ambiguous and controversial life situations specific to Western cultures—generated point scores, which were then interpreted to define our personality types from a codebook that we were not privy to beforehand. When the results were diagnosed, many members of the group became quite upset with the conclusions drawn. Apparently, as explained by the trainers, one particular character type, among the many others with useful characteristics, was considered to have the best potential for effective leadership qualities. On hearing this, participants were visibly angry

Myers-Briggs, with years of experienced trainers implementing this magical formula test in America, obviously had a monopoly in determining leadership qualities worldwide.

Then Andreas, our rebel leader, asked the question on everyone's mind: "Are these test results confidential? If not, can we have them back? If so, how will they be used by headquarters and to what purpose?"

The trainers dodged the question at first, then claimed ignorance of how the test results would be used by CI management. We kept on probing until, hours later, one of the trainers let on that the results could possibly be used as one tool for determining promotion and country assignments. The group went ballistic with protests. The organizational credibility of CI, not to mention the trainers, was suspect from that point on. For the rest of the week, at lunch and coffee breaks, over dinner and at a reggae bar on Key Biscayne, we organized informal gatherings, without the trainers, to share our work problems as a more productive way to understand strategies for managers in the aid industry. Word got back to headquarters that the training had not gone as planned. During that week, I had got a crash course on all the things *not* to do in training staff to improve their skills.

On the last day, hours before the new CEO showed up for his half-day meeting with us, the trainers confirmed that the Myers-Briggs test results, though not to be returned to participants, would no longer be used to determine relocations or promotions. Furthermore, it was strongly suggested that we not bring up this issue at the meeting with the new CEO. As a last resort to salvage the credibility of the test, the trainers handed out to all of us a book, 'Fed-Exed' overnight from Washington, that explained the complete rationale behind Myers-Briggs. Ironically it was entitled *Please Understand Me*.

ॐ

On my way back to Thailand, at Miami Airport, I was told by Air India that my connection from Bombay to Bangkok had been cancelled and that the next available flight was some thirteen hours later. Great! I thought. I can get a taste of India for the first time in my life by exploring Bombay. On a whim, I called my father in Vancouver for the address of my aunt in Bombay whom I'd never met. Not having seen her since he left India in 1928, all he could tell me was that her name was Sakina Hooda, that she lived in an Ismaili housing complex in Andheri, a suburb of Bombay, and to please give her some money from him if I found her.

On the plane, I was all hyped up about the day in India—birthplace of my father, home of my mother tongue, and cultural center of my heritage. I landed at Sahar International Airport at the ungodly hour of five in the morning. The first problem was at Immigration.

"American passport. No Indian visa? Impossible to visit Bombay," said the officer on duty. He seemed adamant.

"Can I please get one now?" I asked.

A CHAMELEON'S TALE

"Not possible. Must go to Indian Consulate in New York. But you're Indian, yes?" He shook his head as if looking for a solution.

Switching to Hindi, I pleaded ignorance about needing a visa and explained how I was returning home after twenty years to see my sick aunt who needed urgent help.

The conversation went back and forth for another ten minutes until he took pity on me and finally said, "Only one solution. Must leave passport here at airport for pick-up at departure time. Temporary pass will be provided."

Somewhat apprehensive about this option, I studied the small slip of paper he called a "temporary pass." It had my name, a semi-official stamp with the date of arrival, and a handwritten note at the bottom stating my flight departure details. I hesitated. I must be mad to believe this man. I'd probably never see my passport again. Yet I was desperate to get a taste of my ancestral homeland. I looked into the man's eyes. No empathy, but no malice either. I took a chance, praying that I wasn't being stupid.

Daylight was approaching as the taxi sped away from the airport, further and further from my passport. Sood, the driver, explained that Andheri was too big an area to explore without a specific address. I repeated my lost aunt story, which luckily perked up his sleepy eyes. He asked my name and religion, and I told him my family background.

Sood agreed to be my guide for the short time I would be on Indian soil. He turned off the taxi's meter, and when I pressed him on what flat rate he would charge for his time and fuel, he insisted, "*Aap khi marjee, bhai saaa-hib.*" 'Up to your goodwill, brother sahib.'

Go with the flow, Mojo. Have faith in your own people, I said to myself.

Bombay was just waking up to the day, but already the streets were clogged with people, taxis, rickshaws, scooters, carts, and all kinds of other vehicles. Food vendors were setting up their mobile

kiosks. The sounds and smells brought out a nostalgia long forgotten
. . . Sunday evenings on Kampala Road when Indian families paraded
in droves on their day of leisure before the weekly Bollywood movie.
In pre-Amin times, Sunday was a good day for the African vendors
on Kampala Road. The Asians, usually tight with their money in their
businesses, spent freely on their families on their weekend holiday.
The Muslims favored the grilled sheesh kebabs marinated in curried
spices; the Hindus opted for vegetarian snacks like *bhajias* and *dhokras*
dipped in green chutney; while some of the Sikhs preferred *nyama*
choma, grilled beef served with a spicy cucumber and onion salad.
Since the Indians always came in family groups, any given Sunday
would make up for slow business during the week for all the vendors.
I told Sood about this flashback, and he informed me that Andheri
was one of the three main Bollywood sites. Now I expected to spot
actor Shashi Kapoor or singer Lata Mangeshkar, both favorites of
my mother, strolling along the street.

We stopped at a roadside teashop to eat and ask directions.
The breakfast of hot rotis with omelets spiced up with onions and
chillies, close enough to Ma's version, gave me a second wind from
the jet lag. The teashop owner, along with two early bird customers,
brainstormed with Sood and me on how best to proceed in search of
my aunt. The consensus was that we should head to a mosque a few
streets away, locate the *imam* there, who might be able to help us find
the right Ismaili mosque, where we would repeat the same procedure
until we found my aunt.

The *imam* at the first mosque did indeed direct us to an Ismaili
mosque, where the *mukhi* was only too happy to interrupt his breakfast
to help a fellow Ismaili from abroad. He started off, in Gujarati, by
asking me to recount my father's family tree. I gave the names of
Bapa's three younger brothers, who he brought over to Uganda; the
grandpa who died in India before I was born; and the grandma who I
used to walk to mosque with on Fridays in Kampala. Twenty minutes

later, from the aunt's name and the family history, we narrowed the search down to four women named Sakina living nearby. I sensed I was getting closer when he gave me the house numbers.

The first of the four Sakinas was not at home, and the second turned out to be too young to be my father's sister. The third, a lady in her fifties in a plain white sari with her hair tied in a bun, though suspicious at first, patiently listened to my by now well-rehearsed story. In a soft voice, she grilled me on my family tree, to which I rattled off answers without hesitation.

Her eyes lit up upon recognizing some of the names of my brothers and sisters. She broke out into a big smile as tears welled up in her eyes. "*Andar aowo, betah.*" 'Come inside, son,' she said in Gujarati, and led us into the house.

Her humble home had bare walls except for a framed picture of the smiling Aga Khan with yellow garlands around his neck. Sood and I met her aging husband, now almost blind from glaucoma. Over yet another breakfast that she insisted on cooking up, I gave them news of all my family and their lives in America and Canada. She, in turn, told us of their life in Bombay, recalling stories of my father's youth as best she could: how my philosophical, meditation-at-dawn father once used to drink and gamble; how he was always the teacher and the Hindi-English translator in the family. She then talked fondly of Grandpa, who died when my father was fifteen, making it necessary for Bapuji to cancel his college plans and support the family. She cried again when I described Grandma's funeral.

At lunchtime her two sons, Karim and Jahangir, showed up from work to meet the unexpected family member from America. More hugs and more food. Since the family had moved residence within Andheri two years before, the brothers wondered how I had found them, chuckling at my explanation of how Sood and I had tracked them down in this teeming city of millions. Karim, three years younger than me, took the afternoon off to show me around

Bombay for the rest of the day, and see me off at the airport. Despite having known these long-lost relatives for just a few hours, it felt like a homecoming. Before saying my farewells, when left alone for a moment, I placed fifty dollars worth of rupees under a book on a dresser. Bapa would be pleased.

Driving around Bombay with Sood and Karim, I was like a boy in a candy shop, wanting to stop everywhere to taste foods I recognized and hadn't eaten for years—*kulfi, pakoras, bhel puri*. When I saw boys playing cricket in the street, I had to join in and make a few strokes. Sood drove us down to Chowpatty Beach, in the southern part of the city, for a taste of Bombay life. The scene, right out of a Fellini movie, had me mesmerised. Kids rode horses and elephants on the beach, and I had to be one of them. A card shark tricked me into forking out a few rupees over a card game I'd first seen on the streets of Kampala. A monkey danced to his owner's flute, and the man played Indian songs from my childhood for a few more rupees. I rejoiced in the thrill of jousting in my own language, mimicking hand and eye gestures only these people would understand. I was re-living my youth, with both Sood and Karim having more fun just watching me have fun. At a bookstore on the way back to the taxi, I stopped to buy a copy of *Midnight's Children* for Karim, who had never heard of Rushdie.

Only when heading towards the airport for check-in did I remember my fear of never seeing my American passport again. I told Karim about my entry into India, but he said nothing. At the airport, he helped me find the designated spot where I was supposed to pick up my passport. A different Immigration official heard my story and then opened a drawer at his desk. "We've been expecting you," he said as he handed me my passport. I felt like a fool about all my insecurities.

During our farewells, when I tried to pay Sood for his services, he simply refused. I kept insisting. Finally, he pointed to Karim and said,

"Tip-top sahib." Unbeknownst to me, Karim had already paid him and wouldn't tell me the amount. *"Aapna desh ma chokas aowjo pacha,"* Karim said. 'Be sure to come back to your country soon.'

I knew I would. For much longer than a few hours.

০৪

In July 1987, when my two years in Khon Kaen were almost up, CI asked me if I was willing to transfer to El Progreso, Guatemala, for three years as country director. The Guatemala field office, established soon after the 1976 earthquake, had gone through four rotations of directors and had a local staff of 120 working with some 40,000 people. El Progreso town, one and a half hours northeast of Guatemala City by car, was described as small but quaint. I deliberated. I had requested a post in Asia, but was told there were no rotations expected there for another six months and that I had to respond to this offer within a week. Apparently they had determined that since I was single and spoke good Spanish, I would be ideal for the posting.

Despite my apprehensions after what I'd experienced with vice president, Bill, and the Miami training fiasco, it was quite apparent to me that CI did give more program autonomy to their field directors than most other agencies in the aid business. During my journey through South America, a decade before, I had spent three wonderful months exploring Guatemala, loving the country and its people. Steve in Khon Kaen had been a good boss, but we did have our differences on acquiescing to head office demands, some quite ludicrous in my opinion. This offer would be a chance to prove my worth in a language I knew and in a country where the poverty, much like in Africa, was more acute. Flying to America and Canada during holidays to see my family, cost- and time-wise, would now be possible as an added bonus. I accepted the posting and within two weeks was halfway across the globe on yet another mission. Little did I know then, that ten years would pass before I would return to Asia again.

The flight time helped me make the mental shift from the Asian to the Latin world. In Guatemala, there would be no room for the non-confrontational Buddhist approach to life and work. Latinos speak their mind, and expect the same from their bosses. I would no longer need to avoid emotional displays. Unlike Asians, Latinos express their feelings freely. This would be a welcome change, since I often ran into problems with Asian friends for being too passionate about both work and play.

ॐ

In Guatemala, the gap between the *mestizos* and the *indígena* cultures, almost half and half in terms of overall population, is huge in terms of wealth distribution and economic opportunity. *Indígenas* got the short end of the stick. CI's operation in Guatemala had a 2.2 million-dollar annual budget. It was the only international aid agency in El Progreso, and thus wielded a lot of power and influence throughout that province. The 1976 earthquake had caused massive devastation, but scores of schools, village health clinics, feeder roads, multi-purpose community centers, and maize silos had been rebuilt over the years by CI staff. Money was never an issue; there was plenty of it. The downside? Almost all the projects built with CI money had required little or no contribution from the local people, not even for physical labor. So much so, that a financial and mental dependency on hand-outs was now well entrenched in the minds of most villagers. To shift that mentality to one of improved self-sufficiency was part of my mandate and challenge.

In this context, four episodes stand out as worth mentioning. The first was in education.

Staff alerted me, early in my first year, that the drop-out rate of village children in the first and second grades of primary school was extremely high. Evening sessions with the villagers, after they came home from the fields, revealed the reason. During the bi-annual corn harvest, children were pulled out of school to work in the fields.

They missed too many classes to be able to catch up, thereby failing their grades, which then led to drop-outs initiated by the parents. Furthermore, with little or no homework help from illiterate mothers or fathers, the children often got discouraged with schooling.

"What if the children were able to pass the grades?" I asked a group of villagers at a meeting one night. "Would you then keep them in primary school?"

"Yes, of course," replied the village headman.

"And during the harvest?"

"*Jefe*, if we know they are doing well in school, we would not worry about money wasted on uniforms and books. We would make sacrifices, including keeping them in school during harvest."

"Sure? Do I have your word on that?"

They all nodded in agreement.

A month later, we chose seven villages in the province for kindergarten programs. The concept of kindergarten schooling was non-existent in El Progreso. CI hired and trained local teachers and provided supplies and textbooks. A new curriculum, with greater emphasis on agriculture and child learning development, was devised. Meanwhile, people in all seven villages constructed basic school buildings and made simple furniture for the classrooms. Twenty children were chosen by each village project committee to attend the school. Any absences or drop-outs, including for emergencies, had to be reported and explained to CI staff. The village leaders took on the responsibility of admonishing the mothers for inexcusable absences. Upon advice from my staff, I negotiated a 'memorandum of understanding' with the provincial education officials, that the ministry would take over the project, including all expenses, within two years, and continue it for an additional five. The cost to CI for two years was a mere 17,000 dollars.

The project took off, probably because my staff had listened to the villagers; because I, in turn, had listened to my staff; and because the villagers had invested their own time and money in the project. By the time I left, three years later, El Progreso had 27 kindergarten schools teaching 500 children. Drop-out rates in first- and second-grade primary school had been reduced by nearly eighty percent.

The second episode had nothing to do with villagers. I had hired Carlos, a humble farmer from El Progreso, as a handyman-cum-gardener to care for and watch over my residence when I was away on village work or in the capital city for meetings. Over time, he became a trusted confidant, teaching me about Guatemalan culture, village agriculture constraints, and the theological turf wars between *Catholicos* and *evangelicos* (the latter converted by Bible-thumbing American missionaries) that were destroying the fabric of village culture. I shunned the missionaries' invitations to collaborate on projects, knowing their hidden agendas.

One morning, before heading to Guatemala City with the CI procurement manager, Juan Jose, to make some large purchases for a big agricultural project, I showed Carlos the three quotations that Juan Jose had come up with. Surprised at the inflated price quotes, he told me where to go for much cheaper products of the same quality.

In the city, I let Juan Jose take me to the three places on his list before asking him to take me to the place that Carlos had recommended. The price was indeed much cheaper and the quality of the products comparable. I ended up buying from Carlos's place—despite vociferous protests from Juan Jose—saving CI 28,000 dollars in the process.

Back at home, Carlos revealed that, country-wide, procurement managers traditionally received a 'commission' for purchasing goods and services from 'select' stores. The higher the purchase, the higher the commission. From that point on—after Juan Jose was asked by me to leave CI—Carlos became my unofficial auditor, reviewing all quotes given to me by the new procurement manager before I signed

163

off on the purchase. Over the period of two years, Carlos must have saved CI thousands of dollars. When I offered to pay him for his clandestine auditing services, he responded, "Señor, the work you and the agency do is all for my people. For sure, God will pay me for my little help."

The third episode involved a solution for reducing the massive deforestation going on in the province. With no electricity in most villages, women cooked with firewood cut from trees in the *campo*, a practice that had gone on for centuries. The scarcer the wood became, the higher the men climbed the mountains to cut. When the trees disappeared altogether in some areas, families had to pay hefty sums to "*coyotes*"—middlemen in the business of selling wood from other provinces. This practice, along with massive logging by contractors in cahoots with corrupt government officials, had eventually led to many parts of El Progreso turning into desert with little or no arable land.

Leopoldo, a CI staff member who had studied conservation in America, alerted me to an experimental project for cheap, easy-to-make solar cookers as a viable alternative to firewood. Sunshine was one commodity that El Progreso had in abundance.

California Bob at Solar Cookers International agreed to come to El Progreso to train villagers how to build the cookers from cardboard boxes with aluminum siding. Each one cost twenty quetzals, about three dollars, while most families spent thirty quetzals a week on wood from *coyotes*. The training went well, and the experimental project was started up in ten villages suffering the most acute wood shortage. The women took only one hour to build the cookers, but they had to adjust their cooking schedules to daylight hours and monitor the time for foods like red beans and chicken that took longer to cook than rice or fish. The project took off in other villages like wildfire, and, two months later, the "first lady" of Guatemala, Señora Norma Callejas, visited us to see for herself this new way of cooking.

However, six months later, while this project was being duplicated in many villages of El Progreso, there was a sudden lull in the momentum. Women all over the province seemed to have stopped using the cookers. Village leaders were asked to find out the reason—and it turned out that the *coyotes* had got wind of the project and come up with a counter plan to ensure that their income would not disappear because of this upstart gringo project. Rumors, perpetrated by the *coyotes*, spread among the women that sun rays, reflected from the aluminum siding in the cookers, caused skin cancer. Repeated meetings to convince the women that these rumors were false, and that the *coyotes*—supported by the wood industry—had a protectionist agenda, did little to allay their fears. In addition, fabricated gossip about how women who had died natural deaths were actually victims of "solar cooker cancer" eventually doomed the project to failure.

Known in El Progreso as an 'advocate for culture'—for embracing local customs as the means to work with the poor—I was shocked and disheartened to learn that rumor and gossip were more powerful tools than pragmatism and sound economics. It was my first hard lesson in realizing the shortcomings of that same rural culture I touted so confidently.

The fourth episode also didn't have much to do with villagers. By 1990, a large part of my job as country director involved career development for the seven CI municipality program managers—all Guatemalan, each with fifteen or so community workers under their supervision. After fiscal management training, I gave each of them the responsibility of directly managing an annual budget of 200,000 dollars for the most urgent projects in their municipality. This new, delegated accountability was not appreciated by my two program directors, who supervised the seven program managers from the field office in El Progreso. Although the two program directors, Antonio and Roberto, resisted relinquishing control over project money, I forced the issue by asking them to relocate to the municipality town centers, much closer to the villages where CI worked. I knew quite well that they would not like this.

Antonio had worked for CI since its inception in 1976, and was promoted to program director in 1980. Roberto, with sharper management skills, had been hired as the second program director by the previous country director, seven years before. He was being groomed by me to become the first national assistant director in Central America. Both had excellent programming and management skills, and would be there long after I was relocated to some other CI posting. Antonio would be groomed next, after Roberto's training was completed.

Soon after passing over budget control to the program managers, I visited all seven municipalities to see for myself how effectively my fiscal and management training was being applied. While in San Ignacio—a poor, semi-arid municipality with acute illiteracy and bad harvests—Alfredo, the manager, requested a private meeting with me at a local restaurant. As we ate, he looked around to make sure no other customers were listening, and then, demanding total confidentiality, which I promised, he asked, "*Jefe*, is it okay to sub-contract construction projects for San Ignacio to someone other than Israel Portillo?"

Israel Portillo was one of CI's oldest building contractors, and was a big figure in El Progreso town.

"Why?" I asked. "Is he giving you cheap quality work? Antonio always speaks highly of his work."

"There is a problem. Maybe you know that Antonio's house in El Progreso was built by Israel? They go back a long ways."

"Are you sure? Antonio's been with CI since the beginning. How come you didn't tell me this before?"

"I was scared, boss. Antonio was here last week insisting that Las Anonas be sub-contracted to Israel."

Las Anonas was an 84,000-dollar project to build new homes for 45 families. The money was donated by a philanthropist 'foster parent' from Holland, who visited his three sponsored children in Guatemala annually.

"Ask the other program managers about Israel if you don't believe me. But please, *jefe*, don't tell them I told you about this."

"Are you telling me that Antonio is another Juan Jose?" I asked, now visibly irritated at this alarming news. Brenda, my supervisor at headquarters, who had known Antonio for seven years, couldn't praise his program work enough. Was Alfredo stirring up trouble, or was there fire behind this smoke?

In secret meetings with all seven program managers and senior accounting staff in the field office, I spent the next two months investigating Alfredo's accusations about Antonio and Israel Portillo. I alerted Brenda by phone. She seemed skeptical of Alfredo's accusations, but went along with my investigation. Roberto turned out to be clean as a whistle, but as more evidence was unearthed, more and more rats deserted Antonio's sinking ship.

Israel Portillo had a semi-monopoly on CI sub-contracts in most of the projects Antonio supervised (many of them before my arrival)—at highly inflated prices. When I eventually confronted Antonio with all the documented evidence, he didn't deny any of the charges, and ended up leaving CI after years of dedicated service.

Within a month, Israel Portillo filed a spurious lawsuit against CI for money owed to him for severance pay as a sub-contractor for the agency for ten years—as per Guatemalan labor code requirements. When this claim fell apart after six months of haggling with lawyers and the Civil Claims Court in Guatemala City, he threatened my life. In a small town like El Progreso, such a death threat had to be taken seriously. Brenda was alerted to this and, without visiting El Progreso, made the decision to transfer me to another post, requesting that I clean up the mess as best I could before leaving.

I was to be transferred to Cali, Colombia. Yet, I couldn't stop thinking about all the years that had gone by while Antonio and Israel Portillo skimmed the CI coffers under the very noses of four country directors, including me. How much longer would this scam have gone on if I hadn't decided to transfer budgetary control from people like Juan Jose to people like Carlos, from people like Antonio to people like Alfredo. Would Alfredo turn into another Antonio one day?

A week before leaving for Cali, Peace Corps Honduras suddenly offered me a job as program and training officer in Tegucigalpa, the capital city, with more training responsibility and much more money. I took it. Training people was what I was good at, and I was tired of playing fiscal cop for CI in the name of the children of the poor.

∾

Tegucigalpa ("Tegoose") is a nondescript, noisy city nestled in a bowl-shaped valley, surrounded by piney mountains. Compared to Guatemala City, it boasts no Latin character except for a couple of exquisite old churches left over from the Spanish period, a few museums, and some old houses with Spanish architecture. The outskirts of the city are mostly slums: row after row of ramshackle huts where the poor eke out a living. Downtown, the American Embassy on Avenida La Paz stands out as a monstrous concrete fort. Every morning, alongside one of the rampart walls, a mile-long line of Hondurans patiently waits in the hot sun to be rejected for a tourist visa to America. (Some who had gone before, never came back.)

At Comayagua army base, two hours northwest of the city, there had been a heavy build-up of American troops during Ronald Reagan's administration, to protect US interests in the banana industry (where the US owned 75 percent of Honduran land) from the socialist revolutions going on in Nicaragua and El Salvador. By 1990, that US presence was on the wane. The "Contra" war, fought from Honduran soil, was quickly forgotten after elections in Nicaragua ousted Daniel Ortega and the Sandinistas. But American influence was still everywhere, despite the Latino saying, "*Lejos de Los Estados, gracias a Dios*"—'the further we are from the US, the greater the thanks be to God.'

In my haste to leave CI, I had forgotten that I'd be working directly for the US government—which had both its perks and consequences. Coming from one-traffic-light El Progreso, I must admit I succumbed to some of the perks. The embassy housing committee determined where employees would live (for safety reasons), and my three-bedroom house in upscale Colonia Palmira had motion detectors in every room, iron grilles on the windows, jagged glass embedded atop the compound walls, and direct radio contact with the 24-hour Marine guard at the embassy. The use-it-or-lose-it housing allowance of 13,000 dollars a year was more than my annual salary at CI.

The American commissary next to the embassy (available to Americans and employees only) sold American goods, shipped in from Miami, at subsidised prices in American dollars only. A liter of Bacardi rum, costing twelve dollars in American supermarkets, cost me four. Access to the ambassador's swimming pool, tennis courts, and cocktail parties at his twelve-acre hacienda in El Hatillo was permitted as long as I signed up in advance at the Marine guard station and submitted to car bomb checks at the entrance. Diplomatic luxury, under the guise of health and safety precautions, was certainly considered to be good use of American taxpayers' money.

The embassy's American staff, most of whom spoke little or 'kitchen' Spanish, lived in a climate of self-imposed fear. They dared not venture outside of the city unless with a military escort in bulletproof vehicles with tinted windows. As second in command at Peace Corps, my work with the embassy involved weekly inter-agency meetings, chaired by the ambassador, in a soundproof 'bubble room.'

Mostly, I was informed about updated security measures and which latest Honduran minister had been co-opted to think and trade the American way.

In sharp contrast, my work with the Peace Corps volunteers— fresh graduates full of idealism—was to organize and oversee their three-month training cycles. They learned Spanish and acquainted themselves with the culture while living in very basic conditions with Honduran families in Santa Lucia and Valle de Angeles, small towns half an hour from Tegoose. Family home stay for all three months of training was now compulsory for all volunteers.

During breaks between the three cycles per year, I facilitated "close of service" (COS) conferences with volunteers who were finishing up their two years of service. Cycle after cycle, COS after COS, I saw these naïve ambassadors of goodwill metamorphosize from green idealists to enlightened souls, often embittered at the level of local suffering—some of it induced by the effects of American foreign policy. Just like I had, back in Thailand.

For five years, I played the role of 'mind molder' to help channel their newfound views to some good use—either in America to help convert others, or abroad to work with the poor. Sometimes I lamented that I had not had my own 'mind molder' to help accelerate my own learning curve during my days with the Peace Corps in Thailand. That's when I would remind myself that people like Ajaan Uthai and Monk Marut in Thailand, Nguyen and Sayeed in the camps, and Don Crucito and Carlos in Central America, had indeed been my mind molders. I should be glad to have the opportunity to repay them by molding American minds in turn, even if there were many more blindfolded 'bubble-room bureaucrats' than volunteers in Honduras.

∞

When my five years with the Peace Corps were up, I had to leave Honduras. So I left Tegucigalpa and headed to Washington, D.C.

for my 'debriefing.' At its inception in 1961, the Peace Corps had instituted a policy that no employee could work for them for more than five years—in order to prevent entrenched bureaucrats holding on to power for too long. But when I got to Washington, I discovered that this excellent policy, unique only to the Corps— still the most liberal, bipartisan agency in the US government—was sadly undermined by the fact that senior management positions in Washington were mostly "Schedule C" positions. Such plum, well-paid appointments can only be made by the US president, and were thus usually reserved for friends or election campaign contributors: people who had no clue about the Corps' worldly mission. These positions of power, overseeing a 200-million-dollar budget, led to a nepotism that has politicized the agency—despite the bipartisan rhetoric—to this day.

It was also during my time in Washington that I first heard about the "Beltway Bandits." Beltway 495 is a bypass route that circles Washington, D.C. Conveniently located all along the Beltway are the headquarters of some fifty or more NGOs, whose main purpose for being there is to schmooze, wine and dine, and suck up to government staff at USAID, the 'Midas' of money for the American aid industry. Each year, USAID doles out millions of dollars for projects in developing countries, and each of these NGO bandits desperately fights to get their hands on some of it.

Using what they call "relationship networking," the bandits get advance notice for overseas project proposals requested by the Midas, which they then crank out, sometimes overnight, using glossy pictures of poverty and suffering, and the latest buzzwords of the aid industry ('self sustainability,' 'results-based performance indicators,' 'child rights advocacy,' 'gender sensitive staffing patterns'). Like hungry dogs, they sniff out every single money and programming tip, whispered by the Midas agents over fine meals and wine, so they can undercut budgets and tailor-make proposals to easily win the bid.

This is considered an open and transparent process, just in case the auditors come poking around.

The one consistent action that most of these bandits do *not* take is to consult with field staff about the viability of a proposed project—if they even have any staff at all in the countries where the money is earmarked for. Many do not. Nor do they actually visit the intended project sites to talk to the beneficiaries in whose name they inherit millions of dollars. What they *do* ensure is that there is always a minimum seventeen percent 'administrative overhead' reserved for their salaries, perks, and junkets to conferences in Bali, Phuket, or Cancun. The system works like clockwork—a beautiful, symbiotic marriage of Midas and the Beltway Bandits, usually at the expense of the poor masses in the southern hemisphere. I met bandits far more ethically degenerate than CI vice president, Bill, with his McDonald's marketing approach to the Hmong children. These people were the norm, rather than the exception, in this Mecca of fund raising.

At the end of my time in Washington, I left in a hurry for Vancouver, Canada, anxious to spend time with my parents, now in their eighties.

శు

In 1995, in Vancouver, I received a phone call from a Peace Corps headquarters staffer who knew of my refugee background and work experience. He had recommended me for a three-month position at the US naval base, Guantanamo Bay ("Gitmo"), Cuba to help with the unexpected arrival of thousands of Haitians and Cubans.

The "*balseros*" as they came to be known, fled their repressive governments and attempted the crossing to the Florida coast on rafts, truck tires, any makeshift vessel. Many died from starvation or drowned, yet thousands more kept coming. They were a Caribbean version of the Vietnamese boat people. Picked up by the US Coast Guard (in an operation dubbed "Sea Signal"), they were taken to

Gitmo as a temporary measure till the Clinton administration could decide what to do with them. I was to be a "conflict resolution negotiator" liaising between the US joint forces running the camp, and the refugees.

Refugee work again. In communist Cuba. I was up for it. One more long phone call with Haitian Jay, the Camp Bravo supervisor in Gitmo, confirmed the appointment. Bravo was already in crisis mode, and I would start in just three days.

After the missile crisis of 1961, the US placed an embargo on Cuba, and American law prohibited its citizens from traveling there. So I was taken to Gitmo secretly on a six-seater plane from a small army airfield in Florida. Gitmo, a gorgeous bay, deep enough for ships to anchor, was leased from Cuba in 1903 and was now the biggest US naval installation in the Caribbean. On arrival at Leeward Point Airfield, I saw soldiers in fatigues transporting heavy military equipment from a ship. A staffer from the Community Services Division of the Department of Justice, my employer, took me to my living quarters—a small cabin aboard a Greek ship in the bay—and then to Camp Bravo on the windward side of the bay. On the way, we passed an exquisite expat housing complex, built American style with picket fences, manicured lawns, and even red-white-and-blue mail boxes with flags. All non-essential American personnel at the base had been evacuated back to America, once the decision had been taken to turn Gitmo into a refugee camp.

Camp Bravo, on the other hand, was a sea of tents fenced off with barbed wire. At the office, Jay explained that I would work with and supervise three Miami Cuban negotiators. Our immediate task was to placate the refugees. Just ten days before, a horde of Cubans had jumped the fence, taken over a McDonald's restaurant nearby, and demanded better food and conditions. They were overpowered by American soldiers and put back behind the fence. More soldiers were on the way from Miami to beef up camp security.

Over the next few days, we discovered that many of the refugees had been professionals back in their homelands. Some were doctors, lawyers, or artists; they were not all criminals (thousands of whom Fidel Castro had allowed to leave Cuba in a similar flight a few years back) as assumed by the army supervisors. The refugees were being fed bland, ready-to-eat meals—shipped in by an American food company at 250,000 dollars a day—when all they wanted was to be allowed to cook their rice or beans, both Cuban staples.

The two UNHCR representatives—in camp to ensure refugee protection—had no authority whatsoever. At night, some soldiers were forcing Cuban women to have sex with them in exchange for unkept promises to help relatives or friends. Black marketing of cigarettes and alcohol was a thriving business for other guards. There was no accountability for the soldiers' actions.

It took days of hard negotiations before the Cubans were allowed to cook their rice and beans. Appeals for reprimands or court martial of abusive or profiteering soldiers went unheard. Requests for updates of decisions being made by US attorney general, Janet Reno, otherwise reported in American newspapers every day, were ignored.

Then, everything changed when communications giant, AT&T, suddenly installed phones outside Camp Bravo. Good old American corporate greed saved the day for the inmates. Refugees with family or friends among the large Cuban population in Florida could now call collect and alert them to the camp situation, which would then be reported in Florida newspapers the next day. The inmates could now receive news of decisions made in Washington faster than the Joint Command staff. Meetings with army supervisors—who now permitted two refugee representatives to attend; one Cuban, one Haitian—turned into political debates on who had the latest information on what Janet Reno or President Clinton had agreed to over the last week.

The tables were turning in favor of the refugees, at least for the Cubans. They, unlike the Asian refugees of the Vietnam War, were anything but passive. The Haitians, far worse off than the Cubans, were less vocal, and were ignored altogether as events in Haiti heated up and the US prepared to invade the country to reinstate Jean-Bertrand Aristede, who had been ousted in a bloody coup in 1991.

So what did the Joint Command do, now that the Cubans had the upper hand? They canceled all conflict-resolution meetings and made our negotiator jobs redundant. I protested, asking Jay for support, but he was silenced by the army officer in command. When I continued to make noise, threatening to go to the American media, I was put on a plane back to Miami.

In Washington, my debriefing report to the Community Services Division at the Department of Justice fell on deaf ears. Since I was neither Cuban nor Haitian, no one had any interest in what I had to say about Gitmo and Camp Bravo.

In May 1995, President Bill Clinton reversed policy and admitted almost all of the Cubans into America. The last group left Gitmo by January 1996. Meanwhile, the US had invaded Haiti and reinstated Aristede as president. (By November 1994, almost all the Haitians in Gitmo had been repatriated to Haiti. They were given forty dollars each to start a new life after having lost everything back home.)

It wasn't long before Guantanamo's bad reputation came under scrutiny again. After the 9/11 terrorist attacks in 2001 and the ensuing American retaliation against the Taleban in Afghanistan, Gitmo became a "temporary detention facility" for suspected Muslim terrorists. Camp X-Ray, on the northern side of the bay, was a holding center for "enemy combatants" who had no charges filed against them, were given no access to lawyers, and were not allowed family visits.

Some prisoners who were eventually released from Gitmo published stories of torture and abuse, which caused worldwide media controversy about human rights issues and the Geneva accords on war conventions.

∾

The Gitmo experience was a turning point for my work in the aid industry. Awakened to people like Bill from CI, the Miami trainers, Antonio in Guatemala, and then the Joint Command at Camp Bravo, I was almost at the end of my rope. If I was to continue to live with my own conscience, I would have to be my own boss. It was that, or get away from this line of work altogether. I returned to Vancouver to spend time with my ageing parents.

During this hiatus, I read two books on the aid industry that would help determine my next move. The first, *Endless Enemies* by Jonathan Kwitny, exposes the seamy side of fifty years of disastrous American foreign policy: 'interventions' from Angola to Afghanistan, from Cuba to Chile, from Honduras to Zaire. The second, *Lords Of Poverty* by Graham Hancock, a journalist who spent three years in Ethiopia during the devastating famine of the mid-1980s, spells out, in intricate detail, the massive damage that agencies like the UN, IMF, and World Bank have done to the poor worldwide.

These books made me realize that I wanted no more part in this gigantic swindle. I had become a cynic, and decided I would be better off training socially conscientious individuals on how to fight this fraud. Opening up my own training agency seemed the only logical thing to do. Focusing on cross-cultural awareness as a way to promote better understanding of work issues with the poor kept me motivated. Despite many ups and downs, I managed to nudge it along for three years. More importantly, I was able to spend lots of quality time with my parents instead of the usual rushed fortnight vacation during a family reunion or wedding. But Canadian clients weren't too keen to give contracts to an individual who had spent most of his life outside Canada, and eventually I moved the agency to Bangkok, where I still had numerous friends and acquaintances. I plodded along for a few more years, sometimes with enough work but more often teetering on bankruptcy, so my cynicism continued to gnaw at me.

But all that changed when Pranee, my Thai girlfriend of four years, and I got caught up in one of the biggest disasters in living memory.

ॐ

It was the morning after Christmas on the picture-postcard island of Surin in southern Thailand. Thirty-two-year-old Pranee, my soul mate, was born in the southern beach town of Songkhla, but was now living in Chiang Mai. Thrilled to be swimming in the Andaman Sea, she was happily snorkeling away in the shallow channel just off Khao Chong Haad Beach, taking underwater photos of clown fish and coral. I was lying on the sand, listening to Bob Marley on my headphones. She told me later that the sudden, rushing appearance of meter-long fish, in shoals of ten or more, had startled her. Something was not right, she thought, as she raised her head and blue snorkel mask above water.

That's when the swirling backwash of the first tsunami wave thrust her violently out to sea. "*Chuay duai*!" 'Help me!' she yelled when she saw other bodies struggling in the water. No one came. I had been swept away by the wave, fifty meters inland, before clutching on to a floating log. That log saved my life.

Pranee, her body sagging, knew she was losing the fight and might drown under the churning water. Have the will to survive; your mother back home depends on you, she told herself. Once more the water thrust her upward. She saw a bright-yellow life vest on a young Thai man, and called out to him. He grabbed her hand before the water smashed them both hard again. Somehow she managed to clutch on to the back of his shirt as he swam towards a rock. Moments later, he had pushed her onto the rock, which she scrambled up on all fours. As soon as she was safe and breathing steadily, he told her he had to search for his missing wife and daughter, and slid back into the water. Weakly, she smiled at him. "He saved my life while his own loved ones were still missing," she told me later.

Only when he was out of sight did Pranee notice another Thai couple, both with life vests on, who were also stranded on the rock. The wife was sobbing profusely, whimpering in Thai that she couldn't swim and they would never be rescued. The husband tried to console her and Pranee held the woman's hand and told her to have faith, as the screams of people still struggling in the water reached their ears.

More than an hour later, when the waves had receded temporarily, a longtail boat driven by a Moken sea gypsy appeared. He took all three of them from the rock and dropped them safely onto the beach. "Get up to high ground. The waves will come again," he warned before speeding off in search of more survivors. Despite the hot sun, Pranee shivered involuntarily as she felt the sand beneath her feet. Only then did she notice that her left leg was bleeding. She had been cut all over by the rocks and coral.

Meanwhile, I was frantic with worry. Dead bodies were being pulled out of the water by the Moken and others, and I wasn't sure if Pranee would be one of them. How would I survive without her? How would I tell her mother she was gone? Would the same Mother Nature that I loved so much be cruel enough to take her away from me? The beach, where we had taken a moonlit walk the night before, was no longer traversable. It was cluttered with debris from lots of fallen tents and shattered buildings. The restaurant where we had eaten breakfast that morning was a pile of rubble. The Audio Visual Room, where we had watched videos of marine life in the Andaman Sea, had collapsed, the roof swept off, with all the tables and chairs splintered and floating in knee-deep water.

I found her after two desperate hours of searching all over the island. I hugged her close to me for an eternity, fearful of losing her again. My heart was beating fast.

All around us, people were yelling out names of missing loved ones, many of them passengers from the cruise liner, *Ocean Princess*, that had anchored offshore just that morning. Pranee refused to acknowledge her near brush with death. She ignored her bleeding leg. "There is much to do," she told me. "That man whose family was missing saved my life. I must help others now with my own *nam jai*."

For the next few hours, she helped tourists look for their loved ones and got children to high ground in case there was another wave. A Japanese woman who couldn't find her husband needed consoling. A Norwegian family of four was desperate for information on how to get off the island. A French woman wanted to know if she'd be able to get an official paper from the marine park authorities to reclaim her lost possessions from her insurance company. Pranee became an unofficial translator. Meanwhile, Moken fisherman and marine-park guides moved floating corpses to higher ground, where we all waited near the water tanks, wondering if we would ever get off the island. Thais and foreigners consoled each other. Then, as daylight faded, word came that the *Ocean Princess* would take us all on board. Her crew, in yellow life vests, passed out water bottles and food in Styrofoam containers to us on the hillside. Pranee exchanged hers with a Muslim woman who feared that the fried rice meal she got might contain pork or non-halal chicken.

As darkness fell, the evacuation by longtail boats to the *Ocean Princess* began. Many of the Thai survivors were scared to brave the sea again. Pranee convinced some of them that the safest place for the night was on the ship, since there was no more food, water, or shelter on the island.

On board, she directed the sick and injured to the doctor and nurse, and only when they had been attended to did she ask the nurse to clean up her leg wounds. She then persuaded the Thai captain to open up vacant rooms for the traumatized. She translated all Thai intercom announcements into English for the foreigners.

"Free buffet dinner is served in the main dining hall for all new arrivals."

"Bathroom and sleeping arrangements will be on the seventh floor."

"There will be a free cabaret show tonight for all on board."

In the dining hall, I caught a glimpse of myself in one of the wall mirrors. I was still in my swimming shorts, had no shirt, and wore two right-footed, odd colored flip-flops I had found on the beach. The waiter didn't blink an eyelid as he served me hot coffee and an assortment of desserts. At the cabaret, a sexy Thai singer sang only upbeat songs to cheer up the new passengers, most of whom were still dressed only in swimsuits. Wearing an equally skimpy outfit herself, she sashayed down the aisles, flirted purposefully, and sat on laps. Amazing Thailand!

The next morning, the Thai captain ordered the rescuers to pick up another hundred or more survivors who had spent the night in the jungle at Mae Ngam Beach, further west on Surin Island. Once on board, they were fed in the dining hall while the boats salvaged bags, clothes, and other belongings from the sea. The ship's reception lobby soon became a mountain of soggy backpacks and cases. Survivors sifted through them, hoping to claim their possessions. My backpack with all our money, mobile phones, and clothes was long gone. "*Mai pen rai*," Pranee said to me. "We have our lives."

The *Princess* headed for Phuket, ten hours south, where the nearest international airport was located. Only when we neared the island in the early hours of the morning did the television channels become audible and visible. Survivors now realized the extent of the devastation in Thailand. But the full magnitude of the disaster would only unfold in the days to come.

Phone signals became operable, and people scrambled up to the highest deck to call their families. Pranee looked for somebody who might lend her a cellphone. She finally got through to her sobbing mother in Bangkok, who was already making plans to travel south to identify her daughter's dead body. She then went to thank the captain of the *Princess* for the crew's generosity above and beyond the call of duty. He smiled and said the army had planes at Phuket waiting to evacuate all survivors to Bangkok.

At the pier, Pranee interpreted for the foreigners and led them to the bus, which took us all to the airport. Two big transport planes were rotating flights to Bangkok.

The airport looked like a scene from *M.A.S.H.* Stretchers with patients on IV drips lay in one corner. Coffee and snacks were being handed out. Volunteers helped lost survivors as they straggled in from the buses. Soldiers, who hadn't slept since the tsunami struck, told us stories of their rescue attempts at Patong Beach. A large pile of emergency clothes, rushed over by Phuket townsfolk, arrived for those who needed them. Pranee took a shirt and shorts to put over her two-piece blue swimsuit she had worn for over 36 hours now. I put on a pair of pants and a clean shirt over my swimming shorts.

Just before dawn, when the plane landed at the domestic terminal in Bangkok, Pranee and I led all the foreigners to their respective emergency embassy kiosks. Free phones to call abroad were available. We wished them well before they went to talk with their loved ones. I called Vancouver and alerted the family that I was safe. They had no idea that half of Asia was in turmoil.

The American kiosk was nowhere in sight. When I finally found two representatives at the international terminal a kilometer away, they were lodged in a comfortable room with their legs up on the table, complaining to each other about having to miss the Christmas celebrations at home in the city. Oblivious to my state of mind, they took one look at my appearance and told me that my lost passport would only be replaced during normal working hours at the embassy itself. Two-inch photos were required at my own expense.

Only when we were in Bangkok proper did Pranee let out a long sigh. Only then did she think of going to the nearest *wat* to make merit, to give thanks for our lives. I went with her.

೪

Hundreds of thousands of people were dead, as many more were missing, and millions were left homeless from Thailand to Tanzania, the land of my birth. The New Year celebrations, a week after the disaster, were subdued everywhere.

In Thailand, the whole country mobilized to help. Inter-faith vigils and last-rites ceremonies were held by Buddhist monks, Christian priests, Sikhs and Muslims. The king and queen of Sweden, grateful for the help given to hundreds of Swedish victims and survivors, paid a special visit to thank the people of Phuket and other hard-hit resorts. International celebrities visited the disaster zones and emptied their pockets. Children in Antwerp, Belgium baked cakes to raise money. A brothel in Berlin donated profits to the tsunami survivors. In Aceh, northern Sumatra, and in the Tamil areas of Sri Lanka, ceasefires were declared between separatists and government forces. For a while, the world came together.

Sure, there were those who used the tragedy to make a profit: corpse looters, store thieves, and profiteers. In southern Thailand, no attention was paid to the 1,000 dead and over 3,000 missing illegal Burmese workers, their families too scared to announce their lost ones for fear of deportation. There were tsunami T-shirts, videos, and other souvenirs.One vendor even came up with the idea of selling ice in tsunami wave shapes to increase sales.

Six months after being caught up in the tsunami, I went back to Phuket to see how the relief effort was coming along and to look for my old Indian friends, Ravin and Narin. Through another Sikh family, I tracked them down, alive and well, at Patong Beach. Their family business—originally just the one tailor shop on Thalang Road—had grown into three beach resorts, two more tailor shops, and one Subway sandwich franchise, most of them at Patong. Ravin's Subway shop that was scheduled to open the week after the tsunami struck, had suffered minimal damage, and luckily the food and drinks machines had been delayed in delivery. However, Narin, now with a wife and two daughters, was caught in the waves in his two-story house at Patong. The family was just waking up after a birthday party for their nine-year-old daughter the night before. The waves came flooding into the ground floor, trapping them upstairs. They were lucky to escape to the roof to avoid the rising water. The before-and-after pictures that Narin showed me of all his damaged properties sent shivers down my spine. He told me that now, every time he opens one of his water-logged accounts ledgers salvaged from the devastation, the smell of tsunami mud in the pages brings back the nightmare all over again. His daughter refuses to put a foot into the sea at Patong Beach, and she said that she doesn't want to celebrate her birthdays ever again.

ॐ

Despite the massive relief effort, thousands of survivors across Asia still suffered. According to a report published by the UN's 'tsunami watchdog committee' a year after the disaster, ninety percent of the most affected victims remained homeless. In most of the ten countries hit by the waves—particularly Thailand, India, and Sri Lanka—corporate land grabbers, with the connivance of government officials, got their hands on prime ocean-front property that was once owned by fishermen, farmers, and vendors. These mostly poor and powerless people simply had their ancestral land stolen from them, as big business and governments conspired to manipulate local property laws.

Vast sums of money were donated to aid charities and the UN itself, but most of it remained unspent and unaccounted for. Rather than getting money and aid to those who most needed it, these 'lords of poverty' busied themselves with on-site evaluations—costing thousands of dollars in consultants' fees—not on actual relief projects, but on figuring out why most of the money never got spent and where it disappeared to.

After reading the report, my cynicism, subdued during the few months when the world did unite, was back again, stronger than ever before.

7. On The Road

When women go wrong,
men go right after them.
Mae West.

In Uganda, if an African girl liked you, she had to have you and made no bones about it. If she didn't, God have mercy on you if you were stupid enough to persist hanging around her. Simple as that. The Indian girls played games with their men till they drove them half crazy or turned them into mush. On the other hand, white girls from colonial or expat families were forbidden territory. We could look, fantasize, and jerk off at night, but never touch.

As a teenager with raging hormones, I went the African way, with dancers of the night at Susannah Bar in Kampala. *Waragi*—sugar cane juice fermented into forty percent alcohol—was the appetizer. *Dumbulo* dancing (butt to butt) was the main course. Panting and squeals of pleasure, usually in the back of my car, was dessert. At home, there was always plenty of love and affection to go around. As a child, I remember often laying on my mother's lap in a room full of guests convinced that the stomach rumblings in her belly was radio static. Any achievement or good deed earned hugs and kisses from brothers and sisters in our house. So passing on all that affection in my adult life came naturally to me.

It wasn't till I was eighteen that I met a Muslim woman in Kampala who tickled both my body and my brain. Born in the Congo but educated in Brussels, Zainab was a veteran chameleon, donning skimpy miniskirts at Friday mosque and culottes to Saturday night dances. She didn't give a damn who thought what of her, and she became my mentor in bed for tantric yoga positions I'd never discovered. We fucked in broad daylight on Persian carpets at an English teacher's house in Buziga, hidden from the religious puritans and their morality sermons. She read to me from Émile Zola's *Nana* by candlelight. Once, on a national park safari trip, we writhed together behind a flame tree to a setting African sunset. The Asian exodus split us apart. Seeing each other during vacations would be neither enough nor practical for both of us. So we both moved on.

As I grew older, on-the-road relationships became the norm and always brought out the best in me. Knowing that both my travel partner and I had the freedom to wake up on any given day and announce that one or the other was going to a different town, or even a different country, made the time we had together that much more immediate and intensely honest. Since my partner and I knew that we may never see each other again, no emotional layer was too sensitive to unpeel, no confession too personal to expose, no language too difficult to overcome, no cultural trait too bizarre to put up with. We lived in the moment. Whether it was a day, a week, or months, I loved the impermanance of these fleeting relationships.

At the Pink Floyd show in London, I met exchange student Ursula from Basel, Switzerland. Our relationship became one long, continuous, sensuous dance. During vacation, we hitchhiked the back roads of England and ended up at Stonehenge on a September afternoon. Imagining ourselves to be Druids, we danced among the 5,000-year-old monoliths, in and out of the inner circle of the sarsen stones, till the evening twilight brought on an autumn chill. That night, on sleeping bags laid out in this ancient power spot, we made passionate love to each other. The half moon peeping through the lintels shone on our naked bodies, creating a halo around Ursula's wavy red hair as her head rested on my heaving belly. Our dance came to an abrupt end by Christmas, when her year in England was over. She was back home skiing in the resort of Zermatt by New Year's Day. My letters across the continent over the next few months never got any replies.

At Albion College in Michigan, I met Jewish princess Lynne from Scarsdale, New York. She was sure that the only way to secure peace in the Middle East was to fuck every good-looking Arab she could find. Although I wasn't Palestinian or Arab, I was close enough to fit the profile. She liked my tongue meandering around her ear lobes just when she came. I liked our morning hot-water shower fucks with scented soaps before we trudged off to class in the winter snow. At Hanukkah she never asked me home to meet the family in New York, and I never reciprocated with invites to Idd-el-Fitr in Vancouver with my folks. We understood each other's limitations perfectly, but still there was no everlasting peace in sight in the Middle East.

In the cobblestone streets of San Miguel de Allende, Patricia from Guadalajara beat me to the last bag of *empanadas* at my favorite Sunday market stall. To make up for my loss, she agreed to cook up *sopa Azteca* for me that evening. The next day, I made her a beef curry using tortillas as rotis. She taught me how to drink Jose Cuervo with limes and salt. I taught her how to rid herself of Catholic guilt after sex by playing naked bull-fight games in her hacienda courtyard at night—two brown bodies horning each other in the Guanajuato desert starlight.

Patricia thought I was mad to go on the peyote hunt with the Huichol Indians in the cacti desert outside Tepic. Yet, on a full moon night, I talked her into climbing to the top of the Pyramid of the Moon at the Mayan ruins in Teotihuacán. When I asked her to sleep up there among the stars with peyote in our brains, that's when she drew the line. Wasn't surprising then that when I asked her to join me for the journey from San Miguel to Machupicchu, Peru, she confessed that she wasn't as wild and crazy as me and preferred to go back to her simpler family life in Guadalajara.

Over time, I realized that the only women who would stick with me for long periods of time had to be those who saw the open road as a home in itself and not just a way to get home. Like me, they would have to love living in that zone where love and sex in Nature were all part of the same energy. Was I doomed to burn out my chameleon fires all alone, or would the lizard gods find me a partner who would rekindle the embers every time they needed stoking on the road to nowhere? I needed to find another Uta—one who didn't have to go home at the end of the summer holidays and one who felt at home in every culture she came upon as it if it were her own.

ॐ

"Use the gel to grease his hair back," said Eva as she rolled up a pack of Marlboro cigarettes in my T-shirt sleeve.

"This green frat jacket will be perfect over his skin-tight T-shirt." Dila chuckled.

"His shoes have to go," piped in Beckie, sipping more wine. "Where can we get some old sneakers? You know, the kind they wore in *West Side Story*."

Eva, a buxom red-haired girl from a small town in western Ohio, had become my American culture chaperon over the first few months at Albion College. The Midwestern girls were having a ball dressing me up for the fall semester "homecoming 50s party" that Saturday evening in 1974. Transforming a long-haired, mustachioed, hairy-chested, brown-skinned African-Asian into James Dean was no easy task. But these gorgeous gals, dolled up with their pigtails and bobby socks, were not to be deterred. The gallon of white Gallo wine was more than half gone, Sha Na Na was blaring out "At The Hop" on the stereo. As they added the finishing touches—a dab of rouge on their cheeks, more padding inside the bra, more gel in my hair—they were all psyched up for the shindig at the Sigma Ki frat house. And I, the African hippie, totally ignorant of the 1950s era, was the perfect guinea pig for their fantasies.

The party was in full swing by the time the girls and I got there. Kegs of beer flowed freely. Boys in tight T-shirts and skin-hugging blue jeans eyed up girls in high heels and poodle skirts as they jived across the dance floor to the wild piano of Jerry Lee Lewis. I noticed that none of the hippies had gone so far as to chop off their locks into quiffs or crew cuts. Instead, like me, they tied it in a ponytail tucked underneath their T-shirts or jackets.

In some of the nooks and crannies, couples were making out, feeling each other up to see whether they would end up in bed together or not. Upstairs, in one of the bedrooms, there was the ganja crowd trading joints and watching Captain Kirk save the universe from the Klingons in "Star Trek." I took a few puffs and decided to skip the impending disaster on the starship *Enterprise* for some funky dance moves downstairs instead.

Eva grabbed me and we slid onto the dance floor. She taught me how to jive properly as Bill Haley's Comets made us rock around the clock. When Buddy Holly came on the stereo, she became my Peggy Sue and nuzzled her head into my neck. The rouge on her cheeks, smudged by now, was all over my penciled-in cleft chin, but she didn't care. I held her tight and yet my mind was elsewhere, as if I was looking at the scene in front of me from the ceiling above. I was seeing the decade of feel-good America being re-enacted live, and

I'd been asked to join in as if I was one of them. Their nostalgia was infectious, and even though I wasn't part of that history, the ganja and beer sucked me in. The scene made me drift into my own world to reflect on what the 50s were like for me. . . .

Back then, us Indian kids and the African boys who lived in the wooden shacks on the dirt road across from Madras Gardens played together most days after school. Luwanga, who was killed during the Amin coup, was one of them. Our simple games needed no fancy equipment or uniforms or safety gear—just sticks and stones. One favorite game was called *gili danda*, an Indian version of baseball played with two wooden sticks, one long and one short. The longer one was used as the bat and the shorter one as the ball. The batsman would place the short stick in a v-shaped groove dug out of the dirt. Using the 'bat' to flip it spinning into the air, he would then try to hit it again, in mid-air, as far as he could from this one and only home base. Three missed strikes on the short stick, or a catch by any of the fielders, and the batsman was out. When all the batsmen were out, the teams changed sides. The team with the most points, measured with the long stick from the point where the short stick landed to home base, won the game.

Other times, we were busy zapping cicadas with catapults after the rains, or catching grasshoppers at streetlights during their migration season. We always played barefoot—*gili danda*, soccer, cricket, or marbles—and when jiggers, parasitic black insects, burrowed into the soles of our feet, there was always a gang member ready to take out the wiggly invader using a safety pin to carve around the skin. The African boys were far better at this skill than us Indians. Luwanga always got rid of them for me.

When we tired of playing or stealing fruit, we sat down by the favorite *pafu* tree to pig out on a picnic. We Indians brought cassava chips and *chevro*, a spicy snack made of peanuts and puffed-up sesame seeds. The African boys were in charge of bringing roasted cassava and fruit in season: mangoes, custard apples, or cashew fruits from the trees in their yards. The winning team would get the lion's share of the picnic goodies hung up on one of the tree branches.

This was how I remembered passing my 50s decade.

I stirred from my reverie to find Eva kissing my neck as we drifted to a slow song. Could America and I ever understand each other? Even with Eva, the gap seemed as deep as Lake Michigan. Yet she couldn't care less. Americana was all she knew, and as long as I was willing to go along with that, her acceptance of me was both forthcoming and genuine. So, we went on scavenger hunts at Easter and somersaulted down sand dunes into Lake Michigan in summer. At Halloween, dressed up as blood-dripping witches and wizards, we petrified little children who were 'trick or treating' from door to door. For the winter, in woolen long johns and duck-down parkas, we skied cross-country on frozen lakes and camped around fires, roasting marshmallows on wooden sticks.

But, not once during that whole year did Eva ask me about my African past or Indian heritage. As if neither had ever existed. When I did attempt to reveal some of my past, Eva's reaction was usually apathetic, and this finally prompted me to end the relationship.

If I wanted to get my past acknowledged, I had to go to the black neighborhoods of Albion itself, on the other side of the railroad tracks, where forty percent of the town's population lived. There, the residents took me in as their token African, to jam with the Lord at Sunday church, to wolf down juicy spare ribs at weekend lakeside barbecues, or jiggle my butt at music bars in Motown. During those times, Karen, with short curly hair and jet-black eyes, became my Afro-American chaperon.

Karen and I loved going to the theater. In the college production of Lorraine Hansberry's play, *A Raisin In The Sun*, she played the rebellious black daughter who fell in love with my Asagai, the visiting African student who stays with her American family. When the three shows were over, she and I pretended that the curtain never went down. In bed, we would spontaneously break into roles. She became Diana Ross as Billie Holiday in *Lady Sings The Blues*, while I recited the title character's soliloquy of hell in *Sizwe Banze Is Dead*—a nightmare depiction of apartheid Soweto by South African playwright Athol Fugard. Roles from my Indian heritage, and impressions of Bollywood actor Shashi Kapoor were not to her liking.

The following year, Karen eventually made it to the bright lights of New York and fulfilled her ambition of an off-Broadway role. We went our separate ways. Our farewell scene was one that we had never rehearsed in our fantasies.

Albion, where I stayed for over a year, was my introduction to understanding America. The genuine feeling of welcome from the Midwesterners to this stranger in their midst has never left me. Throughout my time here, I was in and out of both the black and white worlds of the city. I could fit in either of them at my choosing. But never both together. My few attempts to act as cultural go-between always ended up in disaster, so I stopped trying.

The first time I met Kiku was at one of our jam sessions at Balboa Beach in 1975. A Japanese-American with cascading hair that came down to her small, rounded hips, she exuded sensuality in the way she smoked her cigarette, the way she poured a drink, the way she flicked her cloak of black hair from her pale, smiling face. Days later, she and I talked for hours on the phone on issues of culture and intellect. She felt as if she was caught in two worlds—trapped between the confining Asian traditions of her parents, and the individualistic libertarian values of a female growing up in 1970s America. Kiku often dreamed about taking a trip to Japan, to find a way to balance these conflicting views of the world. This is why we communicated so well. She was one of very few people who understood that I lived not in two, but in several worlds, and had been searching for that balance all my life. Our talks about visits to the motherland—Japan for her, and India and Uganda for me—often went on long into the night. Our physical desire for each other was never consummated then, since we both had different partners at the time. Instead, over time, our platonic relationship became as solid as Mount Fuji, one of words and letters from across the oceans that lasted over the next seven years. Kiku became my confessional priestess to whom I could write my innermost thoughts—from the mountains of South America, the beaches of Phuket, the refugee camp in Galang, and the Himalayan villages of Nepal. In return, she bared her soul to me, writing of her southern Californian inertia, and passing on news of our Balboa Beach gang: Wild Man Baser, Green Beast Bob, music maestro Talmadge. Kiku and I made love to each other with our words, put our passions into poems, helping each other through good and bad days—all through the power of a ball-point pen on aerogramme letters flying across the globe.

Years later, when both of us changed addresses and our lives took us down different paths, we lost contact for a while. But in 1992, when I was passing through Los Angeles, we found each other through Green Beast Bob and did finally spend a night together, consummating all the words written over the years. One night of passion with scented candles and the smell of herbal tea. Satiating as that night was, it never replaced the intensity of our words across the oceans.

In 2004, out of the blue, Kiku tracked me down on the Internet and we reconnected again. Thrilled that she had preserved all my aerogrammes from the 70s, torn and tattered by now, I asked her to scan them for me so that I could rejoice in what once was. Re-reading the letters, I realized that, even back then, I was always the wandering gypsy and Kiku the patient recipient of my chameleon ramblings. Nowadays, in our e-mails, we fantasize about how to create 'chameleon children' for the world of tomorrow so that they too, may enjoy the thrill of being enveloped by many cultures.

ꙮ

Wading barefoot through the tidal pools of Laguna Beach was something that athletic Katie and I loved to do early on Sunday mornings. Searching for crabs and oysters at low tide, we would sometimes spot the occasional pair of seals splashing around in the ocean. Born in a rural town in east Texas, Katie hadn't seen the ocean till she came to California for college, and then she couldn't get enough of it. Coming from landlocked Uganda, I too was enthralled by the thrashing waves off the southern California coast, where it hardly ever rains.

After a few hours of beachcombing, we would feast on avocado-and-cottage-cheese omelets, washed down with chamomile tea, at The Place Across The Street From Hotel Laguna—across the street from the landmark Hotel Laguna. Brunch was often followed by an afternoon hike along Route 101, hugging the California coast. At cozy deserted coves we would make love in the sand to the sound of waves bouncing off the rocks.

Unlike Eva, Katie said she wanted to know all about my Indian world, just as much as I wanted to know about her Texas background. So we made travel plans for the upcoming summer vacations. First, we would hitchhike up to Montreal for the 1976 Olympics. Then we would spend a couple of weeks at her family's home before attending an Ismaili wedding in Vancouver.

Travel through America and Canada, party at the Olympics, meet each other's families, and live out lots of fantasies—all in one summer.

Katie and I made quite an odd couple on the road: 'Texas Jane' with shoulder-length blonde hair, pink tank top, and blue shorts exposing slender tanned thighs, and me, Ugandan Tarzan, with a red bandana over my head, black beard, yellow Indian shirt, cut-off jeans, and brown hairy legs.

Getting rides through California was easy. Roadside sleep was intermittent at a truck stop in Nevada. The forty-minute wait for a ride in Idaho was the longest by far. Camping by a river in Glacier National Park in Montana, we woke to the sound of a moose lapping up water as if it were his morning tea. We crossed the border into Canada and noticed the differences immediately. For me, the soft-spoken Canadians, with their touch of British reserve, were a welcome change from their louder American neighbors. It was almost as if the Canadians had taken the best of both cultures and created their own.

The youth hostel in Banff was full of muscled cyclists getting ready for a magical ride up to Jasper through the Rockies. Katie thought we should take a detour along this scenic route, but I resisted since there were just three more days to go before the opening ceremony in Montreal. So we headed east through the prairie provinces. Katie's feline thighs and our handwritten sign that said "Olympics or Bust" easily got us a ride as far as Regina, Saskatchewan. Then the traffic dried up. Seventeen cars passed by the first day, and then only five the next. Now we were desperate. The opening ceremony was the following day. Then, along came an old pick-up truck with cakes of dust on the side and back windows. Alaskan Bryce was summer camping across Canada and was in no hurry to get to Montreal, but he agreed to take us there as long as we bought a case of beer at the next liquor store and shared gas money and didn't hurry him along the way. We jumped in before he could change his mind.

The next few days whizzed by. We went trout fishing at the Ontario lakes, where Bryce made the moves on Katie. Worse still, Katie didn't resist his advances. I was upset. To make up, she fucked me on a lakeside rock the next afternoon while Bryce was swimming in the lake. I couldn't wait to get to Montreal. We arrived on the fourth day of the Games, and Azad—a cousin of my old friend Nizar—gave us his living-room floor to sleep on. Katie found him attractive, too. Or so I thought.

The Games were a welcome distraction, and I was ready for all the action I could get. Scalpers offered last-minute tickets for most of the events at twice the face value, but what few people realized was that half an hour after the event had begun, the same scalpers would practically be giving the tickets away. That's where I came in.

Two million visitors poured into the city for the Olympics, but I was disappointed to discover that 23 African nations had boycotted the Games in protest at the Olympic Committee's decision to allow New Zealand to compete. The Africans were furious about the New Zealand All Blacks rugby tour to apartheid South Africa, where they played test matches against the all-white Springboks. At the last Games in Munich, Israeli athletes had been kidnapped and killed by Arab terrorists. Once again, politics had marred the one event that was supposed to unite the world every four years.

I was crushed that the long-distance runners from Kenya, the boxers from Uganda, and the marathon maestros from Ethiopia wouldn't be there. Neither would we see Ugandan hero, John Akii-Bua, the world record holder in the 400 meters hurdles. But new heroes emerged every day at the Games. Cuban Alberto Juantorena became the first man ever to win both the 400 and 800 meters. Little Nadia Comaneci from Romania made gymnastics history by getting not one but seven perfect 'ten' scores.

I never knew which country to root for at the Games. Should it be Tanzania, my birthplace, or Uganda? This time, I didn't have to worry about either, since they weren't there anyway. That left India, land of my ancestors. Or America, whose passport I held. Or even Canada, where most of my family lived. Heck, why not a Muslim country? No, I decided. Best just to go for either the underdog who tried his hardest, or for the best athlete of a particular sport. I convinced myself that this wasn't a patriotic gathering, but a celebration of humanity.

At night, the city never slept. Thousands of people partied in the streets, some celebrating victories, others commiserating a loss, others, like me, just soaking up the atmosphere. Amid the teeming throng, I was thrilled not at the victory or the loss of any athlete or nation, but at the unique privilege of being one of the many rejoicing at this planetary 'pow wow.'

Most days, Katie was too hung over to bother with any of the events, so we saw more of each other at night than at the Games. One evening, I fell asleep through exhaustion at a Moroccan restaurant. We went back to Azad's place and she disappeared for the night. Things were never the same between us after that. I went to the closing ceremony by myself while she went partying with yet another new friend in Old Montreal. A few days later, I left for New York to see relatives and she went south to Texas. We both did indeed live out our fantasies that summer, it just happened that the open road made sure they weren't the same for both of us.

oঙ

The Peruvian Andes are pure magic! In 1977, I hitchhiked through them, getting rides on top of trucks carrying cases of Inca Cola to villages along switchback dirt roads that criss-crossed the mountains. This was adventure travel before that term became a buzzword; vertical cliffs on one side and 3,000-foot drops on the other. Mountain folk, barefoot and clad in colorful ponchos and pointed woolen hats with earflaps, were my only companions on these long, windy, dangerous rides. On the back of many trucks was a colorful sign that said "*Pasa Condor Pasa*" which, I found out later, was a reference to the mythical "El Condor"—the fastest and most courageous of all Peruvian truck drivers. When he was driving behind you, it was best to let him overtake if you valued your life. When the trucks came up to wooden log bridges on switchback corners, the passengers would get down, walk over the bridge, and then get back on the truck on the other side. I followed suit and asked why afterwards. Just in case the driver—who recited a few Hail Mary's in Quichua and made the sign of the cross—didn't make it across. A few roadside tombstones I had spotted were proof enough of the latter. One local explained to me that during the rainy season, when the logs became very slippery, it was all in God's hands whether the driver lived or died.

At any mountain village that appealed to me, I would stop and stay with a family for a few days. Often I would seek out trails from one village to another, all the time aching for Uta with her broken *huaraches*. Then, the soothing sound of Andean flutes, played by herders to their huge bulls grazing nearby, would echo off the hills and put me into a serene state of mind. In mountain streams, I would bathe naked in the ice-cold water and let Inti, the Incan sun god, dry my body while I perched on a big rock in the river, meditating to the sounds of flutes and cowbells and the mountain symphony. Mighty Nature, my one and only god since Kilimanjaro, was all I needed to be at peace with myself. More and more, using the techniques taught to me by Bapuji, I started meditating regularly. I understood better now the peace that he experienced in his early morning meditations at mosque in Kampala.

So, by the time I ran into blonde Norwegian, Hilde, who was sitting silently by a river on the outskirts of the town of Huancayo, I was already well immersed in the spiritual magic of the Andes. Turned out that Hilde too, enjoyed the serenity of river baths and meditations in the mountains. Since both of us were headed south to Cusco and Machupicchu, we teamed up to travel together. Hilde's smile immediately put me at ease, and we soon learned to enjoy each other's silence, neither of us compelled to fill it up with words, sometimes for hours on end.

At Cusco, once the capital of the Incan Empire, we explored the fortress of Sacsayhuaman, and marveled at how a civilization from more than five centuries ago could have built walls from 300-ton blocks of limestone to such architectural perfection—without mortar to hold them together. For the trip to Machupicchu, the ancient Incan city perched at 2,350 meters, we opted for the four-day trek instead of taking the four-hour train ride.

"Let's do it on our own. We can stop when we like, where we like," said Hilde.

I nodded.

Back then, the trail had no entrance fee, no guides, no signs—just a few backpackers hiking up the narrow path as it weaved through the rainforest, around giant ferns moist from morning dew and mist rising from the ground. The 45-kilometer hike, though gentle in gradient in most parts, went up to 4,000 meters on the second day. Along the way, orchids and hummingbirds kept us company. At night, around small campfires with rocks for seats, backpackers huddled together to play music as the occasional falling star or meteor shot across a star-studded sky. Recalling my days in Yucatan with Maya, and the dancers of Balboa Beach, I taught the lizard dance to Hilde and my newfound campfire chameleons. *Shantih* and *ayinga* were sitting next to me all over again.

On the third day, a couple from Israel gave us some magic mushrooms, which we crushed up and mixed into our tea for breakfast. The morning took on a slower pace as the cloud-forest mist threw colors and shades through the giant ferns. The hummingbirds turned into kaleidoscopes. At a mountain stream that afternoon, after our picnic lunch of tortillas, cheese, *empanadas*, and sugar cane juice, we took a siesta, and watched the clouds turn into celestial zeppelins. Sometime during the break, I must have got up to take a swim, then sat on a rock in the stream to dry off. I remember focusing on a particular spot in the river, trying to concentrate on a single drop of water, trying to watch it move in the current and make it stay absolutely still at the same time, like Siddhartha had done in Herman Hesse's novel. The sun continued to warm my bare back, and my mind wandered away from the river. I felt like I was projected many miles away, into a different place and time, on a journey to a place on the other side of the planet. . . .

The village of seventy or so huts, just past an old Hindu temple on the dirt road, was unusually noisy for an afternoon. Outside my own hut, somewhere in India, I was sitting on a V-shaped wooden contraption with a flat platform for a seat at one end and an iron blade with jagged teeth at the other. Rocking an opened coconut back and forth around the blade, I was collecting the shavings in a tin bowl beneath. From one of the adobe huts, I could hear an Indian woman singing a lament in Hindi about a poor shoe salesman—a song that my sister Leila sometimes sang to me as a child to put me to sleep. Further away, another woman was washing clothes next to a communal water tap that was still running. I could hear the thwack thwack of her wooden stick beating the sari she was laundering. Then, some time later, I heard someone calling my name from a hut, way in the back of the village. "Sachu! Sachu! Anya ahwoh ne Sachu!" 'Sachu, please come here,' the voice kept saying in Gujarati. Nobody but my mother ever called me by that nickname. I stopped what I was doing, washed my hands, and made my way to where the call was coming from. I seemed to be very familiar with the village, knowing what lane to turn at on each corner. On the way, I ran into two teenage girls, one in a red sari and the other in a beige one. Both greeted me with "namastes" and called me by my real name, as if they had known me for years. When I got to the woman calling out "Sachu," it wasn't my mother, after all. The woman, who broke into a wide smile when she saw me, took out three rupees from a fold in her white sari and asked me to go to the knife sharpener and pay him this money we owed him from three weeks ago. I knew exactly what debt she was talking about and where Bhaloo, the knife sharpener, lived. I knew this woman, knew every contour on her face, but couldn't remember her name. On the way to Bhaloo's hut, on the other side of the village, I passed by a small stream and stopped there for a minute. . . .

That's when Hilde roused me from my trance. It must have been two hours that I had been spaced out on that rock, and she thought it best that we move along the trail to the next camp-site before darkness was upon us. I rubbed my eyes and told her about my journey, somewhere in India, where it seemed as if I knew all the residents and all the lanes of the village.

She nodded in approval and asked, "Were you born there?"

It was still 1977 and I had never yet set foot on Indian soil. It would be almost another decade before I would land in Bombay for the first time to look for Aunt Sakina in Andheri, whom I had never met before. India was calling me, I realized, as we resumed our climb. I had all sorts of unanswered questions about my 'dream.'

On the final day of the trek we were heading downhill, as Machupicchu is concealed at almost half the elevation of the highest pass on the trail. Although perched on a mountain of its own, it is surrounded by valleys below, and higher mountains above. We started off at four in the morning, and it was pitch black except for a circle of light from the torch bobbing up and down the path. Then, at about six in the morning, as the sun came up over the hills, we got our first distant glimpse of the majestic city on the mountaintop. Sunrise over Machupicchu was just as spectacular as at Kilimanjaro. Instead of the glistening white snow, we saw deep valleys and cultivated terraces carved into the lustrous, steep green mountains on all sides. The intricate walls of the ruined city rose from clouds of mist, as if reaching out to the sun god Inti in celestial homage.

Thrilled to be in the city itself, Hilde and I marveled at the glorious views from the Sun Temple; from the observation point where, down below, the gushing Urubamba River carved its way through a massive gorge; and from Intihuatana, the stone column that 'tied the sun down' during the winter months to keep the residents warm. At this last spot, we thanked Inti for the precious warmth he gave us that day at this high altitude.

The day went by quickly as we explored every nook and cranny of this magical place. After the train tourists from Cusco had come and gone, we befriended Manuel, a Quichua Indian, who was the lone night guard of the city. Half an hour later and minus a few hundred pesos, I had convinced him into letting me and Hilde sleep the night in a stone bath in one of the ancient dwellings. With no roof above except a galaxy of stars, and only sleeping bags to cover us, we lay awake as the ancient spirits of the Inca roamed the city at night. Sleep, when it eventually came, was intermittent. Once, during a waking moment, I thought I saw a formation of blinking lights in the sky around a circular disc that looked more like a UFO than a cluster of stars.

The dawn mountain mist brought a chill that sent shivers through our bodies. Hilde and I held each other tighter in the sleeping bags. Then, the first sunrays of Inti, accompanied by the sweet sound of Manuel's Andean pipe, brought a welcome heat that permeated our bodies.

Manuel woke us quickly, worried that we might get caught in the bath by the day's first visitors. We got up quickly, sorted our packs, and then the three of us shared coffee, tortillas, and *empanadas* for breakfast. The first backpackers arrived soon after. Later that morning, we said our farewell to the magical city with a final meditation.

"*Vaya con Dios!*" 'Go with God,' Manuel said before we left to get the train heading back to Cusco.

We arrived just in time for the Inti Raymi Sun Festival in the ancient capital, and the re-enacted rituals of sun worship and sacrifice. We danced in celebration of the sun for two more days until the hordes of tourists got to us, prompting us to leave the city.

Hilde and I traveled south by train to Puno, and then hopped on a late afternoon boat to traverse the immense, 12,500-foot-high Lake Titicaca. We got off at Taquile Island, just before the Bolivian border, as the last of the Uru fishermen in their reed boats were bringing in the day's catch. This scene, against the backdrop of a brilliant pink and orange sunset hovering over snow-capped peaks, was a perfect welcome. We stayed with the kind Uru people for a week and meditated among the Incan ruins facing the lake each day before breakfast and dinner. One night, the father of the family we stayed with took us night fishing on a reed boat, on this sacred lake from where the legendary founders of the Inca were sent down to earth by Inti.

We moved on to Copacabana in Bolivia, from where we made our way by bus to the Valley of the Moon (after overnighting in La Paz). This amazing badlands of hills and rocks eroded into fantastic shapes and gulleys is not actually a valley at all. Like Joshua Tree National Park in California, here was another fabulous place where a Quichua god had carved colossal sculptures from the rugged rock. Amid this lunar landscape, Hilde and I said our goodbyes, for she—just like Uta—had to return home now that summer was almost over. That serene, soothing, peaceful smile of hers still lingers in my mind.

☙

Right after the ill-fated trip to Pakistan in 1984, where I almost got scalped at Gilgit Airport, Corazon and I decided to go trekking in Nepal instead. October is the start of the climbing season in Nepal, when the mighty Himalayas open up their foggy skies for a three-month window. Coming from Gilgit, we both carried winter gear and had already acclimatized to high altitude. So why not go for the dream trek of them all—along the snow-capped ridges of the roof of the world? Having quit our jobs in Galang, both of us had time on our hands. So we hopped on a flight to Kathmandu.

In Kathmandu, we checked into a guesthouse near Durbar Square. First task: get rid of our Pakistan attire. No more *chador* and long-sleeved shirt and pants for Corazon, and no more interview clothes for me. We switched to climbing shorts, parkas, and hiking boots. I had marveled at Corazon's *bahallanah* 'go-with-the-flow' attitude throughout our Pakistan travels. Not once did she complain about the subservient role that women played in rural Gilgit, indeed throughout the country. That she had shown subservience herself, when circumstance thrust it upon her, impressed me even more—because I knew how self reliant and independent she was deep down.

Outside, the square was bustling with activity. Street vendors, backpackers, hippies, shrine worshippers, mountain climbers, Sherpa porters, rickshaw drivers, and crowd gazers all jostled in confined alleyways and shops amidst a cacophony of noise and bartering. We rented two old rickety bicycles—the kind that still had bell rings—to take in the sights around the Thamel district, still full of hash-smoking hippies and old bakeries. On the way to the Monkey Temple, we got our first clear glimpses of the breathtaking Himalayas. From chatting with vendors, I soon realized that numbers in Nepali are the same as Hindi. Indeed, there were many similarities between both cultures: the religion, the reverence for the mountains, the social intercourse and bargaining before any purchase, and, of course, *masala chai*—tea drinking as a gesture of hospitality and respect. Nepal felt like home in many ways.

After checking a few moutain-trek companies for guides, we settled on thirty-year-old Anand, who spoke both Hindi and Nepali, as our man for the climb to the Annapurna Sanctuary. With his help, we secured permits, two porters, climbing and sleeping gear, and all the food needed for the two-week trip. I spotted Mars Bars in a shop and, recalling my cravings for them at Kilimanjaro, I bought two dozen to make sure I wouldn't run out on the trek.

The 1959 jeep that took us from Kathmandu to Pokhara, on the only road west out of the city, was the kind that the driver had to start by winding up a crank handle just above the front bumper. It finally sputtered to life after a few false starts. Ten people found space for themselves, half of them clinging to parts of the vehicle outside as we rattled off at snail-slow speed. Corazon snatched a window seat, with me hanging by her on the outside. On both sides of the road, glorious peaks stared back at us from a crystal blue sky and, a few hours later, we got our first glimpse of Machupichare, Fish Tail Mountain with its double peaks, which would stay in sight for the next few days. To the north, Dhaulagiri and Annapurna II peeked their heads out of the Sanctuary. At Bagar Bazaar, outside Pokhara— where the centuries-old trading trail along the Kali Gandaki River starts—Corazon and I put on our packs and blessed each other for the trek with a bear hug. She said, "*Sigue nalang*"—'Lets go for it' in Tagalog—and I clasped my hands together to *wai* to the mountains that I came to visit them in peace. Two porters carried woven bamboo baskets on their backs, with ropes around their foreheads as support. They zipped ahead barefoot on the trail, as they would set up camp at the end of each day. Anand walked behind us to ensure no mishaps went unnoticed in this rough terrain.

The next ten days became a spectacular collage of images that jogged all five senses: the bottle-green Kali Gandaki River roaring in my ears; balancing Corazon's pack before crossing a log bridge over a gushing mountain stream; smiling Hindu women with broken teeth drying rice on mats outside huts in the village of Hyangja; hot tea and biscuits at *bhatti* teahouses; dusty yak traffic jams at a switchback corner on the trail; Anand singing Hindi songs, with me doing the back-up chorus; Corazon taking pictures of me shitting among the bushes; *dahl bhatt* (rice and lentil) campfire dinners under Milky Way skies; "*Sahib, chai pio . . .*" the wake-up call from one of the porters; *masala chai* in our cozy tent; fresh meat from the Sunday auction at Chandrokot village; Machupichare's double Fish Tail peaks much clearer as we turned another switchback corner; hot bucket showers at the Gurkha Captain's Lodge in Chomrong (heavenly for two dollars' worth of firewood to heat the water); Anand purchasing a live chicken for a meat delight one evening, with spicy tomato pickle to liven up the dinner; the vegetation constantly changing as we got higher, from rice fields to green hills to Spanish-moss rainforest to bamboo forest to blinding snow; hiking with woolen gloves and wind pants in the heart of the Sanctuary; the colossal amphitheater, with gleaming snow and burning rock all around; the nine Annapurna summits encircling the bowl, each over 20,000 feet; hashish day hikes along panoramic ridges within the Sanctuary, followed by rainbow sunsets, followed by starlit night shows; the *click-click* of more 360-degree photos; snow drifting off Annapurna IV, causing a minor avalanche; an early morning climb to Annapurna I; slow, heavy breathing . . . more zinc oxide on roasting skin . . . baby steps to the top . . . relief and rest . . . a quick meditation on the summit . . . more grateful *wais* for the privilege of seeing the nine sisters in all their majestic glory; down, down, down, back to base camp for food and energy; Mars Bar celebrations with tanned Corazon and smirking Anand; the long hike back to the Captain's Lodge for another hot shower, a warm meal, and a soft bed; the dawn hike up to Ghorapani and on to Poon Hill for a sweeping view of the central Himalayan peaks at sunrise; a lone Buddhist monk in a maroon robe turning a prayer wheel; on to Tatopani Hot Springs to soothe aching muscles in the bubbling streams; down, down, down . . . agony on the knees . . . passing a stone cairn in memory of those the mountains have devoured; spotting a mountain man with a bundle of wood on his back speeding down a ridge, yelling wildly at the sky, his cries reverberating all around us; the same man smoking a hookah pipe at Hyangja village, saying he'd been yelling with joy because he was home from wood collecting; back to Pokhara and thanks, bear hugs, and gifts to the porters and Anand; yak steaks and cold beer and a second helping of frosted chocolate cake; and then sweet, sound sleep in Corazon's chocolate-brown arms. *Ayinga. Shantih.*

Kathmandu's cacophony was much harder to tolerate after the serene silence of the mountains. Both of us were ready for some sun and surf on a deserted beach. We celebrated our last breakfast in Nepal with more Mars Bars and the dregs of a Grand Marnier bottle, before boarding a flight to the Philippines, where we would visit the white-sand beaches of Moalboal that Corazon had raved about ever since I met her. We had spent the last few months together in Muslim

Indonesia and Pakistan, and Hindu and Buddhist Nepal, so it seemed only reasonable to her that we now explore the Catholic Philippines and scuba dive in Cebu, the Visayan island where she spent most of her youth. I was keen to know the Filipino culture, meet her family and discover her origins, to see if I would fit into her world or not.

On the plane, I thought about the whirlwind intimacy that had enveloped us over the last few months. Unlike many of my other relationships on the road, I was more at ease with Corazon because she seemed so at ease in all the cultures that we had experienced so far. Was this going to be yet another travel fling or would it turn into something more serious and permanent? I wished for the latter, but was apprehensive about bringing it up for fear of rejection. I didn't want to ruin the perfect travel bond that had developed between us. It would be best to discuss this after I had seen her world and she got more of a taste of my chameleon nature.

❧

The first sight that jarred me at Manila Airport was a kiosk called "Coney Island Ice-Cream Corner." It would be the first of many leftovers of Americana that I would see in this country colonized by the United States after the Spanish-American War of 1898. The jeeps left by the Americans after the Second World War had been turned into colorful "jeepneys," now used to transport commuters all over the congested city. Christmas carols at city malls and straw models of the three wise men of Bethlehem somehow seemed out of place in Asia. Fast-food restaurants were everywhere I looked. Ermita's red light district was packed with go-go bars, where bikini-clad girls hung on the arms of sailors from Subic Naval Base (America's largest naval facility abroad). No wonder some local politicians demanded full American statehood be granted to the Philippines.

There was music everywhere in the city. Kids with guitars strummed their hearts out on the streets, while at the fancy hotel lounges, local jazz bands played faultless renditions of all the standards. At a Saturday-night party at Shakey's pizza parlor, a Beatles look-alike band played "Fab Four" songs to perfection. The famous Hobbit House—a co-operative run by dwarfs and midgets—boasted live music every night, with big names like movie singer, Lea Salonga. The night we went, Corazon and I were privileged to watch Freddie Aguilar, the Filipino Bob Dylan, singing *"Bayan Ko"* ('My Country'), just one month after the Filipino courts had declared the assassination of former senator, Ninoy Aquino, at Manila Airport in August 1983, as a military conspiracy. The country was on the cusp of ousting the reviled Ferdinand Marcos, an Asian Idi Amin who had long been supported by four American presidents. By February 1986, events spiraling one after another against the government culminated in the bloodless "People Power" revolution that would topple the Marcos dictatorship and install Ninoy's wife, Corazon Aquino, as the new president of the country. The Reagan administration would back the Marcos's up to the very last minute, and then fly Ferdinand and his ludicrous wife Imelda to Hawaii on an American plane with millions of dollars on board. Only then would Freddie Aguilar's *"Bayon Ko"* become the new, unofficial national anthem of the country.

Before heading to Moalboal, we took a side trip to the refugee camp in Bataan, three hours northwest of Manila, to visit some mutual friends and see the camp for ourselves. Set up like a college campus, with the wreck of a Vietnamese boat at the entrance, the camp was located on land where the Niak tribe once lived. In 1980, Imelda Marcos, designated as the official commander of the camp by her husband, ordered the displacement and relocation of the tribe to make way for her pet project. In the camp, living conditions were good, and freedom of movement for the refugees was much more liberal than at either Galang or Phanat Nikhom. The night Corazon and I spent at the camp, we were treated to an impressive staging of the musical *Jesus Christ Superstar* put on by the Filipino staff with some of the Christian Vietnamese. It was an early Christmas celebration.

The costumes were elaborate and the singing superb. At one point in the show, while looking at the huge audience of Vietnamese, Cambodian, and Lao refugees, I whispered to Corazon, "Wonder what all these Buddhists think of Jesus as a singing superstar?"

"I know!" she said. "And a flaming *bacla* at that!"

Bacla is the derogatory Filipino slang word for 'homosexual,' and the gay 'actor' playing Jesus had put on a particularly camp performance. I wondered if the refugees watching the show knew.

My impressions of the educated teachers in camp, mainly Filipinas, was that they were fun-loving and quite open with their thoughts and feelings—much more so than the Thais and Indonesians I had known in the other camps. Their historic exposure to American and Spanish colonizers must have added to that openness, I guessed. Bataan, as it turned out, was not only the most liberal and the biggest of the three RPCs in Southeast Asia, it also employed the highest number of foreigners from Europe, Australia, and the United States. This melting-pot campus spread over a few acres of Niak land—'Chameleon College Three'—was the most cosmopolitan of them all.

After returning to Manila, Corazon and I took the SuperCat ferry to Cebu, winding our way through the picturesque Visayan Islands. Back-to-back Hollywood movies played on the upper-deck TV, while the previous year's American NBA basketball finals were on the next lowest deck. On the sleeping mats of the cheapest deck, a group of less affluent Filipinos was playing mah-jong while picnicking on *pancit* noodles and real Oscar Meyer's hot dogs. I walked over, keen to know how the game was played. However, Corazon, after exchanging a few sentences with the group in the Visayan language, dragged me away quite firmly. When I asked what had happened, she seemed reluctant to explain until I insisted. That's when I learned the derogatory Visayan word for Indians is *mumbai*, and for Arabs *marubu*—both or either of which the mah-jong crowd was convinced I belonged to. More boxes to be caged into. What bothered me more though, was Corazon's reluctance to tell me what they had said until I persisted. We had been honest with each other so far, and yet our openness had always been in neutral countries where neither of us had a cultural identity at stake.

Christmas dinner with Corazon's family in Cebu was a sumptuous feast of *lechon* (a whole pig roasted on a spit), barbecued chicken, *pancit* noodles full of healthy vegetables, grilled seafood kebabs, and *kinilao*—raw seafood cocktails in a vinegary sauce. All washed down with chilled San Miguel beer, which Papa certainly enjoyed, but Mama obviously didn't touch or approve of. Then someone served sticky rice with mangoes and chocolate sauce instead of coconut milk. Thai dessert with a Filipino flavor.

One evening, after dinner, Mama got into a heated discussion with me on the subject of religion, and that's when I realized that she was a fanatic Catholic who was convinced that the only way to success and happiness was through Jesus and the Lord's prayers. My desertion of Islam and interest in faiths like Bahá'i and Buddhism didn't go over too well with her. My perception of Nature as my only god was sheer blasphemy to her. Worse still, it upset Corazon that I did not believe in a god or a religion I could call my own. While she didn't agree with most of Mama's obsessions and prejudices, she still very much wanted God to bless her children through Baptism and the Holy Communion. We never resolved the issue that night because we left the next day for the beach. In retrospect we should have resolved it right there and then, that night.

Scuba diving was fun at first. I was thrilled at spotting my first manta rays and electric eels diving down the coral reef drop-off not far from the shore. Corazon chose to laze on the beach and hook up with old friends instead of diving with me. At night, the warmth I had felt in Corazon's arms earlier in our travels now turned cold and clammy, as if some switch in her head had been turned off for good. My attempts to talk her through our differences, to find a middle path, met with a wall of resistance and silence. Over the next few days, the wall turned into a sheet of glacial ice. She was like a lionfish about to release its poisonous barbs on me. She spent more and more time with her old friends and was less and less eager to spend time with me. Eventually I left for Thailand, distraught and disillusioned that I hadn't been successful in making her see the middle path. She had already made up her mind and there was no talking her out of it.

ॐ

More than a decade would pass before I would let a woman get as close to my heart as Corazon had once been. My relationships switched back to 'on-the-road' mode whenever there was compatibility. I became the clown, generating laughs as a ploy to hide my pain. On the few occasions when I did open up, I was always wary of my vulnerability, my fear of hurting and being hurt.

Then, in 1999, in Bangkok, along came educated Pranee, the best of all nurses, to mend this wounded chameleon's heart.

Pranee was a genius at making any broken-down hovel of a place into a cozy home. She was such a good home maker that all my old habits—including the fervent need for one more slice of the wild nightlife in the city—began losing their appeal. I even cut back the visits to my favorite bar, Adhere, when she moved in to live with me. Night after night, she cooked up mouth-watering Thai meals: spicy chicken with cashew nuts; tangy salads with Isaan sausages and wild herbs; carved tropical fruits with passion-fruit ice-cream or mocha almond fudge. When I craved *farang* food for breakfast, she improvised with spinach bagels topped with cream cheese and blackcurrant jam, and fresh squeezed orange juice; or Chinese dim sum dipped in soy sauce, served with Chinese tea laced with lime. She knew that the quickest way to my heart was through my stomach.

Typical of most Thais, Pranee was obsessed with personal cleanliness. She insisted on cutting my nails her way, popping blackheads with her thumbnails, cleaning the sleep out of my eyes, snipping nostril hairs, and ensuring we were both spotless before making love. Sex was only okay when she was in the mood for it. But hugs, snuggling, and a '*hom*'—the uniquely Thai version of kissing by a quick, affectionate sniff of the cheek—were okay any time of the day or night.

Her own Thai world—of family responsibilities, merit-making at the temple, celebrating Chinese New Year (since her father was a Chinese Malay)—was a place I was not allowed to enter. Like Dr. Jekyll and Mr. Hyde, she could slip out of one world and into the other, and no one except me would be the wiser. She realized the limitations of Thai society in contrast to more 'worldly' cultures and hated the fact that she couldn't express herself fully without being criticized by other Thais for being too opinionated. As a reaction to the confines of traditional Thai culture, her desires to master the English language, to learn the *farang* ways of eating, to express political opinions, to enjoy intellectual or cultural evenings, became obsessive at times. This was where I did come into the picture. Whatever I imparted to her, she became better at it than me. It didn't take her long to learn and then beat me soundly in Chinese checkers, or bed wrestling, or even lap races in the swimming pool. She was convinced that the two worlds she lived in, the Thai and the *farang*, could not meet. She was the perfect secretive chameleon.

We decided that the best way to test the waters of our relationship was to travel together. On a trip to Sydney and Melbourne in Australia, we were happy and compatible during the day, strolling through the Opera House and Darling Harbour in Sydney, and the numerous art museums and the colorful Royal Gardens in Melbourne. Pranee was like an excited child at a fairground. At night, however, the food had to be spicy and the venues free of drinkers or smokers—which she would have nothing to do with. When I had to explore the nightlife on my own, we became distant. After two weeks in the cities, she flew back home for work and I did what I really came for—exploring the Great Ocean Road in Victoria, and the east coast all the way up to Cairns. My side trips—diving in the Whitsundays, camping with dingos at Fraser Island, and sunset meditating at Uluru—made the experience unique for me. The rugged raw beauty of the Australian outback captivated me. But it wasn't till I got talking to Aborigine families at Uluru (Ayer's Rock to the colonial Aussies) did I realize that this amazing country has a tragic history just as racist and bloody as that of my once precious Uganda.

Sadly, during these six weeks, I didn't miss Pranee once. Travel had exposed our underlying differences, and given me a sign of things to come.

In so many ways, Pranee was the opposite of me. She didn't like partying or socializing, and dancing was only for the home stereo. She thought our differences could be resolved through actions, and found my need to talk a burden, unless on her terms. She responded to my sadness over unpleasant events or circumstances with a *mai pen rai* 'don't-worry-about-it' attitude, which wasn't always a solution for me. And when that didn't work, she would resort to feeding me a good meal or scrubbing me in the bathtub till I forgot my woes.

And what about her woes? Well, her role during the tsunami clearly revealed her inner strength. She was as strong as the Rock of Gibraltar. And she could nurse herself when she needed to. Even more strongly than she did others. She didn't need to talk things through. For her, it was kept inside; there was nothing so terrible that couldn't be cured with a good cry or a hot bath or a good spring-cleaning around the house. I eventually realized that it was only a matter of time before she wouldn't need me at all, this nurse of all nurses. The one who stole my heart from all those on-the-road relationships; the one that came closest to getting me to settle down. She was the one who brought me out of my cocoon. For that I will always love her.

8. Safari Jumbani

A modern day Odysseus, upon returning home,
may find that Penelope is in New York and
Telemachus has applied for refugee status.
Pico Iyer.

It has been three and a half decades since Idi Amin inadvertently
broke the yoke of culture and country around my neck. That
circumstance of my history gave me the accidental freedom to roam
five of the seven continents of my planet. Little by little, whatever
was left of my cultural baggage was thrown out in towns and villages
in each country I visited, till I was left with a solid core of personal
values that became my personal lens for looking at the world and the
myriad ways that humans survive in it. It has been a long journey over
many waterways and through the cultures that live on their shores.

Languages have been my key for unlocking those cultures. I am
lucky with languages. I soak them up like a sponge and spout them
out like a parrot. As a boy, I spoke Gujarati at home, English at
school, Swahili in the streets, and Hindi with many of my friends.

Learning Thai from Ajaan Uthai and the Thai people was easy for me. Living with a rural Isaan family and striking up friendships with characters like Noi and Monk Marut did the rest.

While living and traveling in other countries, my new friends also became my teachers. In Indonesia, my badminton partners in Galang taught me how to woo Indonesian girls. In San Miguel, Don Crucito and Patricia were my eyes and ears into the Latin world. During our travels through the mountains of Pakistan and Nepal, Corazon taught me some of the Cebuano language, embedded with a lot of Spanish words after 400 years of colonization.

Whenever I ran into people who spoke Swahili, Gujarati, or Hindi—languages not often heard on the road—I would take the opportunity to practice with them for as long as I could. It was always a two-way street, as both speakers were delighted to recall a bit of home with a stranger who spoke the same words.

Working with refugees and non-profit organizations for almost two decades gave me the chance to travel much further and deeper into countries that I fantasized about through the books of my youth. Places like the three 'chameleon colleges' warmed my heart. Characters like Marut in Phuket, little Nguyen in Phanat Nikhom, Tranh the vendor in Hoi An, and Carlos in Guatemala made me realize I could get along with anybody, anywhere, as long as they had compassion in them for fellow human beings. All of them, except one, came from the East. Asia, more than any other continent, threw me many fine straws with which to build my nest and call it home should I choose to.

Travel brought me into contact with many others who live in or are caught in two or more worlds. There are many more of us than I imagined. All with the same primeval need to belong. Music became a liberator along the way, but a life partner in one nesting place I might call my own still eluded me. Was it that unrealistic that I wanted a travel partner like Uta, a dancer like Ursula, an intellectual mirror like Kiku, a trekker like Corazon, and, yes, even a nurse like Pranee—all in one? Was I asking too much? Or was it the search itself that was holding me back? Did I really want it to stop? Before I could find the answer to this last question that had been eluding me all my life, I had to fill in more gaps, search in a few places that hadn't been properly explored.

Before I could fully replace Idi Amin's yoke with a necklace of custom-made values, in a place of my own, I would 'inadvertently' make three trips into the past. Each would be a roller coaster of emotions, and by the time they were over, years apart from each other, I would realize that I had completed my search in this journey of three and a half decades.

One journey was to Vancouver, Canada for the fiftieth wedding anniversary of my parents, which all my family and their kith and kin showed up for. The second was a long-overdue trip to India, to the birthplace of my father. And the final one was a journey back to East Africa to revisit Singida and Kilimanjaro, and to roam through the wild plains of the Serengeti before returning to Uganda.

ଔ

In June 1983, when I was at Galang in Indonesia, I received a letter from Canada that demanded my presence in Vancouver within a week. The family was planning a surprise party for my parents' fiftieth wedding anniversary, and everyone was required to attend. Brothers Amir and Phiroz, now settled in New York City with their families, would be there three days before the event. Brother Ba, who had just spent two years teaching in Kano, Nigeria, would arrive with his family the night before the party. Sultan, now in Toronto and married with two children—Arif and Shakufe—was bringing her whole family. My other four sisters and their families lived in Vancouver and would all be there. I was expected, too—no matter what. The party had also been timed to coincide with a *khushali*—an

Ismaili celebration for special events or occasions in the calendar. Three days after our own family festivities, many of my Ugandan friends in Canada and England would also be coming to Vancouver for the Ismaili gathering. I had to go.

Within two days of receiving the letter, I was in Singapore (after some tough leave negotiations with my supervisor). At Changi Airport, I kept envisaging the moment of hugs and kisses with all my siblings, and seeing new babies that I had not laid eyes on. The last time I had been there was in 1979, just before leaving for Thailand. Eighteen hours later, on a glorious sunny morning, quite disoriented by jet lag, I saw Vancouver (dubbed "Raincouver" in winter) from my airplane window seat. The port city, nestled among ocean inlets and snow-capped mountains at the mouth of the Fraser River, never looked so beautiful. Smack in the city center, which is connected by steel bridges to the residential suburbs, stood fabulous Stanley Park, with its beaches, botanical gardens, fountains, and soothing ponds where swans and geese jostle each other for food. Across from the Strait of Georgia, a series of "First Nation" totem poles, surrounded by seagulls, stood tall, guarding the city entrance with the ancient spirits of the first settlers. Once a British frontier settlement, this cosmopolitan city now boasted a strong Asian population with its own Chinatown and Little India—not far from where my sister Shamim now lived.

I took a taxi to her home to meet up with her family and others who had already arrived. When I walked in unannounced, there was a whooping cry of joy from everyone followed by hugs and kisses. Both Amir and Phiroz sported bushy black beards just like mine. Little Shilo, now a gorgeous woman, had an Ismaili boyfriend named Akbar. Brother Ba and his family were due later that night. Everyone was hanging out in shorts and T-shirts, getting ready for a family picnic at Sunset Beach in Stanley Park, but I had time to wolf down a full plate of beef biryani, mango pickles, and samosas. Ma and Bapa's dinner, the following night, would be at a posh Indian restaurant, owned by a fellow Ugandan friend of ours, at Lonsdale Quay in North Vancouver. As for the anniversary couple, they were at home in Burnaby, oblivious to all the last-minute preparations going on for them.

I just had to hear Ma's voice, despite the objections that the surprise would be ruined. So, from a quiet room, I talked with my parents on the phone, pretending I was calling from a friend's home in Singapore. Bapa asked if the Muslims in Indonesia were treating me well. Ma wished that I were in Vancouver to celebrate the *khushali* with them next week. I almost let the cat out of the bag when I replied that "miracles could happen."

That afternoon, at Stanley Park, with more than forty members of my extended family around me, I couldn't help but marvel at how far our family had come since Uganda. In Vancouver, Nisha and Leila had good jobs; Shamim was a radiologist at BC Cancer Center; and Gulshan had a thriving family business rebuilding Japanese car engines. Sultan had a steady job with the provincial government in Toronto. Pediatrician Amir, and health insurance inspector Phiroz—like all five sisters—had also settled down and bought suburban homes for their families (in New York). House mortgages, credit-card payments, and decent schools for their children were now their priorities. It dawned on me that brother Ba, who had always been an inspiration for my travels, and I were the only two globetrotting gypsies left in the family. A small part of me yearned to be with the family in the comfort and open space of a gorgeous city like Vancouver.

Next evening, Shamim was appointed to drive our parents to Lonsdale Quay and bring them into the room where we had all gathered to surprise them. All they knew about the evening was that they were going to have a quiet dinner by the waterfront with their daughter. When they walked in and saw their whole family—the women in colorful saris and the men in suits and ties—my father gaped speechless and my mother kept blinking as if to wake up from dreaming. Only when the hugs felt real did they both smile and ask how we pulled this off in total secrecy. That one of Bapa's brothers in England, Uncle Badru, and Ma's two nieces from Edmonton had shown up for the occasion made it that much more special for them. The tears flowed freely that night. Ma, not amused that her Sachu had fooled her into thinking he was calling from Singapore the day before, smothered me with kisses anyway.

Then the celebrations began with sitar and tabla music and mounds of food—a panorama of spicy Indian dishes made Ugandan style for the older guests, and some Western salads and blander Indian dishes for the younger ones with a decade of growing up in North America. For dessert, *masala chai*, sweetmeats, and betel leaf pans to help the digestion. Throughout the meal, jokes in Gujarati and anecdotes of life back in Uganda flew back and forth, some quite exaggerated. I noticed that the younger ones, who knew little or no Gujarati, felt a little left out.

Then, with typical Indian sentimentality, began the praise for the two citadels of the Ismaili-Indian culture, now in their seventies and surrounded by 57 members of their extended family. The first of the speeches—mostly in English with key Gujarati and Swahili words thrown in for effect—was given by eldest brother, Amir, who was responsible for the idea of this reunion. He recalled the years of hardship in Singida, the move to Kampala—into one dingy room for ten family members that we struggled in for five years—and finally the step up to Madras Gardens. He thanked my parents for giving up their little sundries shop so that he could set up his *daktari ya watoto*, pediatric clinic, on Nakivubo Road that eventually helped us get out of poverty. He ended with how proud we all were of the younger generation growing up in North America, fluent in English, educating themselves in Western ways, and pointing the way to the future of our family.

In other speeches, my siblings reiterated the sacrifices that our parents had made and how it was time for us to repay that tenfold now that we had the means. Despite the jet lag, brother Ba, dressed in a Nigerian *kanzu*, was eloquent about our former life in Africa. None of them brought up our exodus from Uganda or the horrors of Amin—almost as if it had never happened and was best forgotten. Yet, in my world of Galang, I was reminded daily of refugee suffering.

In my speech, I wanted to publicly thank Amin once again for freeing me to roam the world, and thank my parents for passing on the travel gene that defined my life. But I did no such thing. As the youngest of the nine siblings, I was expected to share the same dreams of suburbia as them. But I was the fish out of water at Lonsdale Quay. I was the prodigal son who refused to come home and join the fold, despite being implored to do so by many in the family; the Indian black sheep who had strayed from the flock. To bring these things up on this occasion would be taboo; it would let loose emotional responses that might alienate me from those close to me. So instead, I praised my parents for the love and affection I received, joked about making my mother dance to Jimi Hendrix at Madras Gardens (laughter from the younger ones; most of the elders didn't understand), and prayed that one day soon I could take them to travel in places where they might be reminded of the many beautiful things left behind in East Africa. The applause was mild and subdued. However, little Arif, Sultan's twelve-year-old son, did ask about my life in Asia, later on.

The after-dinner dancing, a combination of Indian *garba* and rock 'n' roll, culminated in the highlight of the evening—73-year-old Bapa dancing belly to belly with a hired professional belly dancer. Ma was laughing so hard that, with her weak bladder, the sisters had to take turns to whisk her to the bathroom before she peed in her elegant silk sari.

My parents' anniversary celebration turned into much more than that. It was a celebration of arrival and success in a new land, and the coming together of the whole extended family for the first time since Uganda.

Later that week, the family trip to Little India—brown people everywhere shopping for food, saris, jewellery; travel agents and tailors all along Main Street—brought on renewed feelings of alienation. At Canada Place, some 10,000 Ismailis gathered for the *khushali*, celebrating with *dandya* stick dancing to an Asian band named Jambo, with members from East Africa, Pakistan, and India; Kampala celebrations in the heart of a Canadian city. On the way out, I couldn't help but notice the eyes of the white parking-lot attendants gawking at this Indian parade of silk saris, suits, and Mercedes Benzes. Some reflected awe, but most showed resentment at this new immigrant group—the *wabenzi* of Vancouver—that had become so successful in just over a decade. I did run into a few classmates from Aga Khan School. We went down memory lane briefly and then ran out of things to say. Most of them had settled well in North America or the UK, working in professions that afforded them the luxuries of Western lifestyles. Neither Nizar nor Zainab showed up for the gathering.

The week in Vancouver was a whirlwind of emotions that left me unsettled. On the plane back to Indonesia, I lamented again on whether I was wrong to leave the family for the open road. But the bigger part of me still lusted for the countries yet to be explored, the work yet to be done in refugee camps. I felt much more at home bantering with the street vendors of Bangkok, playing music in the ruins of Yucatan, or hiking up Machupicchu. To fill the hole left within me since Uganda with a suburban home, manicured lawns, and two cars in the garage just didn't seem right. Working and living in countries with people who had much less than me somehow satisfied a longing that just hadn't been fulfilled in North America. That calling gave more meaning to my life, even though it prevented me from seeing my nephews and nieces grow up. It was as if I needed to replicate the atmosphere of Uganda wherever I went. I wondered if the new generation would follow in the same footsteps as my siblings.

ↄʒ

Circumstances over the next twenty years would make the dreams I wished for in my speech to my parents, both spoken and unspoken, come partially true. The reunion in Vancouver became the first of many that spanned two more decades. After Lonsdale Quay, any and every family event—a fiftieth or sixtieth birthday, or a marriage of a nephew or niece—became a perfect excuse for another reunion and one more opportunity to thank our parents for all they had done for us.

In 1993, while working for the Peace Corps in Honduras, I attended Amir's surprise sixtieth birthday celebration in Ossining, New York. After the party, I convinced my parents, now in their eighties, to come and stay with me in Tegucigalpa for a month. On the plane to Honduras, it dawned on me that my mother, with her weak knees, would not be able to walk down the stairway that usually greeted the passengers upon arrival at Tegoose Airport. For a moment, I panicked, imagining all the complaints I would receive from my siblings if my parents had to return without setting foot on Honduran soil. In Spanish, I asked a stewardess for help, and she promised to talk to the captain in the cockpit. An hour went by with no word from her. Now I was sweating and cornered her again. She told me that the captain had talked to the ground crew over the radio and to not fret about it. I wasn't quite sure what that meant.

Upon landing, the stewardess advised me to stay behind with my parents. When all the passengers had disembarked, two hefty men boarded the plane with a high chair that had a safety belt strapped on. At our seats, they picked up my mother and gently got her into the chair. Picking up the chair, with my heavy mother in it, they walked down the aisle, down the stairway, and got her into a wheelchair on the bus taking us to the terminal. Inside the airport, they whisked her though Immigration and Customs and patiently waited beside her till I arrived with my father. On the car ride to my home in Tegoose, my mother turned to me and said, "If you'd told me they'd treat me like a queen here, I would have come much sooner." Relieved, I laughed. Then, turning to my father, she added, "See how well my Sachu takes care of me." In my head, I thanked Honduras for all of its strong macho men and the Latino concept of *para servirle*—'at your service.'

Our trips to places that brought back memories of Uganda made me grin often. At the fruit market in Tegucigalpa, Ma and Bapa tasted guavas, custard apples, and cashew fruits after having forgotten them for so long. Bapa recalled my Sunday morning walks with him, at age five, to Nakasero Market in Kampala, my tiny hand curled around his big forefinger. In the villages, Ma chatted with women (with me translating from Gujarati to Spanish) grinding cassava with a mortar and pestle, just like Suleimani once did for her back at Madras Gardens. At home, Ma taught Juanita, my housemaid, how to cook rotis and *khima* (minced beef) curry so her son could have Indian food whenever he desired. One weekend, at a hot springs resort, Ma even cooked boiled eggs, just to recall the sensation of having done the same at Wamba Hot Springs on the outskirts of Mbale in Uganda. That's when she recounted a 1951 trip from Singida to Mbale, with Bapa, to visit her younger brother, Remu, to discuss the prospect of moving to Uganda, which they eventually did in 1953. She left the best part of her story for last: when she had boiled the eggs at Wamba, she was five months pregnant with me in her belly.

CB

By the 1990s, many of my nephews and nieces—in their teens during my parents' fiftieth anniversary—were in their twenties and searching for their own identities in North America. To my great surprise, some of them—eight to be exact—came to visit me in the exotic places I lived and worked in. At different times, nephews and nieces explored with me the villages of Guatemala, the coral reefs of Honduras's Caribbean coast, the blues bars of Bangkok and Jakarta, the white sandy beaches of southern Thailand, the hilltribe villages on the Lao border, and the ruins of Angkor in Cambodia. Another family member, Zubin, a student at Boston University, hiked with me in the canyon lands of Utah, and spent a summer exploring Palawan in the Philippines and the mountains of northern Thailand. It thrilled me no end to see the travel genes I inherited from my parents passed on to their grandchildren. In some strange way, these travels with the new generation vindicated my wayward lifestyle with my disapproving siblings. The chance to guide the young ones in their travels, so that they too could get a taste of the world I lived in, was one I never dreamed possible. A chance to continue a legacy started in the 1920s by a young man from Gujarat on his way to East Africa to start a new life with nothing but his faith and courage.

Then, in October 1997, while I was living in Bangkok, came the opportunity of a lifetime. Little Arif, now in his mid twenties, was working with a non-profit law agency in India and wanted me to meet him in Delhi for his birthday, and then travel together through India and East Africa for the next three months. Since I wasn't busy at the time, I jumped at the chance. Ever since those precious thirteen hours looking for lost Aunt Sakina in Bombay, I had been aching to go back to India. As for East Africa, now that Amin was long gone, the doors had been flung open for Ugandan Asians to return. The government had even offered the additional incentive of returning property that was lost after the expulsion.

ଓଝ

When I met Arif at a guesthouse in Delhi's Connaught Circle, he had just come back from an Indian music awards show where

British musician, Sting, one of his favorite artists, had made a special appearance. Over birthday beers, he recounted how Sting, dressed in a white *kurta*, sang with *bangra* dancers in the background—the latest craze in the Bollywood movies. The blending of cultures through music had captivated Arif, and I knew then and there that we would make good travel partners. Born in Toronto, this Canadian Ismaili who hardly spoke any Gujarati or Hindi, was searching for his place in this land of our ancestors.

The next day, Arif took me to the Qutub Minar, Delhi's best-known landmark and the oldest Muslim monument in south Asia. The 238-foot, five-story sandstone tower was built between 1199 and 1368. Inlaid with carvings and verses from the Koran, it remains unknown whether it was built as a victory tower or a minaret for a neighbouring mosque. After this excursion, we went to his favorite Ahmadabadi biryani restaurant in Old Delhi, and then braved the special office for tourists at the massive train station, where we booked computerized tickets to various destinations ending up in Bombay. Arif had everything organized. Before leaving the city, we hunted out cricket grounds and places where boys played *gili danda*, so I could re-live my childhood. I became the language interpreter and the cultural historian. We made a good team. On the road, locals often mistook us for an Arab father and son team. Once, Arif was even mistaken for an Israeli. When the inevitable question was asked, "Where are you from?" Arif would immediately reply "Canada," while I would opt for Uganda, much to the surprise of the inquirer.

At the grounds of the Taj Mahal in Agra, we played banana-hide-and-seek with the monkeys at dusk, as the jewels encrusted in the marble of the great tomb began to reflect brilliant colors from the half moon in the sky. I taught Arif how to respond in Hindi, so that beggars and souvenir hawkers pestered us much less as we zipped around on the rails. We soon felt at home away from home—wherever that was.

On the train ride to Rishikesh—made famous when the Beatles visited in the 1960s—we met up with tanned Alena from Melbourne, who wore a sexy Indian dress. She had studied classical Indian dancing, loved India, and wanted to swim in the Ganges at Rishikesh, one of the few places where it is still clean and blue instead of dirty brown. Upon arrival, we found that half the city, including transport workers, was on strike in protest against low wages and poor work conditions. While walking with our packs from the station to the nearest guesthouse, we were alarmed to notice that all the food places were closed down, too. We were ravenous from the long train ride. After checking in, we wandered the streets looking for something to eat. Next to a tape cassette shop blaring Bollywood movie music, we found a vendor selling *chai* and biscuits to tide us over. Arif, recognizing a hit song from a Bollywood movie he had seen recently, jumped up on the street and launched into the dance sequence. Alena and I joined in, much to the amusement of the boys hanging out at the cassette shop. Within minutes, a crowd had gathered to watch the crazy brown tourists lip-synching and street dancing to all the latest hits. Alena was in top form and put on a very convincing routine. One of the locals, in all seriousness, asked me if Alena was a Bollywood actress, to which I nodded. When the show was over, food mysteriously appeared from one of the houses nearby—for the honored visitors from Bollywood. Apparently we had earned our dinner, despite the strike. The next day, during our swim at an isolated bank on the blue Ganges, the same man who thought Alena was an actress found us and wanted her autograph.

At the Pushkar Palace Hotel in Rajasthan, the room wallah informed me that I should feel privileged that the room I would sleep in that night was the same one that actress Kate Winslet of *Titanic* fame had slept in when making a movie in Pushkar. Luckily he didn't charge extra for the privilege. In the evenings, when the townsfolk came to bathe and make *puja* by the holy lake, I preferred to chat and smoke ganja chillums with the untouchables of the town, generating more than a few glares from the higher caste locals. Later, at a hat shop in town, Arif decided to buy an untouchable's hat for the road, despite the vehement objections of the hat seller. When the desire to eat meat and drink beer in alcohol-dry, vegetarian Pushkar overtook us, I found out the whereabouts of a Muslim restaurant four kilometers out of town. The place was packed with local customers eating delicious buttered chicken and *nan* bread. We ordered the same and washed it down with beer served in brown paper bags. Two cultural rebels inventing new habits in an old town of worship.

Breakfast at Bapu's Place—on the rooftop of the ancient fort in Jaisalmer, overlooking the Thar Desert—consisted of spicy curried omelets with *parathas*, and piping hot *masala chai*, just like Ma and Sultan made. Guesthouse owner, old man Bapu, turned out to be a wonderful host, treating us as his sons. A three-day camel safari into the sand dunes resulted in very sore butts, but gave us spectacular desert sunsets. Around the evening campfires, the camel drivers and guides sang Hindi songs with us that brought back memories for me of Bollywood parties at the drive-in in Kampala. However, when I let slip, in Hindi, that Arif and I were Ismailis, then the racial jokes about Ismailis from Gujarat began, some of them provoking resentment in me. Amused, the guides said we should be charged more for the trip just because we were Ismailis. I was incensed and refused outright when I realized that they were serious. We were in the middle of the desert with no idea how to get back to Jaisalmer. Eventually we came to a compromise for the return journey. I was glad that Arif was oblivious to most of the cruel jokes and the consequential price hike.

Jaisalmer is the last big town on the edge of the Thar Desert— through which runs part of the border with Pakistan. Tensions between the two countries because of the decades-old territorial dispute over Jammu and Kashmir were simmering as usual. Indian soldiers in khaki uniforms patrolling the streets marred the image of this beautiful city of pink sandstone buildings and ancient ruins. In 1998, a year after Arif and I left, the Indian government would detonate five nuclear devices in the Thar Desert, thereby provoking Pakistan to conduct tests of its own. Global concern over the possibility of a nuclear arms race in south Asia, as tempers flare in beautiful Kashmir, remain to this day.

Arif and I moved on to Gujarat, to visit the birthplace of both Mahatma Gandhi and my father. At the train stop in Ahmadabad, two young men entered our sleeping compartment pretending to be passengers, just before the lights in the whole train went out. When the lights came back on a few minutes later, the two men rushed out of the train, causing Arif to check our belongings on the top rack. Gone was his knapsack with his camera and all his journals about his time in India. Arif could live without the camera, but was furious that he'd lost all his diaries. He pleaded for us to get off the train to search the station, just in case the thieves threw them away as useless notebooks. The frantic two-hour search was in vain. When the station police were alerted, they were sympathetic but said they could only take action if we gave them written statements for the loss in three languages—English, Hindi, and Gujarati. Hours later, they came up with a suspect, whom they proceeded to beat with batons in a back room to induce a confession. Shocked, Arif and I begged them to let the man go, since he looked nothing like the two men on the train. Disgusted with the whole scene, we hopped on the next local train heading southwest to Rajkot, just north of Gondal, Bapa's birthplace.

Bapa had left Gondal as a teenager, soon after his father died. Now in his eighties, his recollection in a phone call from me about the location of his birthplace amounted to "not far from the river and a fifteen-minute walk from the Riverside Palace." The exquisite palace, a remnant of colonial times with gorgeous gardens, antique furniture, and terrace views of the river, was easy to find. For the next two days, in the area nearby, I recited my father's history to anyone who cared to lend a sympathetic ear to my search—monks, *saddhus*, elders, city officials. It was obvious to us that many of the Hindus seemed less eager to help than the Muslims. Twice I thought we were close to the mark, but both leads ended up as false trails. Finally, on the third day, frustrated and disappointed, we boarded the train to Bombay, unable to locate Bapa's house—if it still existed— or anyone who knew of his family in Gondal. The long train ride to Bombay left us in a somber and muted mood.

Little did we know then, that in 2002, racial riots between Hindus and Muslims would explode in Gujarat. A train fire causing the deaths of over fifty Hindu passengers was falsely attributed to Muslims. As a result, some 2,000 Muslims were slaughtered while the police, nonchalant, watched it all happen. In 2006, the local courts sentenced nine Hindus to jail for their part in the massacre. Yet another tragedy in India's seemingly intractable sectarian divide.

At the train station in Bombay, I optimistically kept an eye out for Sood, the airport taxi driver who had helped me find Aunt Sakina in Andheri, on the remote chance that he was doing the rail route as well. Of course, he was nowhere to be seen. The two days with Aunt Sakina's family was a mini family reunion. Arif had never met any of them before. Karim helped me find a dirt-cheap round-trip flight to Nairobi via Dubai. Unfortunately, it flew only once a week and the next flight was the day after. Arif had previously arranged for a different itinerary to Kampala. He was meeting up with his father, Lutaf, who was flying in from Toronto the following week. I would be flying on my own and would hook up with them in Mombasa before Arif and I continued our travels around East Africa. Once again, the sights and sounds of Bombay would have to wait for my return trip.

The few weeks in India had been a whirlwind of memories, good and bad. I knew I would come back to visit again and again. Yet, the familiar food, childhood games, and languages were not enough to entice me to live there for a longer time. This time, I realized that the Indian way of getting things done was not one I particularly cared for. Besides, my long anticipated return to East Africa was a stronger calling right now.

 os

On the Emirates flight to Nairobi, the first surprise was being served free gin and tonics on an Arabian airline. When the hostess realized that I'd keep asking for more, she brought me three airplane bottles of Beefeater and two cans of tonic so she wouldn't have to keep coming back. This suited me just fine. At the duty free Mecca in Dubai, I bought liters of rum and vodka to keep me lubricated in Africa. I landed on African soil elated from both the booze and the anticipation.

At a cheap guesthouse in the seedy part of Nairobi, my Kenyan roommate warned me to beware of *kondos* roaming the streets in daylight to scam unsuspecting tourists. "*Hatari sana*" ('Lots of danger') he kept repeating. Just two days before, he had been mugged and lost his month's salary to one of them. The city, once a hopping hubbub of African nightlife, was now rife with crime and deserted at night. I carried my money in my shoes when I went to buy a train ticket to Mombasa, where I was to meet with Arif and Lutaf that week. On the overcrowded *matatu* minivan to the station, the few Kenyan notes in my right pocket mysteriously disappeared anyway.

I left for Mombasa the next day. Some fifty kilometers before reaching the city, the train broke down at a small village, forcing all the passengers to get off with their luggage, and negotiate inflated prices with minivan drivers who miraculously appeared out of nowhere. "*Haraka, haraka!*" the drivers pressured all the passengers, who were at their mercy. So much for the *Hakuna matata* welcome.

The minivan dropped me off at the Aga Khan Hostel on Bamburi Beach, on the outskirts of Mombasa, where I would meet with Arif and Lutaf, who I hadn't seen since my parents' anniversary in Vancouver. The beach—the very same deserted one I had slept on during my first ever trip to the ocean in 1967—now had wall-to-wall resorts full of German and Scandinavian tourists on Christmas vacation. The contrast of tanned European bodies in bikinis against Arabian women in black *bui buis* from head to toe was inescapable. Lutaf's sister, Najma, who was still living in Mombasa, had rented a seaside cottage in this secluded hostel compound, open to Ismailis only. She had graciously cooked up a mountain of Indian food for the reunion, since Ramadan was in full swing and food was hard to find during the daytime. Her *kuku paka* was heavenly, as were the beef samosas. Come evenings, while Lutaf and Najma went to mosque for evening *Dua* prayers, Arif and I drank iced rum *madafs* mixed with coconut milk and slices of ripe coconut, and flirted with the rebellious few scantily-clad Arabian girls cruising the tourists at the beachfront bars. The generational clash between young Arif and Lutaf and Najma was very evident. Me? As usual, I was caught in the middle.

A few days later, Lutaf flew from Mombasa on his way back to Toronto to resume work. Arif and I continued north by bus to Malindi and took the ferry ride to the island of Lamu, where my mother was born. We hoped to be more successful in finding Ma's house than we were with Bapa's in Gondal. Najma had given us the shop address of the one and only Ismaili still living on Lamu to start us off.

Lamu, an idyllic island paradise with Arabian *dhows* sailing on turquoise waters was a hippie hang-out in the 1970s. We checked into the Pole Pole Guesthouse, with its rooftop affording spectacular views of Lamu and the Indian Ocean; Arab women in *bui buis* and men in colorful *kanzus* everywhere. The muezzin called for prayer five times a day during Ramadan. On the beachfront, Petley's Inn, established by a British retiree in the nineteenth century, boasted luxurious divan sofas to wine and dine on, with Kikuyu hookers to spice up the atmosphere. Lamu also happens to be the donkey capital of the world. In the narrow alleyways of Lamu town, donkeys have the right of way, causing many an accident with the unsuspecting visitor, especially at nighttime with no electricity. *Karibuni!*

The search for Ma's house began in earnest on Christmas Eve. The Ismaili clothes vendor with the Arab wife, though courteous, was keener to make a sale than to listen to my story. But nearby, a friendly young shop owner, Mahmadi, from whom we bought tie-dye shirts, suggested we talk to the town elders, of whom there were four. He promised to seek one of them out at prayer that evening. Over the next couple of days, word got out in the small town about the two Muslim men who were looking for their mother's house. Now Arif and I were brothers. The next day, for two hours, we talked with 72-year-old Mzee Suleiman, who really didn' t remember much. He recommended we have a meeting with the other three elders. Chief Abdullah, now in his nineties, would surely remember something, he said. Getting them all together would take some time, but he promised to let Mahmadi know when and where to meet.

That evening, Arif and I pieced together all we knew of my mother's family. We joined the Christmas dinner celebrations at the posh Peponi Hotel—a feast of various meat dishes complete with cranberry sauce and plum pudding. We checked in with Mahmadi every morning before going on day trips to local villages and snorkeling around the island. Then, on the last day of Ramadan, we got word from Mahmadi that the meeting would take place that evening over dinner to break the final fast. We seemed to be edging closer, but I wasn't getting my hopes up only to be let down, like in Gondal. That evening, the four men, including Mzee Suleiman and Chief Abdullah, showed up at a local restaurant, all dressed in white *kanzus*, two with salt-and-pepper beards. Mahmadi and his friend, Ahmed, had ordered food for all of us: mutton curries with rotis and marinated *miskhaki* kebabs with cucumber chutney.

During dinner, the questioning began in English mixed with Swahili. When the elders switched to Arabic, Mahmadi translated for us. Family names? Family business? Names of brothers and sisters? How old was Fatima (Ma) now? What did she look like when she was young? When did her family move from Lamu to mainland Kenya? Time went by and yet nothing. *Halva* and *witumbwa* desserts were served with Arabica coffee. Show us the pictures again. Are you sure the brother's name was Rahimtullah? On the last question, I mentioned that Ma used to call him Remu for short, recalling her story about Wamba Hot Springs.

"Remu? Remu? Did he have a large black mole on his right cheek?" asked Chief Abdullah.

"Yes! That's him!" I replied, recalling his birthmark from seeing him at Idd-el-Fitr in Kampala.

Minutes after Remu was identified and remembered, Chief Abdullah had recognized the family and pinpointed the house. Cheers all around. He remembered Remu as a fun-loving businessman, but couldn't recall any stories about older sister Fatima. Mahmadi would take us to the house the following day. *Bismillah*! Hugs, photos, profound thank-yous, and smiles all around. Outside, in Lamu town, the end of Ramadan celebration was in full swing. Music was playing everywhere—a mix of Bollywood, Arabian melodies, African samba, and even reggae.

We hardly slept that night. My *gado-gado* dreams were back, more jumbled than ever. Next morning, on New Year's Eve, Mahmadi took us past a few alleyways to Ma's house, which was now a Kenyan Customs office with staff working. Mahmadi explained our situation and the kind supervisor agreed to let us look around and take photos. We took pictures of every room, including the decrepit bathroom, and then more from the balcony that looked over a small square. Mission accomplished. Ma would be ecstatic when she received the pictures via e-mail from Dar es Salaam, our next destination.

In the evening, with Mahmadi and a group of his friends, we took a *dhow* to Manda Island, where the Peponi Hotel had set up a dance party on the sand-floor restaurant. All of Lamu was there: backpackers, visitors from Mombasa and Malindi, even the donkeys. We ushered in the New Year dancing the night away. At dawn, I woke up Arif, who was napping in a dug-out canoe on the beach. Sunrise on an Arabian *dhow* sailing through the blue Indian Ocean, with Mahmadi and me singing reggae songs, was a perfect way to start off 1998. Donkeys braying by the pier welcomed us back before sleep took over.

ഇ

The short flight from Mombasa to Dar es Salaam plunked us into Tanzania. It was a joy to hear pure Kiswahili spoken all around us at the airport. Amid the bustle of the city, I was thrilled to come upon a billboard-size painting of the first president of Tanzania, Mwalimu Julius Nyerere, the revered statesman responsible for the ousting of Idi Amin in 1979. In 1985, he would become the first African politician to voluntarily step down from power. I recounted to Arif a summary of the *ujamaa* socialist education policies of his administration, the subject of one of my thesis papers at Ohio University. Like Mandela, he was now one of the elderly peace negotiators for regional conflicts in Africa, including Uganda. Sadly, he would die of natural causes in 1999.

Keen to get to my birthplace of Singida and then make our way to Arusha for Kilimanjaro and the Serengeti, Arif and I stayed just long enough in Dar to send the Lamu pictures to Ma and to stock up on fruits at the Kariakoo Market for the train ride early the next day.

The ten-hour journey afforded panoramic views of the countryside; of farmers tilling land and women picking tea and cotton in the fields. At the tiny Singida Station, a group of dancers, probably celebrating a local holiday, made us feel welcome. The first task, after checking into the only hotel in town, was to dress up well and locate the Ismaili mosque, where we hoped to find someone who knew the Tejani family. It wasn't hard to find in the town with one market. At the mosque entrance, imagine our elated surprise upon finding Bapa's name on a wooden plaque displaying the names of all the mosque clerics since 1946: "Hadimohamed Tejani, *Mukhisahib* 1951-52"—the year of my birth. I had no idea that Bapuji had been a *mukhi* here. The plaque would be our icebreaker with the people inside. Some twenty odd Ismailis had just finished *Dua* prayers, and many of them looked up in amazement at the two strangers who just walked in.

Bapuji's name was all that was needed for introductions. The current *mukhi*, Salim Nagji, now in his fifties, remembered Bapa and Ma from when he was a boy growing up in Singida. He rolled out the welcome carpet for us. Dinner would be at his home that night, no arguments. He introduced us to Amir Ladha, a 64-year-old man who turned out to be brother Amir's classmate at Singida Secondary School, where Bapa was the headmaster—another tidbit that I had forgotten about my own father. Not only did this man know the house I was born in, he promised to show us the actual classroom where Bapa taught him and brother Amir. Over half a century after Bapuji had left India for Africa, his son and grandson had arrived home to pay their respects to the town that stored a vault of memories of my parents and all my siblings.

That wasn't all. At dinner that night, we met Salim's 84-year-old mother, Khadeeja, visiting from Toronto, whose babysitter for her sons had been none other than my sister Nisha. She reminisced in Gujarati about the huge cookouts that she and Ma used to prepare for the community during *khushali* celebrations. She told us of life in Singida in the 1950s, when hyenas used to roam the area that is now the Singida Market, of the growl of lions in the jungle that made my siblings cry in their sleep. I translated everything she said for Arif, so he could share the emotional high I was experiencing in hearing her stories. She remembered Sultan, Arif's mother, as a shy, quiet teenager who didn't say much. Khadeeja, this historian of Singida, even cried when she heard that Dadima, my grandmother, who taught her how to sew, had passed away in Kampala in the early 1960s! To make her feel better, even though it was dark outside, Salim ordered the houseboy to cut down a bowl of *jamburas*—the sweet black fruit found only in East Africa—from their backyard tree.

The next day, we went to the school. There was a new annex building, but the old dilapidated classroom where Bapa taught was still standing, with a cracked blackboard and rickety furniture. It was now used for storage of school supplies and gunny sacks of rice. Ever the clown, Arif convinced me to attend class by sitting at a broken desk. Amir Ladha lectured from the blackboard while Arif took pictures of us from different angles.

The emotions kept piling on when, later that day, we went to the house where I was born. Mr. Faud, a sick-looking Arab who lived there, was taken aback by the unannounced visitors, but he opened his door for us when Amir Ladha explained why we had come. It was a simple, two-bedroom house with a long corridor leading to the terrace in the back that now boasted a TV satellite dish. A sign in capital red letters on top of a tightly packed white gunny sack in the kitchen caught my eye: "*UNGA WA MUHINDI.*" 'Indian wheat flour.' Amir Ladha explained that, at one time, two families lived here: my parents with nine children, and Uncle Badru's family of six including Dadima. I wondered how we had managed in such cramped quarters. I recalled Ma telling me in Vancouver that my birth—I was delivered by a midwife in one of the rooms—was quick and easy, and that she was back at her housework within a week. I bounced up and down on the beds in the two rooms, imagining what it must have felt like to be rocked to sleep by Ma or my sisters amid these cracked walls with peeling paint. Before we left, Arif and I finished off a full roll of film, capturing every nook and cranny for posterity. I put my hands together for a Thai *wai* of gratitude to the house and its new owner as we said goodbye to sickly Mr. Faud. Amir Ladha told me later that he was suffering from typhoid.

The days went by so fast. Salim took time off from his trucking business to show us the surrounding areas of Singida: jumbo rock formations that were similar to Joshua Tree in California; salt lakes teeming with herons and storks; and the *shambas* of tamarind and mango trees—all wonders of Nature that none of my siblings had ever mentioned in their reminiscences at family gatherings. Salim's gracious wife, Salma, insisted on filling us up every night with her delicious home cooking. The spicy *masala* fish with rice pilau and fresh grilled corn with *tui* (an Indian coconut-milk sauce with turmeric) was to die for. Ismaili small-town hospitality that I would never forget.

On the morning we were to depart for Arusha, I was lugging my backpack from the hotel lobby to the minivan waiting outside to take us to the bus station. That's when I saw it, on the front entrance wall, near a frangipani tree. I gawked at it, my mouth wide open. It just stood there motionless and camouflaged as if pasted on the beige concrete wall. I had just seen my first real chameleon. In Singida of all places.

ভ

The sight of Kilimanjaro from the bus approaching Arusha took my breath away. There she was, serene as ever, with that mound of snow beckoning me to the rooftop of Africa once again. I had to remind myself that, at the age of 46, I was no longer the athletic jock that survived Outward Bound at Loitokitok. In Arusha, we decided that Arif would make the five-day trek to Uhuru Peak from the Tanzania side, while I arranged for park permits and a safari into the Serengeti and Ngorongoro Crater. The Kilimanjaro climb now cost 100 dollars per day, a commercial enterprise that would never live up to my experience of Outward Bound. Arif left the following day for the mountain, probably fed up of my incessant instructions on what to do when and where, and what pictures to take.

At the Park Permits station, realizing that Tanzanians paid much less than tourists for the expensive entrance fee, I whipped out my torn and withered Tanzanian birth certificate in the hopes of getting a discount. With some soothing words in Swahili to the ranger on duty, I pleaded my case. The trick worked, and I paid one tenth of the price that Arif would end up paying for entering the Serengeti. My Tanzanian birthright was put to good use for once. Of course, a baksheesh of Tanzanian currency was included with the application form I handed in.

Arif came back five days later, pumped from the climb. Kili had been kind to him, and the weather permitted him to make the final sunrise push to Uhuru Peak. At the summit, instead of the iron book I once signed my name in, Arif saw a Tanzanian flagpole with a quote from Nyerere congratulating the climber on being at the highest point in Africa. I was very proud of him.

(In April 2006, brother Phiroz's son, Amir, would climb the same peak while traveling with his father on an East African pilgrimage much like the one Arif and I were enjoying now. It seemed that the rite of passage to manhood, by climbing Kilimanjaro, was alive and well in the new generation of Tejanis.)

The trip into Ngorongoro Crater and then to the Serengeti, in an open-roof jeep with a young Polynesian couple from Hawaii, was stupendous. The switchback dirt road into the crater was dry, as the rains were still a few months away. It meant that Arif would miss the spectacle of the wildebeest migration, but the wildlife was as abundant as ever. Hippos, their jaws gaping wide, yawned in the Grumeti River. Lions, some with radio transmitters on fitted collars, studiously ignored the few jeeps spiraling around them in the park. At one spot, after waiting for hours, we were spellbound as a lioness killed an impala. Our guide and driver, Jomo, a wildlife connoisseur, knew exactly where and when to wait for what. He was also a walking encyclopedia on birds, so I pestered him to find us some crested cranes, Uganda's suave national bird with its yellow Mohican crown. When he did eventually find me a group of three females, striding across the plains on their stick-thin legs, I burst into a celebratory but out-of-key version of the Swahili song "Malaika."

The side trip to Olduvai Gorge and the Louis Leakey Museum to see the remains of *Zinjanthropus*—"Nutcracker Man" with his large molars—was a journey down memory lane. Back in 1966, at this same museum with my family, Leakey's African assistant had given us a step-by-step account of the actual discovery of this ape-like skull. Leaky's 1959 find—proved later to be almost 2 million years old—had prompted a heated debate on human evolution.

Another place that Jomo took us to was a Masai homestead off the tarmac road. We would pay extra for this privilege, but one peep inside the compound was enough to disgust me, as a horde of park tourists gawked at the dolled-up Masai men and bare-breasted girls putting on a dancing show like animals in a circus. While the rest of our group toured the compound, I played checkers outside with a Masai elder who was using Coca-Cola bottle tops as pieces on his hand-drawn cardboard set. He won the first game, but I won the second. Halfway into the third, three teenage Masai boys appeared in black loincloths with white markings on their faces. These marks indicated that they had recently gone through the circumcision rite into manhood. I joked with them in Swahili about the pain. One of them asked if I wanted to pay to take pictures of his healing penis. I replied that I would show him my own circumcised penis as a trade off instead. The old man, sitting opposite me on his haunches, laughed so hard that he almost fell over backwards.

On our very last morning in the park, meters away from our camp-site, in a grassy patch just off the tarmac road, we came upon a cheetah mating ritual. Four lustful males circled around a female in heat, all purring and yelping loud, attempting to claim the first coupling. The female, irritable and impervious to their pleas, was playing hard to get. She wasn't about to give way or choose her first mate until she was well and ready. The chase went on for almost an hour before the female sauntered away to a secluded spot, pursued by all four suitors. Jomo said that he had never come across such a sight in all his seventeen years in the park. *Ayinga. Shantih.*

Arif and I left our group at Ndabaka Gate, at the western end of the Serengeti, to flag down a bus to Mwanza, where we hoped to catch a ferry across Lake Victoria into Uganda.

ᘓ

In Mwanza, we found that the ferry to Port Bell, Uganda was no longer running because of a horrible accident a few years back, and the recent menace of water hyacinth—an aquatic weed whose intertwined roots formed a net that was almost impossible to navigate through. The weed, introduced in the 1980s from Asia, was apparently now at plague proportions on the Ugandan side of the lake. What to do? A kind Sikh man in Mwanza advised us to take a ferry to Bukoba, within Tanzania, from where we could make our way overland into Uganda.

We did so the next day. Lake Victoria, the second largest freshwater lake in the world—where thousands of Ugandans had been fed to crocodiles during the Amin regime—was teeming with bird life. On the ferry, Arif hooked up with a couple of Canadians who had flown to South Africa, bought a decent Land Rover, and were driving across

Africa in it. One thing led to another and they agreed to take us all the way to Kampala as long as we shared the gas money. On the ride from Bukoba to Mutukula at the Ugandan border, Jimi Hendrix's "Are You Experienced?" was on the tape player. What a perfect song for the return home. At the Customs point, the visa officer smiled at us—"Velkom to Uganda"—as she stamped our passports. Once inside Uganda, instinctively I knelt and kissed the red clay soil.

In Masaka, at the restaurant we happened to stop at for lunch, the owner turned out to be a Vancouver Ismaili who had come back temporarily to help rebuild the Aga Khan Mosque in Kampala (destroyed during the Amin years) and had decided to stay. On the way to Kampala, when we came to a monument of two cement circles with a big sign saying "EQUATOR," all four of us got out to take pictures with one foot in the southern hemisphere and the other in the north. Not often you get to have a foot in both worlds. Across from the monument, at a fruit stall overflowing with mangoes and pomegranates, women dressed in bright *basutis* haggled in the Lugandan language—not Swahili, to my surprise.

Next stop Kampala *mukade*. Good old Kampala. A quarter century had gone by.

The Canadians dropped us at Mahmoud's place in Bugolobi, late at night. Mahmoud, a distant relative from Vancouver, whose family had returned to Uganda to start a filtered water business, had visited me in Khon Kaen, Thailand on one of his travels. He was thrilled to take us in. Cold Tusker beer and *matoke* was waiting for us after we had showered off the red dust from the road, and Mahmoud told us about his business in Uganda and the problems he was having with his local staff. When we called it a night, from a shelf in my room I picked up a book called *Throne Of Gold*, a new account of the Aga Khan dynasty that revealed as many achievements as scandals about our two religious leaders over the past century. I fell asleep with the book on my lap.

We explored Kampala over the next few days. After two decades of civil strife and looting, the last decade of President Yoweri Musoweni's administration had turned my city into a reconstructed, thriving place. Yet, a lot had changed. City folks preferred to speak Lugandan instead of Swahili now that the monarchy had been restored (though with no political power). Rubaga Cathedral and the Bahá'i temple were still intact. My Susannah Bar was no more, but there were new discos, nightclubs, and casinos. Bands played live music at fancy hotels while seedy dance bars with names like Al's and Capital stayed open till dawn for the ever-increasing expat community. Makerere University was alive with students again, some of whom weren't even aware that a quarter century ago, some 80,000 Asians lived in their country. City restaurants served food from many countries, but Greek Kristos was now an Internet café, and the food at Krua Thai, a Thai place on Nakasero Hill, wasn't nearly spicy enough for me.

The market on Nakivubo Road was still bedlam, as it always had been, with taxis and traders packing the huge space. Here, one could still buy all sorts of contraband goods. Further up the road, our sundries shop that Amir turned into a pediatric clinic was all boarded up, but the Aga Khan Mosque did indeed look splendid at night, with all the minarets lit up. One evening, at the mosque's adjoining annex with its badminton court, I talked Arif and Mahmoud into playing a few games, just like in the old days. At night, coffee houses on Kampala Road, lined with frangipani trees, stayed open till the last customers left. The Indian Sunday parade on Kampala Road no longer took place, of course. The city was safe from the Lord's Resistance Army, the Islamic anti-government insurgents who had been operating in the north since the mid-1980s.

During breaks in our sightseeing, Arif checked tourist agencies that advertised white water rafting on the Nile, safaris to national parks, and rainforest treks to see the silverback gorillas. Meanwhile, now that the government was returning lost properties to the deported Asians, I chatted with some of the Asian families who had returned to start up new businesses—to find out more about reclaiming some of our family's houses. I learned from them that brother Amir's posh house in Kololo was now, ironically, the British Embassy.

Oxford School, where I once taught, was now an empty, dilapidated ruin. "Should we even bother going to Aga Khan School?" I asked Arif, disheartened. He convinced me to go. It was a holiday break at the school, but the Muslim headmaster at work was delighted to show us around. The school courtyard, where our theater group once performed Arthur Miller's *The Crucible*, was still the same. I backed away from entering old McCourt's office, where I was caned repeatedly. The classrooms did bring back a flood of memories: Miss Renee, who taught me to read Émile Zola in French; cruel history teacher, Mrs. Goldman, who had McCourt suspend me for three days for "unacceptable behavior." During her class on East African history, I had kept insisting that British explorer John Hanning Speke did not discover the source of the River Nile at Uganda's Ripon Falls in 1862 since Africans were already living there. My father had to take time off from work to complain to the Ismaili School Board, who then had me reinstated the next day. I asked the current headmaster about where the teachers came from. He said that they were mainly African, and the students were from all over Uganda. On our way out, the headmaster took us to the new "sewing skills lab" and gave us souvenir school T-shirts with a picture of a crested crane on the back. Touched that he wouldn't accept any payment, I made a donation to the school kitty instead.

On the way to 8 Madras Gardens from the school, I retraced all my steps down the once very familiar road. The Indian lady's shop where I used to buy strawberry lollipops for ten cents after school was now an African kiosk selling *mandazi* and *chai*. I bought some anyway. The "Madras Gardens" sign at the entrance to the triangular

Indian compound was still there, though tilted now with a crack down the middle. I was relieved to see that my house was still there, and the favorite guava tree was still bearing fruit. The house looked occupied. As we approached, I clasped Arif's hand, wondering who lived there and if they would let us in.

When he heard my story, the African man who opened the door looked worried. Before he would let us in, I had to reassure him repeatedly that all we wanted was a quick tour of the house and nothing more. Then I understood why, when we finally got in. The balcony from where I saw Luwanga shot by Amin's soldiers and the living/dining room where we deliberated over our exile had been turned into one big classroom. Behind the wooden desks, barefoot African boys and girls were busy writing in their notebooks. When this teacher introduced us, they all stood up fast and chimed in unison, "Good aftanun, sah!"

Despite the initial shock, I was pleased that the house had been put to good use.

We moved on. In one of the three bedrooms, a stack of English grammar textbooks was piled up high. The other two had people living in them, with dirty clothes all over. On the back veranda, a girl was washing clothes next to Suleimani's old room. Looking up, she stopped her chores and appeared scared to see these two brown strangers. I greeted her in Swahili and reassured her with a calm smile.

Suleimani's room was stacked full of gunny sacks with no labels on them. Moments later, in the bedroom where his mother Sultan used to sleep, Arif pulled out his camera to take pictures. The teacher was now horrified, convinced that we had indeed come back to reclaim the house. He was adamant in his refusal to allow us to take any pictures. Our pleading fell on deaf ears and he suddenly wanted us to leave immediately. We had to be satisfied with pictures of the house from the outside after we left.

The patch of ground where the Kampala Kudus played marbles and other games was now overgrown with tall grass, but the *pafu* tree on the dirt road was still standing tall.

മ

When Arif left a few days later—for a trip to Egypt and the Middle East—I stayed on in Kampala and entertained the idea of finding work with one of the many non-profit agencies now operating in the country. While some were interested in my history, most thought I had been away too long to make a meaningful contribution to the rebuilding of Uganda. I should have known better.

One Saturday evening, I went to Al's Bar for a few drinks and some *dumbolo* dancing. The place was packed, standing room only. For every African and expat male present, there must been at least two hookers hovering around for free drinks and, hopefully, a trick for the night. King Sunny Ade blaring from the speakers got me onto the dance floor. My chameleon dancing and butt-rubbing jigs with the sensuous ladies of the night went on till just before midnight. Cellphones ringing in their back pockets kept interrupting the great music. On a whim, I decided to change venue and walk over to the Capital Bar. Three minutes after I left, there was a thunderous explosion behind me. I turned back to see people screaming as they fled Al's. Minutes later, there was another explosion, much louder than the first one. More people fled the bar, some with blood on their bodies. "*Bomba, bomba!*" a man yelled as he flew past me. A hysterical hooker told me that two bombs had blown up the front part of the bar. The scene turned into a nightmare as people dragged out bodies from the wreckage and shoved injured ones into taxis bound for the hospital. I made my way back to Bugolobi quickly, reeling from the realization that I had escaped possible death by just three minutes.

The next day, the Kampala newspapers reported that the Lord's Resistance Army had exploded two bombs at Al's Bar, killing 22 people and injuring many others. Over lunch with Mahmoud, I told him that the incident had shaken me enough to want to leave Uganda soon. As luck would have it, one of Mahmoud's Indian friends was headed to his coffee *shamba* in Busia on the Kenyan border that same afternoon. Mahmoud made the phone call to confirm the ride and the pick-up from his place. Within two hours, I was packed and on the road to Busia, keen to get to Nairobi to catch the flight back to Asia.

Epilogue

Ma passed away in Vancouver in 1998 after a knee operation that proved fatal. I was the one who found her lifeless. Four years later, Bapuji, now living at Phiroz's new home in Pennsylvania, said his goodbyes to the few family members that prayed around him. I was not one of them. A few months later, brother Amir, on a college reunion trip to India, died in his sleep in Bombay, in the very same house where he got married to sweet Nergesh.

At my parents' funerals in Vancouver, and Amir's in Ossining, New York, with tears pouring down my cheeks, I thanked them all—through poems about their lives—for all that they gave me. Fearless Bapuji's journey from Gondal to Bombay to Singida to Kampala to Vancouver had taught me that the world was mine for the taking, be it out of choice or out of necessity. Ma's limitless ability to shower love, wherever she was, had given me compassion for my fellow human beings and the understanding that Nature, with its *yin-yang* beauty and destruction, served as my spiritual guide. Brother Amir was laid in the ground in a non-Muslim cemetary with a copy of the *New York Times* and surrounded by all of his extended family, womenfolk, too (which is a taboo in Islamic funerals). Amir, the family nurturer, taught me to appreciate the world outside of Islam and Uganda. The rest was up to me.

One summer, in my teens, in Kampala, when I asked permission to hitchhike around East Africa, my parents flatly refused, claiming that it was too dangerous. Instead, they let me and Nizar go on a weekend trip to Jinja, the next big town, fifty kilometers away. We had nothing but pocket money to survive the weekend on. On the road out of town, past Lugogo Stadium, we decided to hitchhike anyway. Our first ride took us all the way to Nairobi, where an Ismaili family at mosque took us in for the night. Worried, they forced me to make a collect call home. I told Bapa I was in Kenya and would return home in two weeks, to please inform Nizar's family, and then put the phone down quickly before he could give me an earful. It took us two more days to get to Mombasa. On the way, in Voi, the only free place to spend the night was a jail cell at the police station. The policemen gave us *mandazi* and *chai* for breakfast. In Mombasa, we slept on the beach at Bamburi. That deserted beach. That first trip to the ocean. When we did get back to Kampala, ten days later, I asked the family for forgiveness, but still insisted that I wanted their blessings and money to travel around East Africa again that same summer. Ma and Bapa knew then that they had to let me go.

From then on, travel to forlorn and out-of-the-way places and the experience of new cultures became my school of life. The more I traveled, the clearer it became to me that I could survive anywhere I went. The fear of the unknown eventually left me forever. Idi Amin made it much easier. Over the next three decades, the needs prevalent in most humans—to gain possessions, a house, a family of their own, to eat familiar food—became less and less important. Now, I am just as comfortable sleeping in warm beds in hotels and rented houses as I am on the beach in Bamburi, the traveler's hut in Chiapas, or a hammock outside a shack in Ollantaytambo. Over time, my tastes in food have adjusted to the mouth-watering dishes of all corners of the world—like the field mice in Nakhon Nayok, or the *empanadas* in San Miguel, or even the bacon and eggs in England. Comfort food is a concept I no longer understand. When I do yearn for cassava or guavas or samosas, I always manage to find some somewhere, sooner or later. More often than not, a book or two in my backpack—to pass the time while waiting for a truck or bus or train—suffice as my only possessions. My own family is all around me, all over the globe.

Cultures continue to fascinate me. Dining with people of many nationalities always makes for a great meal. Dancing to the many different instruments and musical styles of the world has made me come up with new moves for my body. From each and every culture, I have picked up norms I thought best and left all the rest for others to fight over. Traits that I don't understand become learning tools on how to be more tolerant of strange behavior. When I do come across behavior that upsets me, like racial discrimination or violence, I avoid it, move on, leave quickly, not quite sure why people need to believe in those values.

Inadvertently I have created my own hybrid culture, one that no longer defines me as a Ugandan-Asian but, so far, incorporates three hypens: Indian-Muslim-Ugandan-chameleon (with more hyphens to add over time). This hybrid culture allows me to enjoy eating samosas as much as cassava; dance to Jimi Hendrix in a bar, or Gazaals at a south Asian music party; seek comfort in rivers and mountains rather than some man-made God (with all the accompanying dogma). I am the exile turned immigrant turned Asian diasporic whose metamophosis into a chameleon now comes at will.

The cynicism born out of the injustices I have seen in our world, and the ruses of people in power perpetrated in the name of politics, religion, and race, is slowly being replaced by an inner peace that comes with age—a peace reflected in the actions of the downtrodden who, while continuing the fight for their rights, hold on tight to the axiom: 'if Mohammed [or any other humanitarian for that matter] cannot come down from the mountain, then take the mountain to Mohammed.'

As partners in life come and go, each one teaching me something new and wonderful, gradually I become aware that I can just as easily live on my own. I have learned to keep clean the room I stay in, find partners when the need and mutual compatibility is there. If I am sick or sad or lonely, there are hundreds of fellow travelers on my path who will give me comfort. Indian or Ismaili or African or Western 'therapy sessions'—joking and celebrating with family and friends in various languages—are no longer enough by themselves. I need them all.

Day by day, that demonic fear of solitary death in old age has become less and less of a preoccupation. The need to learn from mentors much further down my road, and teach those not far behind, has replaced the need for an immediate family to see me through to my last breath.

Indeed, there have been many mentors on this road I have taken that I haven't mentioned as yet—all of whom were gracious enough to teach me when I too, was ready to learn. British Julian, my geography teacher at Aga Khan School for four years, who put the early bug for travel in me during many a field trip in East Africa, and who now teaches in the Solomon Islands. German Otto, who cycled from Frankfurt to Pushkar, lived in a tree house that he built by himself in Phanat Nikhom, and who now works with fishermen in Benin. American Rolando in Honduras, who has taught farmers all over the world how to increase yields when the harsh forces of

Nature foil them. These wandering souls of the world—people who have, for reasons of their own, left behind the places where they were born and grew up to criss-cross the globe—have but one mission: to help others make their lives better. These self-reliant nomads, with their simple talismans, have been and are my teachers. Not only do they make me realize that I am not alone, but also that I still have a long way to go down my own road. Every day, more and more, I am slowly becoming one of them.

Like my teachers, I have my own talismans: the Outward Bound badge from Kilimanjaro; my Buddha amulet from Nguyen; a T-shirt with the flags of all countries; Hendrix's "Little Wing" inside my head; a world calendar marked with holidays from all cultures; photo albums of friends and places, jumbled up purposefully to keep reminding me of the whole world and not just a particular place or person.

My search for a home in places like Vancouver, Gujarat, and Kampala has only helped crystallize the realization that home is where I go every single day; that John Lennon was right when he said that there are more and more dreamers who realize that borders and passports are indeed man-made barriers; that from time immemorial, birds and animals, in their annual migrations, have never adhered to these human contrivances. And neither should we.

More and more stories of people struggling to live in two worlds are being written every day now. Intercultural marriages, and the 'third-culture' children conceived from them, are no longer unusual (or unnacceptable in many places). On the contrary, they are the way of the future. How beautiful is the daughter of a Gambian father and a Georgian mother? Or the son of a Chinese mother and a Chilean father? Where will home be for such children? Do we really even have, or need, a traditional home anymore? What if you decide to live in not two but five or even ten worlds in one lifetime? At least that way, you don't have to choose one or the other anymore. Surely it's not the house you live in, or its location, but who and what you put in it that makes it a home.

Sure, everyone needs a base camp once in a while to dump his or her possessions. From time to time, I need a place to have a shower and put up my weary feet. As long as it is a mobile base camp, one I am not attached to and can leave at short notice, then this planet is still mine to enjoy and love.

Thailand still remains that base camp for me. Why? Because Thailand is a chameleon itself, a country where the people, despite strong cultural traditions of their own, are not afraid to welcome those of very different beliefs to live alongside them—at least the ones that don't hurt or offend others around them. Thai cultural ideals like the concepts of *nam jai* (practiced by Pranee) and the non-confrontational *jai yen* (found in Monk Marut) have convinced me of that. Yet, Thailand doesn't possess or consume me. Even with the Thai language, I will always be a brown *farang* here, dealing with two-tiered prices and the haggling over street purchases. I can live with that, knowing that the cost of living elsewhere is much higher, both in terms of money and lifestyle. The age of digital communications—e-mail, chat lines, and cellphones—has arrived here, so I can communicate with anyone, anywhere. English, the Esperanto of our times, with all its wonderful pidgin and creole forms, remains my connector in those communications. So it really doesn't matter anymore where I live.

And now that I know all of this, a great burden has been lifted off my shoulders, ridding me of all the cumbersome categorical boxes that I've been shedding all my life, leaving me with a freedom that no one can ever take away—a freedom I can call my home and family.

I can stop searching now. I know where I belong.

Selected Glossary

Agent Orange—chemical defoliant [used by the US
           military to clear jungle in Vietnam;
           later cause of widespread human
           birth deformities].

Ajaan/*ajaan*—(Thai) professor, esteemed teacher, or mentor.

ao dai—(Vietnamese) traditional female costume of long
           tunic with side splits and matching trousers.

apsara—(Sanskrit) female court dancer, celestial angel.

ayinga—(Swahili) 'let feelings of peace come.'

Baganda—the major tribe in Uganda.

Bahá'í—modern universal religion founded by Bahá'u'llah
           [b. Mirza Huseyn in Persia, 1817; d. Palestine 1892].

253

baila—(Spanish) dance.

Bapuji—(Hindi/Gujarati) familiar name for
        'Father' [also 'Bapa'].

basuti—(Swahili) Ugandan female dress.

Batak—a tribal people of north Sumatra, mostly Christian.

bhel puri—(Hindi/Gujarati) puffed up chapatti with vegetable filling.

bismillah—(Arabic) 'the grace of God's care and forgiveness.'

bui bui—(Arabic) long black garment and veil worn
        by Muslim women in East Africa.

ꙅ *campesino*—(Spanish) farmer or peasant.

campo—(Spanish) countryside.

casa de viajeros—(Spanish) traveler's lodge.

chador—(Persian) headscarf/veil worn by Muslim women.

chai—(Hindi/Gujarati) tea.

compañero—(Spanish) companion.

ꙅ *dada*—(Swahili) sister ['Amin *Dada*' used as a term of
        mockery after Amin described his many wives
        and mistresses as his "sisters"].

dim sum—(Cantonese) steamed or fried
        dumpling [with various fillings].

dugu—(Swahili) brother.

ꙅ *empanada*—(Spanish) pastry filled with beef or other meat.

ꙅ fakir—(Hindi/Arabic) holy man [literally 'poor man'].

farang—(Thai) white foreigner.

fatwa—(Arabic) Islamic edict or ruling.

ꙅ *gunda*—(Gujarati) goon, thug, or henchman.

gurdwara—(Punjabi) Sikh temple.

hakuna matata—(Swahili) 'no worries.'

halva—(Yiddish/Turkish) Mediterranean or Middle
        Eastern dessert of sesame flour and honey.

Hanukkah—(Hebrew) Jewish Festival of Lights
        [held in December, commemorating
        the re-dedication of the Temple
        destroyed by the Syrians, 165 BC].

hermano—(Spanish) brother.

huevos rancheros—(Spanish) fried eggs and salsa breakfast.

ibu—(Indonesian) mother.

Idd-el-Fitr—(Arabic) feast marking the end of Ramadam.

imam—(Arabic) head priest/leader of prayers in a mosque.

IMF—International Monetary Fund.

indígena—(Spanish) indigenous people.

Intifada—(Arabic) Palestinian uprising [first, 1987].

jai yen—(Thai) self-control; keeping one's cool
        [literally 'heart cool'].

jambo—(Swahili) hello.

jefe—(Spanish) boss.

JVA—Joint Voluntary Agencies.

kabaka—(Swahili) king.

kanzu—(Swahili) long male garment with sleeves [usually white].

karibuni—(Swahili) welcome.

khaek—(Thai, derog.) Indian-Thai; person of south
        Asian or Middle-Eastern origin [literally 'guest'].

kikajo—(Swahili) sugar cane.

Kikuyu—one of the two major tribes in Kenya.

kitenge—(Swahili) African tie-dye shirt material.

kondo—(Swahili) thief, criminal.

kulfi—(Hindi/Gujarati) dessert of condensed milk,
    sugar, and spices
kurta—(Hindi) loose, long shirt [and leggings] worn by men.

ଔ *linga*—(Sanskrit) a carved symbol [usually a phallus,
    the symbol of Shiva, but also other figures].

ଔ *madrasah*—(Arabic) Koranic school [in some places,
    associated with the radical elements of Islam].
mai pen rai—(Thai) 'never mind'; 'it's all right'; 'don't worry.'
mandazi—(Swahili) Ugandan breakfast of fried dough
    made from rice flour and cardamom.
masala—(Urdu/Hindi) mixed, ground spices for cooking.
masala chai—(Urdu/Hindi) tea boiled with milk, water,
    cloves, ginger, and one cinnamon stick.
matoke—(Swahili) boiled green plantains mixed with spices.
mesa—(Spanish) flat-topped mountain.
mestizo—(Spanish) person of European and
    indígena mixed heritage.
mor lam—(Thai) traditional popular folk music
    of NE Thailand.
muhindi—(Swahili) person of Indian or south Asian origin.
mukhi—(Gujarati) one of the two head
    priests in an Ismaili mosque.
muzungu—(Swahili) white man.
Mwalimu/*mwalimu*—(Swahili) esteemed teacher.

ଔ *namaste*—(Hindi/Nepali) hello.
nam jai—(Thai) generosity, feeling for others
    [literally 'water of the heart'].
nasi goreng—(Indonesian) fried rice.
NGO—non-governmental organization.
NSC—National Security Council (US).

pakora—(Hindi/Gujarati) type of samosa.
paratha—(Hindi) roti stuffed with potato and spices.
pombe—(Swahili) alcohol.
puja—(Hindi) prayer.

rai—(Thai) land measurement equal to about
     half an acre [or 1,600 square meters].
regalo—(Spanish) gift or keepsake.
R 'n' R—rest and recuperation [US military term
       for recreational Sleave from the front line].
RPC—refugee processing center.

saddhu—(Sanskrit) holy man, sage, or aesthetic.
shamba—(Swahili) plantation.
shantih—(Hindi/Gujarati) peace.
sopa Azteca—(Spanish) 'Aztec soup' [traditional
        Mexican soup, with variations in recipe].
soto—(Indonesian) soup.

tuk-tuk—(Thai) three-wheeled [*samlor*] motor taxi.

UCI—University of California, Irvine.
UNHCR—United Nations High Commission for Refugees.
USAID—United States Agency for International Development.

wabenzi—(Swahili) wealthy Mercedes-Benz drivers.
wai—(Thai) traditional, respectful greeting [in which hands
     are held prayer-like, in front of head, face, or chest].
wat—(Thai) Buddhist temple.
witumbwa—(Swahili) fried dough of rice paste,
       coconut milk, sugar, and spices.

yaa baa—(Thai) methamphetamine [literally 'crazy drug'].

Printed by Chulalongkorn University Printing House
June, 2005 [4908-268/3,000(2)]
Tel. 0-2218-3557, 0-2218-3563, 0-2215-3612
http://www.cuprint.chula.ac.th